Understanding Style

Understanding Style

Practical Ways to Improve Your Writing

SECOND EDITION

JOE GLASER
WESTERN KENTUCKY UNIVERSITY

New York   Oxford
OXFORD UNIVERSITY PRESS
2010

Oxford University Press, Inc., publishes works that further
Oxford University's objective of excellence
in research, scholarship, and education.

Oxford New York
Auckland Cape Town Dar es Salaam Hong Kong Karachi
Kuala Lumpur Madrid Melbourne Mexico City Nairobi
New Delhi Shanghai Taipei Toronto

With offices in
Argentina Austria Brazil Chile Czech Republic France Greece
Guatemala Hungary Italy Japan Poland Portugal Singapore
South Korea Switzerland Thailand Turkey Ukraine Vietnam

Published by Oxford University Press, Inc.
198 Madison Avenue, New York, New York 10016
http://www.oup.com

Oxford is a registered trademark of Oxford University Press.

Library of Congress Cataloging-in-Publication Data

Glaser, Joseph.
  Understanding style : practical ways to improve your writing / Joe Glaser.
    p. cm.
  Includes bibliographical references and index.
  ISBN 978-0-19-537949-5 (acid-free paper) 1. English language—Style. 2. English
language—Rhetoric. 3. Report writing. I. Title.
  PE1421.G53 2009
  808'.042—dc22

                                                                    2008050912

Printed in the United States of America
on acid-free paper

Contents

Preface

Any how-to book that has been in print for more than ten years, as this one has, likely needs sprucing-up. This new edition of *Understanding Style* features the effective and practical approach to writing of the first edition along with a host of major and minor improvements inspired by users' comments. I've updated many exercises and topical references throughout the text, revamped the order of the chapters, and added a new one, "Subjects and Predicates," on recognizing essential sentence elements. Just as important, I've thoroughly reworked the book's website at <http://www.wku.edu/~joe.glaser/style%20home%20page.html>, including pages of analytical aids and sample answers. Throughout the process I've tried to keep the book concise while making it even more clear, practical, and fun to read. I hope I succeeded.

This book concentrates on style in writing because it is style rather than organization or content that most writers find especially hard to master. It seems so subjective. I hope to take some of the mystery out of style, explaining how to craft good sentences and combine them into writing that is clear and readable, no matter what you have to say. Most of the advice in this book is easy to carry out once you see what the goal is—developing a written voice suited to the material and readers you have to work with. The first two chapters discuss effective and ineffective written voices and describe some characteristics of each. Later chapters go back over this ground in detail, offering step-by-step help in developing an effective written voice, or style, of your own.

What goes into an effective written voice? As you can imagine, there is a wide range of possible answers. But to get some sense of the approach taken here, consider this passage from the influential journalist Barbara Ehrenreich:

> I think it's ridiculous to expect employers to provide health insurance, if only because people change jobs so frequently. We all—freelance writers as well as Wal-Mart associates—need health insurance that is not attached to our jobs. Until that glorious day arrives, though, I'll be biting at Wal-Mart's ankles to protest their health plan, which is financially out of reach of half their employees.
>
> WAL-MART DEBATE, *Slate, June 28, 2006*

What makes this good writing? Well, Ehrenreich projects a lively, feisty voice with plenty of rhythmic variety. Her eight breath units—word groups you would speak without a pause—range from two syllables to twenty syllables long, and her syllable/word ratio is a friendly 1.5/1. (Those measurements are discussed in Chapters 1 and 10).[1] Ehrenreich also writes efficiently, making good word choices and not too many of them (Chapters 3, 4, and 5). Over half her grammatical subjects are people, and she showcases brisk actions like *needing* and *biting* (Chapter 7). She focuses narrowly on workers, employers, and health insurance and uses various ways of controlling emphasis to highlight telling words like *insurance, all,* and *jobs* (Chapters 8 and 9). She includes a good deal of grammatical variety as well, using a broad range of constructions, not just simple sentences (Chapter 11). Her unpredictable grammar gives her another way of keeping readers engaged with what she's saying.

As you see, there's a lot going on in even a fairly commonplace passage like this one. But none of it is mysterious. The measures of style discussed here are largely definite and quantifiable. You can use them to improve your writing almost from the moment you pick up the book.

And you should. People judge you by your style in writing just as they do by your style in other things, but good writing does more than make you look good. The questions it raises and the thinking it requires can strengthen and transform your ideas. *What's the best way to say this?* The one that best helps your readers see what you mean. *Who are my readers?* The answer will vary according to the situation, but the harder

---

[1] As you'll see in Chapter 10, people may sometimes disagree about breath units. In arriving at my figure of eight, for instance, I ran together "Until that glorious day arrives, though" as one unit. Other readers might pause before and after *though*.

you try to imagine the people you're writing for and how they will react to what you say, the more you come to see the world with new eyes. Their eyes. Even if you write mainly for yourself, imagining other readers will broaden your thinking. *What do I mean?* At first you may not be entirely sure yourself. E.M. Forster's question, "How do I know what I think until I see what I say?" points to a real truth: the give and take between you and the readers in your imagination will uncover gaps in your thinking and send you looking for fresh information and ideas. It's built into the process. That's why writing is such a powerful learning tool. Use it to the best of your ability and you will find yourself growing not just as a stylist but as a person.

So why are there more useful books on sudoku than on style? For one thing, many key secrets generally go undisclosed because even authors who write on style may not understand them clearly. While all the experts urge you to eliminate deadwood, be specific, and employ a variety of sentence structures (good advice, though they don't always tell you how), few have much to say about the relationship between written style and spoken voices or ways writers control rhythm and emphasis. Yet these are precisely the kinds of issues that give style its reputation as a difficult topic. Would this sentence sound better turned around the other way? Is this clause too long to read gracefully? How do you keep important words from being buried under less important ones? Although questions like these concerning the *sound* of writing are crucial to understanding style, most style books leave them to linguists—who in fact have answers for many of them. Several chapters of this book adapt the findings of linguistic research into detailed writing advice seldom found elsewhere, advice that can give you new confidence dealing with the hidden choices and adjustments that make your style come to life.

Rhythm? Emphasis? Linguistics? Don't worry. Another principle of this book is that you already know nearly everything you need to about the technical features of English. Shakespeare never saw a book on English grammar. Before most speakers are in their teens, they can understand and generate constructions that professional linguists are hard put to analyze and explain. And writers generally don't have to analyze and explain the language they use; they just have to use it, which they do best without stopping to parse every grammatical construction. A great deal of research shows that learning the finer details of grammar has little effect on writing ability. Writers are better off learning to write by absorption, imitation, and practice, just the way they learned to speak.

That's certainly the approach taken here. While technical grammatical terms do appear from time to time, they are printed in **boldface** and defined and illustrated in the glossary at the end of the book. You'll need to be able to identify subjects and verbs (help with that appears in Chapter 6), but beyond that you can pretty well get by on your instincts and experience of English, along with the general language competence you've been perfecting since you put your first words together at about the age of two.

Finally, the writing advice given here is highly pragmatic. Want to begin a sentence with *and* or *but*? No problem. As long ago as 1967, Francis Christensen found that professional non-fiction writers started almost one out of ten sentences with a coordinating conjunction. How long should your words be? Chapter 4 suggests you aim for an average of roughly 1.4 to 1.9 syllables per word in your writing. Those are the syllable/word ratios of the Gettysburg address and the Declaration of Independence, still excellent models of style. Though some of the writing advice given here may be debatable (like telling you to write mostly in **independent clauses** or to delete transitional phrases that readers can do without), it reflects what good writers like Barbara Ehrenreich, Bill Bryson, or Kathleen Parker do most of the time.

Throughout the text you'll find an abundance of exercises to test and reinforce what you've learned. Most of these are open-ended assignments designed to help you explore writing options and have fun doing it. The more time you spend on these exercises, tinkering with style and noting the effects of the changes you make, the better sense you'll gain of how to make language behave the way you want it to.

Again, more help is available at the book's website <http://www.wku.edu/~joe.glaser/style%20home%20page.html>, where you will find texts you can cut and paste when working through exercises based on particular passages, sample answers, word-processing and computation tricks, grammar aids, and links to other useful sites.

I'd be pleased to know what you think of the book. If you want to comment on a feature you liked or didn't like, or if you have a question, please e-mail me at <Joe.Glaser@wku.edu>.

Acknowledgments

Nobody writes a book alone. I came across the ideas at the heart of this one—the chapters on coherence, emphasis, and rhythm—while using Martha Kolln's *Understanding English Grammar* to teach a grammar class. Professor Kolln's book led me to M.A.K. Halliday's systemic functional linguistics and new ways of talking about those "intangibles" of prose style. I'm grateful to both of them, and also to my students that semester and the following ones (hundreds of students by now), who unknowingly helped me work up the materials and exercises presented here.

Anthony English, my first editor at Oxford, had a surprising degree of faith in the book and boosted it along with unflagging enthusiasm and practical advice. Janet Beatty and Cory Schneider, the current Executive Editor and Assistant Editor, have been equally helpful in shaping this new edition. I must also thank the team of reviewers they put together: Victoria Aarons, Trinity University; Kara Poe Alexander, Baylor University; Basil A. Clark, Saginaw Valley State University; Elias Domínguez Barajas, Texas A&M University; Sarah Duerden, Arizona State University; J. Michael Duvall, College of Charleston; Laura S. Garrett, California State University at Los Angeles; John Hagaman, Western Kentucky University; Karen Keaton Jackson, North Carolina Central University; Jennifer MacKenzie, University of Missouri—St. Louis; Tom Montgomery-Fate, College of DuPage; Raul Sánchez, University of Florida; and, Xiaoye You, The Pennsylvania State University. I'm grateful to these expert readers for their suggestions. They certainly made this a better book.

Closer to home, I thank Carol Glaser, my excellent wife, for letting me slope off when I needed time to work on this project and others. All through my career Carol has been my dearest friend and upholder, always ready to help out with any undertaking. I thank Western Kentucky University and Karen Schneider, my department head, for their support, and I'm particularly grateful to my colleague John Reiss, the invaluable first reader of all my books.

PART ONE

What Style Is
Good and Bad Writing

CHAPTER 1

Voices You Want to Listen to
Elements of a Written Voice

It may seem odd to begin a book on writing talking about written "voices" and reading, but writing, reading, talking, and listening are more closely related than people realize. Good writers picture their readers and try to appeal to them personally. Readers read between the lines to get a sense of the person "talking" to them, almost as if they were listening to actual speech. No one would believe what Art Whattadeal said about the mint 2008 Ford Explorer he was selling without considering how he delivered his spiel. Did he talk too fast? Were his words clear or weaselly? Did he sound uncertain or overconfident? Was he bombastic or plain? Written language has counterparts to all these signals. In addition to reacting to what you "say," readers judge the "voice" you create. If the voice is wrong, they may throw out the content. That's one reason style counts so much toward your success as a writer.

It follows that a good first step to controlling the voices that speak through your writing is to become an attentive reader yourself. Although there's no single way writing should "sound," reading with your eyes open to style allows you to see how other writers achieved an effective voice, and this is an essential step in developing your own writing. It helps to notice choices other writers have made, so that when you are reading over something you've written or trying variations on a phrase in your head, you'll have a better notion of what worked for them and may work for you. This chapter explores several of the elements that make up a written voice. By the end of it you should have a better sense of what makes writing sound good or bad and why "sound" is so important to a writer's success.

The **voice** readers hear in your writing is a blend of the **grammar**, **diction**, and **sound qualities** of your language. All of these should suit the **writing situation**, or the nature of your topic and the relation between you and your readers. Like the noise of the tree that fell in the forest, your written voice exists only when it is processed in a reader's mind. But nothing can help or hurt you more. Good writing projects a voice readers trust and respect. Their sense of your personality and intentions colors the way they see everything else in whatever you've written.

Voice and the Sound Qualities of Writing

A powerful but woefully under-discussed influence on readers is the *sound* of your written words, which they hear inside their heads as they **subvocalize**—going through the mental processes of generating speech, but not actually triggering speech muscles or uttering sounds. They "listen" to this mental speech as if it were spoken aloud. What they "hear" is in fact their own voice saying your words, but saying them silently.

Here is a fairly typical sentence. Try reading it silently and then out loud:

It was the Boston Public Library, opened in 1852, that founded the American tradition of free public libraries open to all citizens.

As you read the sentence you should notice a pause in the flow of words after "Library" and "1852" (pauses are marked by an upright bar)[1]:

It was the Boston Public Library, | opened in 1852, | that founded the American tradition of free public libraries open to all citizens.

The words between these pauses are called **breath units** because you say them together at one go before catching your breath at the pause. Breath units divide sentences into segments your readers subvocalize separately.

Slightly more tricky is determining levels of **emphasis**, or the force and clarity with which you pronounce the accented syllables of certain

---

[1] English is a stress-timed language in which breath units usually stretch from one stressed syllable to the next and take the same amount of time to say. This applies to all native English dialects, including regional and non-standard varieties.

words. In the example sentence above you probably put special emphasis on these syllables: "**LI**brary," "eighteen fifty-**TWO**," and "**CIT**izens." You may also have emphasized the first part of "**LI**braries" if you paused after that word before going on to "open to all citizens." If these details seem hard to follow, look ahead to Chapters 9 and 10, where breath units and emphasis are discussed in detail.

Pauses and emphasized words break up written or spoken language into chunks of information that are easy to process. In my reading, our 23-word Boston Library sentence (counting "1852" as two words), breaks into breath units of 6, 4, and 13 words, containing 10, 8, and 25 syllables respectively. Mixing these longer and shorter units creates changes in rhythm. English speakers tend to speak each breath unit in the same amount of time, going faster or slower in keeping with the number of syllables they need to fit in. Try saying "that founded the American tradition of free public libraries open to all citizens" in the same amount of time as "opened in 1852." That's what most people do when they read the sentence silently or aloud.

Differences in emphasis also change the way words are voiced, so that an English sentence goes slowly or quickly and slips over some words and syllables and comes down hard on others, even if it's written rather than spoken. This is one great secret key to good writing. All else being equal, the closer a written sentence comes to the music of a well-formed spoken one, the more human and credible its "voice" seems. Sentence rhythms are not just ornamental. Chapters 9 and 12 show how they can be used to improve the clarity and coherence of your writing.

EXERCISE 1

Say these passages out loud, placing an upright bar (**|**) at each pause you hear. Then circle the emphasized syllables, most often the accented syllable of the last highly significant word before each pause. It might help to de-emphasize differences in speed and accent. Speak the sentences in Martian, "Take-me-to-your-leader" style. Then say them normally and listen for the differences. Be patient. Say each passage over until you really hear pauses and emphasized syllables. If you're still having trouble, look ahead to the examples in Chapters 9 and 10. Do any of the breath here units seem awkward or choppy? Which version sounds best to you? The passage is based on Noam Cohen, "Start Writing the Eulogies for Print Encyclopedias," *New York Times*, March 16, 2008. You'll find a sample answer on the *Understanding Style* website.

1. Sales of *Britannica*'s 32 volumes peaked in 1990. Then they dropped for six years. They fell 60 percent. The company had to reinvent itself online. In 1996, *Britannica* eliminated its legendary staff of 1,000 door-to-door salesmen, already only half what it was in the 1970s. The change was brought on by competition with Microsoft. Microsoft's *Encarta* was readily available on home computers.

2. Sales of *Britannica*'s 32 volumes peaked in 1990, but in the next six years, they dropped 60 percent, and the company moved quickly to reinvent itself online. In 1996, *Britannica* eliminated its legendary staff of 1,000 door-to-door salesmen, already down from a high of 2,000 in the 1970's, in the face of competition from Microsoft's *Encarta* for home computers.

3. Sales of *Britannica*'s 32 volumes fell by 60 percent between 1990 and 1996 and had to be made up for by online sales. In 1996, *Britannica* eliminated its already-reduced staff of 1,000 door-to-door salesmen in the face of competition from Microsoft's *Encarta* for home computers.

EXERCISE 2

Rewrite the following passages to replace long, awkward breath units with shorter, more manageable ones. *Hint: shorten breath units by eliminating unneeded words and creating more sentences*. Aim for units roughly 5 to 25 syllables long. Within that range, a variety of lengths is good. Change the sentence structure however you like, but include all the major ideas of the original. How do your revisions change the writer's voice? You'll find a sample answer on the *Understanding Style* website.

1. In late medieval England armed and belligerent bands of agricultural workers who were incensed over standard of living inequities between themselves and their employers attacked manor houses and burned crops and barns in an effort to frighten the rich into a more equal division of the country's wealth.

2. The problem with corn and other alternative fuel sources boils down to the cost and output of fuels made from switch grass and other non-petroleum sources. Biofuel costs a great deal to produce and delivers a lot less energy than an equal amount of petroleum products would. Crops like corn would also require

that vast areas of farmland be given over to them in order to meet a meaningful percentage of current energy needs.

Voice and the Writing Situation

There are two ways of looking at **writing situation**: in terms of the topic and in terms of the relationship between writer and reader. As topics and the roles of writer and reader change, so does the writing situation. Readers may demand a dry, impersonal treatment of a technical topic or expect a bureaucratic style in a grant proposal. They will forgive a difficult and demanding style if the topic seems to require it. And they accept language from someone they regard as an authority that they would resent from a writer on their own level of expertise. If the subject will bear it, they will even let writers work on their feelings. But the style must fit the topic and the situation if the voice they hear is to be convincing. For instance the **passive verbs**, **impersonal subjects**, and **Latinate diction** of the following passage would be out of place writing for friends and equals, but they are exactly what readers expect in a scientific report.

Cockroaches have conventionally been anesthetized with carbon dioxide before removal of the brain. However, primary data from our laboratory and others (Woodring, *et al.*) suggest that this may add undue stress to the roach and thereby induce the release of octopamine into the hemolymph from neurohemal organs. We feel this potentially confounding effect (i.e., elevated levels due to stress) can be eliminated by rapidly freezing the cockroach in $-72°C$ petroleum ether. After freezing the cockroach, the brains will be removed, weighed, and kept frozen at $-72°C$ pending analysis.

Equally conventional is the measured use of professional **jargon** in this example from a successful grant application:

The algebra institute will focus on how technology, alternative teaching strategies, and new topics can be incorporated into the classroom. Participants will gain hands-on experience with graphing calculators and computer software and will explore new approaches to traditional topics and other topics such as data analysis, geometric probability, and matrices.

Each of these passages is effectively written for its purposes. The writers asked themselves what "voice" their readers would expect to hear and conformed to it, but not blindly. Although some technical and bureaucratic styles are maddeningly hard to follow, both these passages make sure that readers can grasp the main ideas. The roaches will be flash-frozen to avoid being contaminated by their own secretions, and the teachers in the algebra institute will learn about the latest technology and math topics. This comes through even if you don't know geometric probability from a hemolymph.

In writing for general audiences the same principles hold true. Readers weigh the writer's voice—its **grammar, diction,** and **sound qualities**— against what is being said. They expect a sentence about the history of public libraries to be written soberly, with relatively formal diction and syntax. A radically different style probably won't work, except as parody:

> As soon as they cut the ribbon in 1852, that old Boston Library became numero uno, the grandpappy of all American public libraries.

> The 1852 inauguration of services at the Boston Public Library marked the commencement of a novel philanthropic national institution, free public libraries ministering to the populace in its motley entirety.

> Eighteen fifty-two—the number rings through the empty, echoing chambers of my mind. In that year the Boston Public Library started a trend that has a lot to do with what I am today. Oh, those long afternoons in the silent, musty stacks! What would I have been without the fabulous aid of the friendly public library, open to the humblest citizen, open in my preteen innocence even to me!

Although effective written voices vary widely, they all maintain a suitable distance between writer and reader. Readers resent writers who patronize them or make subjects seem harder than they need to be. Two of the last three examples offend in these ways. The first talks down, as if phony slang might entice you to read about a subject you otherwise would never care about. The second is written in the overblown style some writers adopt to suggest they know vastly more than you, whether they do or not.

The third false voice calls more attention to the writer than to the subject, and does it in an unaccountably personal way. When every insight is dramatic and every sensory impression is amplified by a string of particulars, you begin to wonder why the writer is taking on so. Some writing situations justify this highly charged approach. Most do not.

Several passages of effective writing appear in a "Gallery of Voices" at the end of the chapter. Although the writers there found themselves in different writing situations, they all chose an appropriate style and they all got the writer-reader distance right.

EXERCISE 3

Consider the following passages in light of their settings and subjects. How does each violate the writing situation through its sentence structure, diction, and sound qualities? How would readers react to the writer's voice in each case?

1. From a letter arguing that a cancelled insurance policy should be extended for the writer's benefit:

   Pursuant to our correspondence of May 16 it must be noted that although payment to extend my employee health benefits failed to reach your office within six months of my official termination, my notification that payment was due was also delayed until a full two weeks following cessation of my employee status, and so I feel an extension of the deadline is appropriate.

2. From an essay for general readers with no prior knowledge of the writer:

   As I take my first sip of the ruby-red Stag's Leap 2007 Merlot, cradling the thin blown-glass globe of the wine glass in my calloused fingers so that the fragrant wine is infused with the blood-warmth of my palm, I am carried back to my first experience with wine—a sweet, searing swig of Richardson's Wild Irish Rose from the crumpled brown paper bag offered to me by Arlen, my one-time best friend, as we stood with his sister Phoebe in the snowy alley behind Bill Morroni's grocery store one moonless, starlit February night in 2003.

3. From an examination paper in an accounting class:

   Say you're doing an audit of some company and you need to know where the bodies are buried? Well sir, one thing you do is up and make them give you a letter from their lawyers as to how there are no lawsuits they are likely to lose waiting in the wings. That way if legal trouble blows up, at least you've got your own butt covered.

EXERCISE 4

How did each writer in the following exchange violate the writing situation in terms of sentence structure, diction, and sound qualities? Rewrite
each letter so it projects an effective voice. You'll find a sample answer
on the *Understanding Style* website.

A. Gentlemen:

It's 6:35 and company is coming at seven. I check the roast
I have going in the crockpot. It hasn't even started cooking. The
carrots and onions are raw. This is a new appliance. I bought it
just over a month ago. No heat at all. What am I going to feed
the Browards? I had to go out for chicken.

Tell me how a month-old crockpot can go haywire. What kind of
garbage are you selling? I want my $29.99 back and an apology.

Cordially yours,
A. Piedmont Lucas

B. Dear Mr. Piedmont:

I am in receipt of your missive dated 14 November of the present year. I regret to inform you that institutional policy militates
against your final request inasmuch as the information you supply
is not only incomplete but wholly unsubstantiated. To bring
your claim to a favorable termination, my firm will require the
part number and order code of the appliance in question, date of
installation and date of failure. We also require the damaged pot
itself, to be inspected for evidence of tampering or abuse. Should
your claim be allowed, we will reimburse any acceptable pack-
ing and shipping costs.

If these terms do not meet with your approval, address all further correspondence in the matter to our legal department.

Sincerely yours,
Fenwicke O. Hardesty

Grammar and Voice

Think of all the processes that go into reading. Decoding the words themselves is just the beginning: readers also decipher the **sentence structure**

of the material, forming an impression of its relative complexity. For instance, the sentence you just read was rather complicated, with 24 words, 2 **clauses**, and some mildly unusual grammatical features. Your subconscious language-processing machinery recognized this complexity, putting you on notice that something serious and possibly demanding was being explained.[2] While readers don't diagram sentences as they read, their sense of grammatical simplicity or complexity also helps shape the way they hear a writer's voice.

EXERCISE 5

Without worrying about grammatical terminology, rank the following passages from most to least complex in sentence structure. Then listen carefully to the voice speaking in each. Which voice seems most forthcoming and lively? Which seems most distant and cool? Which seems to fit the subject best?

1. Matisse was drunk with color, splashing bold shapes and primary hues across the canvas in brilliant highlights and surfaces that dance forward and recede. The painter's spontaneous creative force is still as evident as if the paint were wet.

2. Drunk with color, Matisse splashed bold shapes and hues— brilliant highlights and surfaces that dance forward and recede— across his canvasses in a display of spontaneous creative force as evident today as it was when the paint was still wet.

3. Matisse was drunk with color. He splashed bold shapes and primary hues across the canvas. His highlights are brilliant; his surfaces dance forward and recede. You feel his spontaneous creative force. It's as if the paint's still wet.

EXERCISE 6

Rewrite the following passages so that the first contains only two long sentences and the second contains four short ones. Change the sentence structure however you like, but include all the major ideas of the original and stick as close as you can to the same language. How do your

---

[2] Of course, not all complicated sentences live up to the implications of their grammar. One hallmark of the **Official Style**, discussed in Chapter 2, is a deadly combination of complicated sentence structure and obvious ideas.

revisions change the writer's voice? You'll find a sample answer on the *Understanding Style* website.

1. Most fossil dinosaur eggs are sterile or contain undeveloped embryos. Fossil eggs that do contain developed embryos can be painstakingly peeled away, layer by layer, to reveal the embryo. This gives paleontologists their best direct evidence of the dinosaur's appearance. All the animal's parts are present in the embryo and connected in the proper manner. But the odds of finding an egg containing a developed embryo are roughly only one in five hundred. And you don't know whether a developed embryo is present until you've carefully peeled away enough layers to see for yourself.

2. When it came night, the white waves paced to and fro in the moonlight, and the wind brought the sound of the great sea's voice to the men on shore, and they felt that they could then be interpreters.

STEVEN CRANE, *The Open Boat*

Diction and Voice

Readers take in other technical features of writing besides grammar. In the passage about sentence structure we looked at earlier, words like "decoding," and "decipher" make it clear that the word choice, or **diction**, of the sentence is moderately bookish. The sentence contains 46 **syllables** for a syllable/word ratio of 1.9/1, not enormously high, but certainly higher than *Time Magazine*'s average of about 1.4/1, which is about par for popular writing. In addition, most of the longer words—*sentence, structure, impression, complexity*, for example—are based on Latin roots. **Latinate** words, discussed in more detail in Chapter 4, generally sound learned and formal, and this feeling of formality also contributes to a reader's sense of the writer's voice. While formality may sound out of place in some situations, at other times—for instance, in a full-dress research paper or business proposal—it might be precisely the effect you need to get a favorable hearing.

EXERCISE 7

Rank the following passages from most to least formal, paying special attention to the diction, or word choice, including one writer's decision to address readers personally. Which writer's voice seems most relaxed and breezy? Which most cool and impersonal? Which seems to fit the subject best?

1. In the tiniest embryos, cells are capable of taking on any role. They have to be. As the embryo develops they must give rise to all the specialized cells the organism will need in order to function on its own. Now scientists have found ways to "trick" specialized cells from adults into behaving like the widely adaptable cells of embryos.

2. In the initial stages of development, embryonic cells exhibit the multi-valent adaptability needed to generate the specialized tissues and organs the individual will need at parturition. It is now possible to return differentiated cells to this state of undifferentiated mutability.

3. Baby cells start off ready to be anything from teeth to toenails. But then they get boxed in. If you're a liver cell, you're a liver cell. Or are you? Now they've found out how to make all kinds of cells start all over and grow into something else.

EXERCISE 8

Rewrite the following passages, reversing the styles so that the first sounds slangy and colloquial like the second and the second sounds formal and restrained like the first. In addition to changing individual words, try adding direct address pronouns (*you, your*) to the first passage and dropping them from the second. How do your revisions change the writer's voice? You'll find a sample answer on the *Understanding Style* website.

1. In 1862, just two years after their marriage, which had followed a long and ardent courtship, Dante Gabriel Rossetti's wife Elizabeth died of an overdose of laudanum, a powerful sedative. Overcome with grief, Rossetti placed the only manuscript copy of his unpublished poems, many of which he had written for Elizabeth, in his cherished wife's casket to be buried with the body. Seven years later, after watching several friends whose work he considered inferior to his own become recognized poets, Rossetti regretted his rash gesture and took steps to correct it, causing Elizabeth's casket to be exhumed, retrieving the handwritten volume, and publishing his recovered poems in 1870 to wide acclaim.

2. The old Roman sculptors had this process they called lost wax to make bronze statues on the cheap. You would slap a lump of clay into about the shape you wanted. Then you would put wax over that the way you wanted the statue to look, being real artistic. Then more clay on top. When the whole shebang was set up hard, you'd pour your hot bronze in there where the wax was. The bronze would melt the wax and go where the wax was. When the bronze hardened, you'd break away the clay inside and outside it. Presto chango, a bronze statue all hollow on the inside!

Avoiding Discriminatory Language

Nothing puts off readers faster than unfair stereotypes and offensive language. Stereotyping is really a problem of thought rather than style and therefore not always easy to recognize. Imagine how your writing will sound to the groups you mention. Don't let your words imply things about them you wouldn't want someone thinking about you.

Even a few dropouts contributed to the fund drive.
[*Can't dropouts have school spirit?*]

I met Dr. Sanchez, her Mexican oncologist.
[*Don't many Mexicans become doctors?*]

When you become a partner your wife is expected to entertain clients frequently.
[*Do only men become partners?*]

Although she was disabled, she was far from bitter.
[*Are disabled people usually bitter?*]

Laurie may be gay, but she's got good sense.
[*Are most lesbians stupid?*]

Those old people know how to have a good time.
[*Are old people generally dull?*]

Just as objectionable is writing that assumes a limited audience, as if no one outside the writer's group could possibly be reading the piece:

We should always be sensitive to the feelings of Jews and other minorities.
[*Who's we?*]

How would you like to be a welfare mother?

[*Who says I'm not?*]

Racial slurs are always hurtful, but the acceptability of other terms changes frequently. Speaking of African Americans, *Afro-American* is out; *African American* is in, and *black* has come back. *Person of color* is admissible, but *colored person* offensive. Homosexuals no longer mind being called *gay* or *lesbian* and may refer to themselves as *queer*, though not so long ago *queer* was a fighting word. *Hispanic* is in the process of being replaced by *Mexican* or *Latino* and *Latina*. For a short while it was polite to refer to handicapped people as *physically challenged* until that expression became material for jokes, as in *fiscally challenged* or *ethically challenged*. *Disabled* is now preferred, but who knows for how long? A writer who wants to get a fair hearing and also to do the right thing must keep abreast of changes like these.

Sexist language is another form of linguistic discrimination that English is sloughing off. For centuries male-centered attitudes showed themselves in words like *mankind* (meaning everybody), *forefathers* (meaning ancestors), and *brotherhood* (which ignored a lot of sisters). While *adventurers* (generally referring to males) adventured, *adventuresses* slept around. *Poet* was a name of respect; *poetess* was condescending. Other words, such as *lady*, simply carried too many unwanted social overtones and needed to be replaced by less specific terms, like *woman*. Now sexist words and distinctions are disappearing from most people's writing, but some terms still require gender-neutral substitutes, such as *chair* for *chairman* or *letter carrier* for *mailman*.

Another sexist trait of the English language was the tradition of "common gender," which required that masculine pronouns *he*, *him*, and *his* be used to refer to singular indefinite antecedents like *someone*, *no one*, *neither*, or *a farmer*, even when the reference could easily apply to women as well as men:

Everyone will need *his* own book.

A farmer often grows attached to *his* animals.

English is still struggling with this built-in affront to women. Proposed solutions have included doubling the reference pronouns to include both genders:

Everyone will need *his or her* own book.

A farmer often grows attached to *his or her* animals.

or using plural reference pronouns:

> *Everyone* will need *their* own books.

> *A farmer* often grows attached to *their* animals.

But both these solutions have problems. Double reference pronouns quickly grow awkward:

> If a student calls, tell *him or her* to bring *his or her* book to *his or her* English class.

And plural references to singular antecedents still sound ungrammatical to many people. A better plan is to avoid singular indefinite antecedents in the first place when you can. Just make them plural:

> All *students* will need their own books.

> *Farmers* often grow attached to *their* animals.

EXERCISE 9

Rewrite the following passages to eliminate stereotypes and discriminatory language. You'll find a sample answer on the *Understanding Style* website.

1. When doctors are in training they have little time for wives and children. Then when they begin to practice, they can make so much money from just one more office visit or hospital round that they put in extra time almost despite themselves. It gets to the point that when his anniversary or child's birthday comes up, the doctor simply tells his nurse to go out and buy something she thinks will make an appropriate present.

2. Though we seldom spend much time there, the poor parts of town are full of physically challenged Afro Americans and Mexican Hispanics who are undereducated and unemployable. How well would you have done if you had been brought up in a family headed by someone with so many problems?

3. Mankind has always worked for the common good. Where would we be today if men of the past had not supported our way of life? The scientist who put in extra hours in his lab advanced our knowledge of natural forces. The parent who taught his children right from wrong promoted a stable society. And the men of the cloth who stood up for Christian values kept our precious faith alive.

A Gallery of Voices

How do you achieve an effective written voice? Not by straining for eloquence, but by matching the sentence structure, diction, and sound qualities of your writing to your subject and readership. It's fine to write one way in a grant proposal, another in a thank-you note, and still another in a sociology paper. If you don't, your voice will be ineffective two times out of the three. The passages collected here show how widely good writers' voices vary. They were selected because they are interesting and because the writing is fairly plain, at least compared to a typical political speech or a letter from your local planning board. They represent a standard of prose within most people's reach.

Try to analyze the writers' sentence structure, diction, and sound qualities on your own before you read the comments on each passage.

From a Non-traditional Student's Essay for a Writing Class

About five years ago when my family moved, one of the biggest adjustments the children had to make was to the rigidly structured classroom environment of their new school. The old school had encouraged creativity through recesses and play, art classes, drama, free reading and other activities. The new school offered few or none of these. My refrigerator, usually covered with the kids' masterpieces, was naked. I saw this as a major problem and asked the school system to at least hire an elementary art teacher. Although my suggestion got nowhere, I was delighted to learn my seventh grader would have a twelve-week art class the next term. I didn't know then that his "art" teacher was really trained in math, put top priority on neatness and comportment, and stifled students' creativity instead of giving it room to flourish.

Patricia Brown, the writer, strikes just about the right note here. Her sentence structure is varied but undemanding, and her diction is generally plain and clear, which is important because she doesn't want to sound like an overly protective mother who would get upset over nothing. Brown's syllable/word ratio is 1.5/1, slightly high for what is essentially a straightforward personal experience. Some of the congestion comes in the second breath unit: "one of the biggest adjustments the children had to make was to the rigidly structured classroom environment of their new school," which is also marginally too long to read gracefully. But on the whole, Brown's voice is nicely suited to the writing situation, down to the excellent detail about her bare refrigerator. This touch might be questionable for a formal research project in education, but it's perfect for a writing class.

From a Student Research Paper

If you want to build strength without bulk, think positive. Translation: when your training emphasizes only the concentric, or positive phase of the exercise—actually lifting the weight—muscle growth is minimal. For maximum size gains, eccentric contractions—the lowering phase, or negatives—are more important. Even though you're often told to lower weights slowly and keep muscles under stress to get maximum benefit, there's no need to do that unless you want extra bulk. You can gain strength without size by lowering weights easily. Just let them down (Sternlight 67).

George Underwood's style is lively. His sentences are long, but broken up by a variety of strong pauses. His syllable/word ratio, 1.5/1, would be much lower without the technical terms he includes: "concentric," "eccentric contractions," "negatives." The rest of his language is commendably plain. His breath units tend to be short. The longest, "Even though you're often told to lower weights slowly and keep muscles under stress to get maximum benefit," is offset by many brief ones: "think positive," "Translation," "are more important." His sentences start and stop like a telegraph: "Translation: | when your training emphasizes only the concentric, | or positive phase of the exercise | -- actually lifting the weight-- | muscle growth is minimal." Unlike most writers, who need short breath units to provide a change of pace, Underwood depends on longer ones for variety.

From Annie Dillard's Memories of Her First Lighted Microscope

I burnt out or broke my little five-watt bulb right away. To replace it, I rigged an old table lamp laid on its side; the table lamp carried a seventy-five watt bulb. I was about twelve, immortal and invulnerable, and did not know what I was doing; neither did anyone else. My parents let me set up my laboratory in the basement, where they wouldn't have to smell the urine I collected in test tubes and kept in the vain hope it would grow something horrible. So in full, solitary ignorance I spent evenings in the basement staring into a seventy-five-watt bulb magnified three hundred times and focused into my eye. It is a wonder I can see at all.

Dillard's sentence structure is simple. If we count her semicolons as equivalent to periods, there are 8 sentences in the passage with only one **dependent clause**. Her diction is plain, with a syllable/word ratio of 1.4/1 and a near absence of learned diction. This makes the exceptional phrases "immortal and invulnerable" and "solitary ignorance," more effective when they appear. The sentences average 15.5 words. But averages can deceive. Dillard's first five independent clauses and the final one total 62 words, for a ratio of only 12.4 words per sentence. The two longer sentences total 35 and 27 words respectively. These large differences in sentence length are echoed in the breath units, which go from short ("to replace it") to long-enough-to-be-risky ("where they wouldn't have to smell the urine I collected in test tubes and kept in the vain hope it would grow something horrible"). The result is a complex word music that is a major factor in Dillard's reputation as a stylist.

From an Explanation of the Way Rivers Shape Themselves

An initial diversion of the stream's course may be the result of a change in gradient, with the stream encountering enough of an upgrade that it seeks a lower bed line around the obstacle. But the stream's tendency is to increase the diversion. As soon as the stream changes direction, the water on the outside of the curve speeds up, and that on the inside slows down—for the same reason you need a differential in your car's rear axle. The slowly moving water on the inside of the curve can no longer carry as much sediment, and drops its particulate load; sand and silt bars always form on the inside of a curve in a stream. The faster water on the outside of the curve carries more abrasive material with more force, and therefore carves out the outside stream bank and carries those carvings away. Curves grow. Curves also migrate downstream by the same process. On a flat, as at a river delta or terminal moraine, a stream will silt up its bed so badly as it slows that it will eventually seek new routes, leaving a braided effect of intertwined abandoned channels. Often it will cut off and abandon an entire curve, forming the familiar oxbow lake. You can spot such lakes on the map of just about any area that includes a flood plain or tidal plain.

The author, John Jerome, writes sentences up to 38 words long. Counting the semicolon after "particulate load" the same as a period, his eleven sentences average 21 words each, yet what he is saying seems to require this complexity. It's hard to imagine the topic being made more clear any other way. Jerome keeps his diction as simple as possible. Though he's forced to use assorted technical terms, his syllable/word ratio of 1.4/1 is the same as Annie Dillard's. His voice is different, though. His longer sentences and Latinate terms—"initial diversion," "particulate," "terminal moraine"—make him sound less personal, more businesslike. But while Jerome's voice is less inclined to fun than Dillard's, it certainly isn't dead. Notice the emphatically brief sentence, "Curves grow." Jerome is listening to his own voice as he writes and knows we need a change of pace. That sentence lights up the whole passage. In his way Jerome is as concerned as Dillard with word music. Halfway through the passage he puts an unnecessary comma after "carry as much sediment" to make us pause where we ordinarily wouldn't. He was worried that the breath unit would be too long without a pause.

From a Software Manual

There is no need to schedule a meeting in advance with Acrobat Connect. You can invite someone to a meeting on the spot, or at a specific time, by simply communicating your meeting URL. For example, you can paste the URL in an instant message or send it in an e-mail invitation. When you are logged in to your meeting room and an attendee uses the URL to access it, you are notified immediately and must accept or deny the request to enter your room. (Attendees cannot access the room unless you are there.)

Who says committees can't write? This little description was produced by some combination of computer experts for Adobe's Acrobat program. It's nicely done. The five sentences show an intelligent mix of sentence structures. The syllable/word ratio is a moderate 1.5/1, and none of the terminology is difficult. The rhythm of the piece varies pleasingly, with short breath units like "For example," set off against longer ones like "you are notified immediately and must accept or deny the request to enter your room." The writers realize they are using the word "room" in a special sense, as the name for a website where several users can view the same images on their screens and interact with each other, so they repeat the term three times, hoping to help it stick. They guess, too, that the room's "owner" might be a bit nervous about other people accessing things on his or her computer. So they provide a final piece of reassurance: ("Attendees cannot access the room unless you are there.")

From "The World's Biggest Membrane"

Viewed from the distance of the moon, the astonishing thing about the earth, catching the breath, is that it is alive. The photographs show the dry, pounded surface of the moon in the foreground, dead as an old bone. Aloft, floating free beneath the moist, gleaming membrane of bright blue sky, is the rising earth, the only exuberant thing in this part of the cosmos. If you could look long enough, you would see the swirling of the great drifts of white cloud, covering and uncovering the half-hidden masses of land.

This passage from Lewis Thomas's *The Lives of a Cell* is relatively ornate, but even here, in the heartfelt opening of a luminous essay, Thomas keeps his style under control. His sentences average 23 words, about the same as John Jerome's. His syllable to word ratio is 1.34/1, the lowest of any writer in this gallery. Much of Thomas's power comes from his rhythms. His first 11 breath units average 6.5 syllables each compared to 12.5 for the last 4, driving the passage along to a crescendo at the end.

Thomas's writing is visual and lively. He plays off the moon—"dead as an old bone"—against the "floating," "moist," "gleaming," "rising" earth beneath its membrane of "swirling" sky. These *-ing* verb forms add visual details, but they name actions as well—two effects for the price of one. The unexpected words *exuberant* and *cosmos* also stand out. While exuberant means "joyful and boisterous" in English, its Latin ancestors had more to do with abundance and fertility—fit associations for the life-supporting Earth. *Kosmos* was a common term in Greek philosophy, where it indicated not just the universe, but the beauty and order of the world. As Thomas probably knew, the word *cosmetic* comes from the same root.

EXERCISE 10

Which of these voices—Brown's, Underwood's, Dillard's, Jerome's, the software manual's, Thomas's—would best suit the following writing situations?

An instruction booklet to accompany a microwave oven
A how-to article for *Seventeen* or *Popular Mechanics*
A report on erosion and farming in Nebraska
An essay on spouse abuse in your town
An inspirational think piece on global warming

EXERCISE 11

Write the first sentence of each of these hypothetical essays, thinking about appropriate sentence structure, diction, and word music.

Your Writing

Choose a piece of your own writing, preferably one you completed before beginning this book. Write a point-by-point discussion of your written voice in the piece, analyzing its grammar, diction, and sound qualities. Include syllable/word and syllable/breath unit ratios of a sample passage in your analysis. Did your writing avoid discriminatory language? How would you describe your own written voice in the piece you've analyzed? Why was or wasn't it appropriate for the writing situation?

◇◇

POINTS TO REMEMBER

1. The sound qualities—breath units and emphasis—of your sentences affect their rhythms and clarity.
2. Readers will register and react to the complexity or simplicity of your sentence structure.
3. The formality or informality of your diction has a major effect on your style.
4. All these elements should be appropriate to the writing situation.
5. You should take special pains to avoid discriminatory language.

◇◇

CHAPTER 2

Voices That Put You Off
Common Modes of Bad Writing

While no one sets out to write badly, bad writing is as common as pocket lint. Strangely, although much of it is simply careless, nearly as much is learned—one form or another of **overwriting**. Overwriters think they are doing fine, even when the results are awful, in some cases, especially when the results are awful. They are proud of every sin they commit. Other bad writers just don't listen to themselves putting readers to sleep with monotonous **breath units** or setting their teeth on edge with ugly, grating prose. If you recognize yourself in the examples that follow, don't be discouraged. The toughest step toward improving your writing may be seeing that something is wrong in the first place. Once you've made that breakthrough, correcting your style is just a matter of practice and determination.

The Professional Terror

Actuaries, accountants, bureaucrats, doctors, lawyers, ministers, professors—professionals in general churn out mountains of bad writing, and many of them delight in it. You hear the self-satisfaction in their voices. Fuzzy, inflated "professional" styles are the number one writing problem in agencies, offices, clinics, and schools. Consider this university memo quoted in Richard Lanham's excellent guide, *Style: An Anti-Textbook*:

> The Task Force is also concerned that it provide the basis for the faculty of this campus to govern itself, rather than being governed by others less understanding of the nature of the

University. Consequently, we are asking you to specify the methods you use to evaluate the effectiveness of your instruction. Likewise, we are seeking your views on the function of evaluation and your suggestions for the implementation of evaluation of instruction on a campus-wide basis. This information will greatly contribute to our recommendations regarding the best possible methods for evaluation of instruction which will at the same time be most acceptable to the greatest number of faculty possible, keeping in mind that diverse forms of evaluation will probably be called for in the face of the diverse functions and characteristics of this institution.

The passage displays fairly complicated **sentence structure** and **Latinate diction**. While its **syllable/word ratio**, 1.75/1, is not outrageously high, its rhythms are atrocious. The breath units leave you wheezing. Only the first two are under 30 syllables, while the longest ("This information will greatly contribute to our recommendations regarding the best possible methods for evaluation of instruction which will at the same time be most acceptable to the greatest number of faculty possible") weighs in at 62. Unless you pause after "Consequently" and "Likewise," there are no short breath units.

Another way of seeing what is wrong with the passage is to realize that everything it says could be said better in a fraction of the space:

We want the faculty to govern itself rather than be governed by others who know less about the nature of the university. How do you evaluate your own teaching? What ideas do you have for making campus-wide evaluation accurate and acceptable to the faculty? In replying please remember that different forms of evaluation may be needed for different areas of the university.

The second version is 62 words, about half the length of the first, yet it includes all the important ideas of the original and is much easier to read.

Putting things briefly when you can and smoothing the way for your readers are hallmarks of good writing. The original memo doesn't try to do either. The writer would rather sound "professional" than communicate effectively. Does the original memo sound professional? In the sense that it could not have been written by anyone but an educational bureaucrat, maybe so. But that doesn't mean it's acceptable to anyone but the proud author. It's still a pain to read. No one looking at the second

version by itself would think it was inappropriate for the writing situation, and everyone would agree it's more efficient and crisp.[1]

EXERCISE 1

Rewrite the following passages so they are only half as long and easier
to read. Change the sentence structure however you like, but include
the essential content of the original. At times you may have to guess
what the writer meant. How do your revisions change the writer's voice?
You'll find a sample answer on the *Understanding Style* website.

1. Taking up a position in near proximity to a radio or similar
   device may significantly improve reception inasmuch as
   degraded radio waves dispersed by reflective surfaces in a
   typical room or enclosure are regularly present in sufficient
   quantity to noticeably degrade signal quality. A body adjacent
   to the reception device acts in effect as a filter to absorb randomly dispersed waves so that the signal selection mechanism
   can better distinguish the strong primary signal and reject the
   diminished number of weaker reflective signals. (83 words)

2. Although environmental activists and scholars, who might
   be termed the environmentally concerned community, have
   evidenced a longstanding commitment to ongoing conflict
   with resource-based industries in the interest of maximizing
   the quality of the environment, it now appears that natural
   resources, especially in the Eastern United States, have
   rebounded sufficiently from serious lows in the past to make
   resumption of some forms of environmentally taxing economic
   activity not only desirable but innocuous. (71 words)

3. Assuming a flat-tax rate of seventeen percent, substantially
   below the current maximal rate of approximately forty percent—coupled with simultaneous cessation of current taxes
   levied and collected on income derived from dividends, interest,

---

[1] In professional writing, it is important to distinguish between your own and other people's styles. By all means make your own style as accessible to readers as you can, given
the situation. They'll appreciate it. But if you work with colleagues or bosses who write
like the memo writer above, critique their styles as you would their children: only when
they ask you to and circumspectly even then. Remember that professional overwriting is
learned behavior and people are often proud of it. You don't want colleagues getting angry
with you for telling them how to write, even if it's clear that someone should.

and capital gains—and also concomitant radical enlargement of basic exemptions from taxation that would effectively render many low-income families tax-free, governmental discretionary and other income appears certain to decrease while the proportionate burden of taxation on middle-tier earners and households appears certain to increase. (78 words)

The memo about teacher evaluation and the examples in the last exercise illustrate, to adopt their own style, a generalized syndrome of dysfunctional verbal obfuscation (all-purpose bumfuzzlement); but much overwriting may more accurately be characterized or classified as essentially discipline-specific. (See how hard it is to stop writing this way once you get started?) Anthropology, computer science, economics, medicine—all have their own leaden tricks of style, which people who master them find irresistible, even artistically satisfying. Many of these are matters of **jargon**, or the specialized vocabularies of various interests. For instance, students of education rarely say *test*. They prefer *assessment*, as in "educational outcomes assessment." Psychologists don't change how people act; they engage in *behavior modification*. When you add in **doublespeak**, pompous language with little meaning, and **euphemism**, or substituting a mild-sounding expression for a more direct one, the possibilities for miscommunication are endless. For years, sociologists took the cake as the worst writers among the learned professions. It takes only a sentence or two from Talcott Parsons, a sociologist legendary for his brain bruising style, to see why:

The mere fact of the presence of certain genes in the gene pool of a species is not a sufficient determinant of their role in the generation of phenotypical organisms. For this to occur, there must be integration of the genetically given patterning with a series of exigencies defined by the nature of the species' life in its environment.

Meaning? Some genes never modify a species because the changes they trigger aren't suited to the animals' environment.

Lately, other disciplines have challenged sociology for the soggy palm. Here is a random sampling from works in several fields:

Management and Information Services

In MCDM [Multiple Criteria Decision Making] we always talk about choosing among nondominated solutions, solutions from which we can improve one objective only by allowing at least one other objective to deteriorate. Even though under certainty with all objectives expressed and measured correctly, we do want nondominated solutions, we may not want this in practice. We may not have all objectives expressed.

STANLEY ZIONTS, *Multiple Criteria Decision Making: The Challenge That Lies Ahead*

Social Work

Much can and has been learned from studying individual families who are in at-risk situations. The primary function of this chapter is to explore the individual family situations of at-risk parents and children, and to share particular insights on how early childhood professionals attempted to engage in empowering relationships with them.

KEVIN J. SWICK AND STEPHEN B GRAVES, *Empowering At-risk Families during the Early Childhood Years*

Physical Education

A dominant factor in the American way of life is the ability of the average citizen to know about and understand sports, if not as a participant, then as a spectator. Therefore, it is beneficial to learn the rules and strategies of various sports. In addition, knowledge of etiquette, safety, equipment, history, values, techniques, and other factors can enhance the enjoyment of watching or participating in team, dual, or individual activities.

DALE MOOD, FRANK F. MUSKER, AND JUDITH E. RINK, *Sports and Recreational Activities*

English [!]

Given the dominance of logocentrism at the time, is it appropriate to analyze Renaissance works by applying the conclusions of deconstruction, which dictates an ontology opposed to logocentrism. As we have just seen, logocentrism posits an objective reality identified as an unalterable, immaterial realm of absolute being and described as a nonpalpable system of numbers/forms/ideas in the mind of deity. In opposition, poststructuralist thought pushes us beyond skepticism and relativism, arriving at a subjectivism that annihilates all else.

S.K. HENINGER, JR. *The Subtext of Form in the English Renaissance*

The writers of all these passages are intelligent people with at least a little something to say, but they trip over their tongues. Why? Probably because they feared they wouldn't sound sufficiently impressive if they wrote plainly or because they thought this sort of writing was required for their professional fields. Unfortunately, they may be partly right about professional expectations. But even in a field largely mired in stuffy writing, you still can be as clear and efficient as possible. For instance, consider this passage from the brochure for a "Team Building Workshop":

> Teams that function at an exceptionally high performance level get there by each team member being an integral part of the team, which is demonstrated by the active involvement of each team member and a commitment to be the best the team can be.

Would this really sound less professional if you let some of the air out of it?

> All members of exceptionally effective teams must be involved and committed to the team's success.

Of course, once you clarify the writer's claim to this extent, you may also notice that it applies just as well to exceptionally poor teams that happen to have enthusiastic members.

EXERCISE 2

Rewrite the social work and physical education passages from the last group of examples so they are only half as long and easier to read. Change the sentence structure however you like, but include the essential content of the original. How do your revisions change the writer's voice? You'll find a sample answer on the *Understanding Style* website.

EXERCISE 3

Find a passage of jargon and pretentious diction from a memo, web site, or textbook. Rewrite it so that it is only half as long and easier to read. How do your revisions change the writer's voice?

EXERCISE 4

Rewrite the following passages in the most overblown pompous style you can invent. Pretend you're a distinguished professor, a CEO, a brain surgeon, or a bishop. Use a thesaurus. You'll find a sample answer on the *Understanding Style* website.

1. You must remember this,
   A kiss is still a kiss,
   A sigh is just a sigh;
   The fundamental things apply,
   As time goes by.

   HERMAN HUPFELD, *As Time Goes By*

2. The growing good of the world is partly dependent on unhistoric acts; and that things are not so ill with you and me as they might have been, is half owing to the number who lived faithfully a hidden life, and rest in unvisited tombs.

   GEORGE ELIOT, *Middlemarch*

3. We say the cows laid out Boston. Well, there are worse surveyors.

   EMERSON, *Worship*

The Creative Genius

In recent years, a detail-laden descriptive style has found favor with some writing teachers and workshops. More often than not it's a formula for bad writing: Be dramatic! Specify every detail as narrowly as possible! Load up on adjectives and modifiers! String each sentence out to include more insights!

> Across the room sat Aunt Marney, her care-worn, calloused hands crossed in her denim-aproned lap with a resignation born of half a century of stubborn toil on the ungrateful land, her head inclined at a weary, humble angle above a wrinkled breast once fruitful with milk for her abundant, rosy, clamoring offspring, now dry and barren as the untilled acres that surrounded her ramshackle, unpainted shanty. (66 words)

If you write this way, don't show Aunt Marney what you said about her. She'd take her care-worn, calloused hands and wring your neck. How to avoid such a style? View modifiers with suspicion, especially doubled and hyphenated modifiers ("care-worn, calloused," "denim-aproned"). And once a sentence is grammatically complete ("Across the room sat

Aunt Marney") escape from it with decent haste. Don't let it drag on through half a page of piled-on details.

The creative genius way of writing is another case in which the writer puts style before communication. Details and sense impressions that might be effective in their place become annoying distractions elsewhere:

> Psychologists (my cousin Beth, for example) often note that people in unsettling, unfamiliar situations—their breathing restricted, palms sticky with nervous perspiration—look around almost feverishly in their churning anxiety to see how others are behaving in order to match their own actions to those of others in a return to the warm, comforting conformity of the herd. (58 words)

It's hard to imagine where such a combination of objectivity (Psychologists . . . note) and sticky perspiration would be effective, but it would never do in a psychology class or any professional setting.

EXERCISE 5

Rewrite the Aunt Marney, and psychology passages so they are only half as long, less overwrought, and easier to read. Change the sentence structure however you like, but include all the essential content of the original. How do your revisions change the writer's voice? You'll find a sample answer on the *Understanding Style* website.

EXERCISE 6

Rewrite the following passages in the most overheated style you can invent. Pretend you're a creative genius of great sympathy and compassion. Use a thesaurus. You'll find a sample answer on the *Understanding Style* website.

1. In most of mankind gratitude is merely a secret hope for greater favors.

   LA ROCHEFOUCAULD, *Maximes*

2. I opened the door, to find a four-foot black snake hanging from a pipe. I'm not much frightened of snakes but I religiously believe in their right to privacy.

   RITA MAE BROWN, *Ariadne's Thread*

3. Time flies like an arrow. Fruit flies like a banana.

   GROUCHO MARX

The Sleepwalker

Sleepwalkers are the opposite end of the spectrum from creative geniuses. Perhaps someone told them to be detached and impersonal; perhaps they never learned to use a variety of sentence structures and rhythms; perhaps their metabolism is just low. Whatever the reason, everything they write is flat as Houston. They aren't pretentious. They aren't overdramatic. Just dull.

> Remembering dead people we have known reminds us of who we are. They also make us remember that we will die one day as well, which is a fact human beings generally forget whenever possible. This has been remarked on by many writers and thinkers like the French author Montaigne.

It's hard to pinpoint the problem with this bloodless passage. Its sentence structure is straightforward. Its diction is fine, if not memorable (syllables/words = 1.5/1). The best indication of what is wrong may be the breath units, which measure 17, 15, 20, and 21 syllables long, to create an unvarying rhythm not suited to the subject. While death and dying are emotional topics, the written voice just plods along at the same dispirited pace. Look how another writer handles this material:

> It is the dead who tell us who we are, not just as individuals (though that too) but as a species of animals that needs reminding. They tell us constantly that life is a rough place and nobody gets out of it alive. Or as Montaigne put it, "Live as long as you please, you will strike nothing off the time you will have to spend dead."
>
> CHRISTOPHER CLAUSEN, *Dialogues with the Dead*

Clausen's treatment gains by its word music. His breath units measure 10, 8, 3, 13, 21, 6, 6, and 14 syllables long, so the voice slows and accelerates, adding interest and variety to the passage. He also creates a nice contrast between Latinate diction ("individuals," "species," "animals") and colloquial words ("life is a rough place," "nobody"). Instead of just mentioning Montaigne, Clausen gives us his words, which—as always—are memorable. Finally there is the matter of emphasis, which usually falls on the last significant word in each sentence or breath unit. The words emphasized in the first version of the passage (**ARE, WELL, POS**sible, Mon**TAIGNE**) aren't clearly related to each other or to the topic. Clausen's set of emphasized words is much more relevant and expressive (**ARE**, indi**VID**uals, **THAT**, re**MIND**ing, a**LIVE**, Mon**TAIGNE**, **PLEASE**, **DEAD**).

Differences between sleepwalking and wide-awake writers aren't always this dramatic, but they are always significant. Here's a stubbornly insipid treatment of a subject that needs all the help it can get, computer programming:

> The computer language C is smaller than several others. It depends on a large runtime library for many operations. The runtime library consists of object files containing machine instructions for functions for a wide variety of services. The functions are divided into a number of groups. Each group depends on a source file containing instructions necessary to use the relevant function. These header files have names that end in the extension *.h*. The standard group of input and output functions is linked to a header file called *stdio.h*.

Not all bad. But *dull*. The breath units go 14, 17, 33, 14, 26, 13, and 23, a string in which the only real variety is provided by the too-long 33 syllable unit, "The runtime library consists of object files containing machine instructions for functions for a wide variety of services." The grammar is repetitious. There's no attempt to vary the diction. The writer's voice would bore a cow. Imagine the whole piece from which it might have been taken!

Here's the same content handled by a couple of writers actively trying to keep readers interested in what they are saying:

> One of the reasons C is such a small language is that it defers many operations to a large runtime library. The runtime library is a collection of object files. Each file contains the machine instructions for a function that performs one of a wide variety of services. The functions are divided into groups, such as I/O (Input and Output), memory management, mathematical operations, and string manipulation. For each group there is a source file, called a *header file*, that contains information you need to use these functions. By convention, the names for header files end with a *.h* extension. For example, the standard group of I/O functions has an associated header file called *stdio.h*.
>
> PETER A. DARNELL AND PHILIP E MARGOLIS,
C: A Software Engineering Approach

In my reading the breath units in this version run 12, 19, 15, 28, 10, 4, 5, 6, 9, 7, 8, 5, 14, 4, 13, 4, 24, providing welcome variety, a lot of which arises from a more complicated grammatical scheme. This passage has 3 subordinate *that* clauses to break up the other one's monotonous succession of **simple sentences**. Further variety comes from the **parallel series** "such as I/O (Input and Output), memory management, mathematical operations, and string manipulation," which also helps the reader understand what is meant by reducing it to specific examples. The slightly unexpected **verb** *defers* in the first sentence and the authors' decision to address readers directly as "you" are two more touches that make their writing more interesting and accessible. All in all, the second passage invites us into the subject, while the first says, "Take it or leave it." The techniques that make Clausen's and Darnell and Margolis' writing sparkle by comparison with the flatter version are detailed in the chapters that follow, but just as important is the approach they take to writing: they're thinking of readers, not just content. *"How can we keep people on their toes, interested, even moderately entertained?"* They know their success as writers depends on meeting this challenge in sentence after sentence.

EXERCISE 7

What differences in rhythm, diction, and emphasis make the second passage in each of the following pairs more lively than the first?

1. Science has a tendency to give naturalistic and verifiable answers to questions posed by religions. When scientific hypotheses are accepted some religious explanations may have to be abandoned.

    Extinguished theologians lie about the cradle of every science as the strangled snakes beside that of Hercules.

    T.H. HUXLEY, *Darwiniana*

2. Artists must please themselves first and take it on faith that what pleases them will please someone else as well.

    I personally make music because I want to ask a question, and I want to get an answer. If that question and answer amuse me, then statistically, there are a certain number of other people out there who will be amused by it, and we will all have a good time.

    FRANK ZAPPA, *On 'Junk Food for the Soul'*

3. People who are outside the mainstream often behave energetically and entertain others, but sometimes they feel alienated and lost on the inside.

> I was much too far out all my life
> And not waving but drowning.
>
> STEVIE SMITH, *Not Waving but Drowning*

EXERCISE 8

Rewrite the following passages to relieve the tedium. Vary the length of the breath units so that some are at least twice as long as others. Experiment with colloquial and formal diction. Try to make emphasis fall on expressive, relevant words. Change the sentence structure however you like, but include the essential content of the original. How do your revisions change the writer's voice? You'll find a sample answer on the *Understanding Style* website.

1. The SS doctor Josef Mengele came to Auschwitz after being wounded on the Russian Front. At Auschwitz, Mengele selected prisoners to be sent to the gas chambers at regular intervals. Among the prisoners he excused from death by asphyxiation were sets of twins he reserved for medical research. Mengele performed a number of medical experiments on these twins to determine what characteristics were inherited. His experiments on the twins included inoculating them with diseases and dissecting them after he had them killed.

2. E.H. Carr was a historian at Cambridge University who was one of the first to ask, "What is history?" Carr thought it was not good enough to say that history is the record of what had happened in the past. He pointed out that most of what happened never gets into history books and what does is interpreted by historians in the act of writing the books. So history is more what goes on in the minds of historians studying the past than it is the past itself.

3. *America 101* concerns two brothers from a small Mexican town. They decide to cross the border and live the "American Dream," but what they get is not at all what they expected. They are double-crossed by a smuggler and abandoned in the desert. Then they make their way to Tucson to support themselves as day-laborers. They wind up sleeping in parks and living as social outcasts.

The Clunker

A tribe related to the sleepwalkers, writers with tin ears are deaf not only to rhythm, but to everything else, producing sentences that are not just monotonous but downright ugly:

> One function of examination coordination would be the implementation of a revision of the examination schedule to guarantee that examiners scheduled for the same examination were free at the hour the examination was scheduled.

Besides gracelessly repeating whole words (*examination, schedule*), this sentence is hobbled by other unintended repetition of sounds (*function* of examina*tion* coordina*tion*...implementa*tion* of a revi*sion* of the examina*tion*). It grates like a rusty hinge, and moves about as briskly, too. Fixing the sentence requires editing out the repetition and breathing a little life into its rhythm:

Coordinating the examination schedule will mean assigning new times. That way we can guarantee all examiners will be free when needed.

The worst offender when it comes to making ugly sentences is the **suffix** *-tion* or *-sion*. Because it converts verbs into **Latinate** nouns, *-tion* causes other stylistic problems as well. But the beginnings of words and internal syllables can also chime against a writer's intentions:

Next, let's in*spect* the *specter* of deregulation in the private *sector*.

The best defense against tin ear is to read your sentences over to yourself silently or aloud, listening carefully to the way they sound. If you have to twist your tongue around the syllables (in*spect* the *spect*er), revise.

Listening to your own prose is not easy at first. Sometimes it helps to record yourself reading what you've written. Another trick is to analyze sentences in a well edited magazine like *Harper's* or *Atlantic Monthly*. Forget the meaning and think about sentence structure, diction, and long and short breath units. Try making good sentences monotonous and ugly. You'll soon grow sensitive to the difference.

EXERCISE 9

What sound problems make the first passage in each of the following pairs sound awkward compared to the original?

1. The declination of each declivity shall be decreased.
   Every valley shall be exalted.

                                                    Isaiah 40:4[2]

2. There's a pervading crusading spirit masquerading as an unfad-
   ing moral superiority and parading its values in a way that is
   grating and degrading.
   Judge not, that you be not judged.

                                                    Matthew 7:1

3. Now the reptile had guile and beat the other beasts by a mile in
   wile.
   Now the serpent was more subtle than any beast of the field.

                                                    Genesis 3:1

EXERCISE 10

Rewrite the following passages to make them sound better. If necessary, vary the length of the breath units so that some are at least twice
as long as others. Eliminate awkward repetition of sounds. Change the
sentence structure however you like, but include the essential content of
the original. How do your revisions change the writer's voice? You'll
find a sample answer on the *Understanding Style* website.

1. Even in the 1950s we had the chemical capacity to make new
   chemicals and distribute old chemicals like never before. We
   could put more of the chemical sulfur dioxide which produces
   sulfuric acid and acid rain in the air than volcanoes do, at a
   great cost to acid-sensitive plants.

2. You know I was clueless until you clued me in to your conclusions on how concussions can contribute to delusions,

3. While paroxysmal trachycardia, or abnormal accelerated
   heartbeat, is rarely fatal, fatalities can be expected if heartbeat
   accelerates to fatal levels.

---

[2] More than any other single work, the "Authorized" or "King James" version of the
Bible established how standard English prose should sound—in general, simple, plain,
and direct.

EXERCISE 11

Rewrite the following passages to make them sound monotonous or ugly. Monotony results from a series of breath units of roughly the same length, usually 15–25 syllables. Ugliness most often means awkward repetition of sounds. Change the sentence structure however you like, but include the essential content of the original. How do your revisions change the writer's voice? You'll find a sample answer on the *Understanding Style* website.

1. I have learned
   To look on nature, not as in the hour
   Of thoughtless youth; but hearing often-times
   The still, sad music of humanity,
   Nor harsh nor grating, though of ample power
   To chasten and subdue.

   WILLIAM WORDSWORTH, *Tintern Abbey*

2. Later that night I loosed my hair from its braids and combed it smooth—not for myself, but so the village girls could play with it in the morning.

   ANNIE DILLARD, *Teaching a Stone to Talk*

3. I've learned that you shouldn't go through life with a catcher's mitt on both hands; you need to be able to throw something back.

   MAYA ANGELOU

Your Writing

Scan a recent piece of your writing for the traits discussed in this chapter. Is the style too complicated? (Syllable/word ratios over 2 or syllable/breath unit ratios over 25 are danger signs.) Is it over-excited? (Watch for doubled or hyphenated modifiers.) Is it dull? (Too many breath units of the same length are likely culprits.) Is it ugly? (Look for unintentional chiming: "Philistine philanderer Phil.") Any of these traits you find may indicate tendencies you need to guard against.

◇◇

POINTS TO REMEMBER

1. Don't put style before substance by trying to sound overly learned or overly creative.
2. Listen to what you've written, if only with your inner ear, to make sure it avoids monotony and places emphasis effectively.
3. Watch out for unintended repetition of words and sounds that can make your sentences ugly.

◇◇

CHAPTER 3

Two Common Problems
Overwriting and Underwriting

While later chapters of this book go into detail about how to craft effective sentences, two general problems of style deserve separate treatment here. Even before you think of subjects like diction and emphasis, you may achieve a quick and substantial improvement by learning not to write too much or too little. Writing too much means including unnecessary words, empty phrases, self-conscious asides, or pointless explanations. Writing too little means overly simple, repetitious sentence structure and the unfortunate defects that go with it: disconnected ideas and stark, monotonous rhythms.

Eliminating Deadwood

The term *deadwood* covers hundreds of needless words and constructions that weigh writing down, clogging its arteries, blocking its communicative force, overwhelming its vitality. Deadwood bloats prose, making it puffy and shapeless. To see what I mean, look at the opening sentence of this paragraph:

> The term *deadwood* covers hundreds of needless words and constructions that weigh writing down, clogging its arteries, blocking its communicative force, overwhelming its vitality.

Like many sentences infested with deadwood, this one gets into trouble by trying too hard. The extra words and phrases muffle the point rather than drive it home as they were meant to. The sentence needs pruning. Why specify that *deadwood* is a term? "Hundreds of" adds nothing. The "clogging," "blocking," and "overwhelming" phrases all say the same thing. Excising this deadwood produces a leaner, cleaner statement, 13 words in place of 24:

> *Deadwood* means needless words and constructions that weigh writing down, clogging its arteries.

In his book *On Writing Well*, William Zinsser, a fierce enemy of deadwood, estimates that most first drafts should be cut by 50 percent. Zinsser knows. He is amazed how much he finds to eliminate from his own writing even after four or five rewrites. For Zinsser, rewriting largely *means* cutting deadwood. He recommends bracketing deadwood in your writing in order to become sensitive to the problem. A passage Zinsserized to highlight unneeded words and phrases might look like this:

> In [*the disastrous spring of*] 1993, [*the Midwest United States experienced one of the greatest natural disasters in United States history. Before conditions improved in the fall of that year,*] 17 million acres of [*productive*] farmland went [*out of production*] under a sheet of floodwater. [*Crop damage and safety were the main concerns.*] An overlooked problem, [*however,*] was [*an increase in*] Zebra mussels in the Illinois River. [*Zebra mussels are*] an aquatic life form like oysters or clams, but smaller. Zebra mussels [*originated in Europe. They came to America on the bottoms of ships bound for the Great Lakes. Until*] recently [*they*] were restricted to the Great Lakes [*and their estuaries*]. Now they can be found much further south in concentrations of a half a million or more. (128 words)

Clearing away the bracketed words and phrases cuts the passage in half:

> In 1993, 17 million acres of Midwest farmland went under a sheet of floodwater. An overlooked problem was Zebra mussels in the Illinois River. An aquatic life form like oysters or clams, but smaller, Zebra mussels recently were restricted to the Great Lakes. Now they can be found much further south in concentrations of a half a million or more. (60 words)

Once you've cut to this level, you often see other ways to save words, usually by juggling **sentence structure** and reducing wasteful phrases like "went under a sheet of floodwater" to one or two words:

> In 1993, 17 million acres of Midwest farmland flooded, releasing Zebra mussels into the Illinois River. Zebra mussels, which resemble small clams, were recently restricted to the Great Lakes. Now they can be found much further south in concentrations of a half a million or more. (46 words)

Now the first draft has been reduced by 65 percent. Free of verbal undergrowth, the remaining ideas stand distinct and clear.

How Much Cutting Is Enough?

A purposeful prose pruner can always find more to cut. The Appalachian writer James Still said his publishers once accused him of trying to eliminate every word in a piece he'd written. Each time they sent back a final version, he'd cut some more. When should you stop cutting? The 50 percent rule is a rough guide. When you've reduced a draft by that much you've probably got most of the deadwood out. Another sign is trade-offs. When cuts begin to affect your style and meaning in ways you're not sure are good, you're cutting muscle, not fat.

Look back at the last version of the Zebra mussels passage. You could combine a bit more, drop another detail or two, and save a few more words:

> In spring 1993, 17 million acres of Midwest farmland flooded, releasing Zebra mussels into the Illinois River. Zebra mussels, which were recently restricted to the Great Lakes, can now be found much further south in concentrations of a over half a million. (42 words)

But these changes cost you the physical description of Zebra mussels and the **emphasis** earlier attached to "Great Lakes" as the last significant word in its sentence. You may not find these compromises worth making to save four words. When you find yourself shaving off only one or two words a sentence and even that changes your meaning, you are getting close to the bone. Your own writing may be the most useful guide of all. Keep a "Zinsserized" first draft of your own on hand. Highlight the bracketed material in a bright color to show at a glance how much deadwood you eliminated. You now have a personalized template showing how much you can expect to cut from future first drafts to achieve an efficient style.

Cutting deadwood out of your writing is hard, demanding work. But it pays. Someone has to put out the mental effort it takes to decide which of the words in your first drafts are wasted. When you cut these words yourself, your readers no longer have to filter them out as they read. A one-page memo becomes a sharply focused half a page; a 20-page proposal is transformed into an efficient ten pages. Your ideas will be clearer and get a more sympathetic hearing.

EXERCISE 1

Rank the following passages from most to least efficiently written on the basis of the amount of deadwood in each. How does deadwood in a passage affect the writer's voice?

1. Bosnia still mourns 68 people killed by a mortar shell in the Sarajevo marketplace in 1994. The bloody scene was televised world wide.

2. My paper is about the bombing in Bosnia in 1994. Sarajevo and the country at large still mourn the 68 people who were killed by the mortar shell that hit the town marketplace. The bloody scene was seen in television programs around the world.

3. I am writing to tell you about the bombing in Bosnia in 1994. It was terrible. Sarajevo and the rest of the country at large are still in deep mourning for the 68 people who were killed by an exploding mortar shell when it hit the teeming marketplace at the center of the town. The tragic, bloody scene went around the world in a series of television programs that projected the painful images for all to see.

EXERCISE 2

Bracket deadwood in the following passages. Then write out the passages without the bracketed words and phrases. As you do that, try to find further ways to save words and make the ideas even clearer. Change the sentence structure however you like, but include all the major ideas of the original. How many words did you save? How do your revisions change the writer's voice? You'll find a sample answer on the *Understanding Style* website.

1. Casinos bring with them the ability to lift poor towns out of poverty. They create an economy. They give the people of these communities something to look forward to. In many of these towns the economy is low, and no one works. When these casinos come in they offer jobs to these people. Although most of these casinos pay only minimum wage or slightly better, the steady employment they offer will transform people's lives. Casinos want to help the communities in any way they can. (85 words)

2. Those that feel that faith healing is faked are understandably infuriated by what they consider to be swindlers. These doubters, however, do not seem to be personally affected with any serious problems stemming from the faith healers' activities, unless of course they take up the hopeless task of trying to disprove that faith healing works as advertised. In this case, because of their beliefs against it they will lead a very frustrated life. After all, someone who believes in faith healing only has to prove one true healing took place. A person going against this particular view would have to disprove every case. (103 words)

3. The story of Hamlet and the murder of his father was not an especially well known tale to many people during the Elizabethan Period, or the reign of Queen Elizabeth. Although the story was available in one or two printed books to anyone who was able to read, cared to read it, and had access to the books in question, it was not often adapted into plays, narratives, or poems, or other popular forms of literature at the time. Moreover, the story existed as a bare, undeveloped plot outline without elaboration in the books in which it appeared, lacking the character development and complication, not only of Hamlet but of the other characters who appear in the story, that it achieves in Shakespeare's version. (124 words)

Varieties of Deadwood

While any word or construction might be deadwood in a given sentence, some phrases rate a red flag wherever they appear. A red flag, not an automatic hook. Each of the following categories produces a lot of the deadwood that often clogs a first draft. When you see words and phrases like these in your writing, weigh each one carefully. Does it make a necessary distinction? Will it really help readers follow your meaning? If so, keep it. If not, whack it out. You'll never miss it.

The examples below show kinds of constructions you should consider eliminating. The clichés discussed in Chapter 5 are also candidates for cutting. Many phrases listed here are highlighted by "grammar" programs for personal computers. If you're addicted to set phrases, one of these programs might help you purge them.

Verbal Filler

Cheap Cuts. Consider crossing out phrases like these wherever they appear.

> I'm considering ~~the area of~~ biotechnology.
> We regret ~~the fact that~~ you were inconvenienced. [your inconvenience]
> ~~It is interesting to note that~~ earlier vowel shifts had occurred.

Redundancies. Illogical repetition of the same idea in different words.

> The consensus ~~of opinion~~ favored soft ice cream.
> Our first ~~and foremost~~ thought was to avoid prosecution.
> Helena's ~~future~~ plans include graduate school.

Needless Complications. Usually a misguided effort to sound impressive.

> ~~At the present point in time~~ (now) we're at a loss.
> Yolanda declined ~~due to the fact that~~ (because) she had other commitments.
> Paula will serve ~~until such time as~~ (until) her appointment expires.

EXERCISE 3

Rewrite the following passages, removing set phrases and verbal padding. Change the sentence structure if you like, but include all the major ideas of the original. How many words did you save? How do your revisions change the writer's voice? You'll find a sample answer on the *Understanding Style* website.

1. Personally, I think Heath surely was one of the most if not the most outstanding alpine climbers in the area of unprotected traverses.

2. The firm's first and foremost future plan is to increase profits and lower dividends for the foreseeable future.

3. It is most interesting to note that the consensus of opinion was on the side of doing nothing until such time as all the evidence proves conclusively that our effluvia are maiming children at the present point in time.

EXERCISE 4

Rewrite the following passages, adding the kinds of constructions you took out of the last group. Try to double the length of each passage. Change the sentence structure however you like, but include all the major ideas of the original. How many words did you add? How do your revisions change the writer's voice? You'll find a sample answer on the *Understanding Style* website.

1. I want to celebrate the moment not long ago when, at his first dog show, my Airedale, Drummer, learned that there can be a public place where his work is respected.

   VIKI HEARNE, *What's Wrong with Animal Rights?*

2. When people look at how hard they would have to work to get rid of the calories in just one piece of pie a la mode (running fast for an hour or sawing wood for 2), not to mention what it takes to lose a pound (walking for 16 hours or swimming hard for 7), many sit down in self-defeat.

   JANE BRODY, *Jane Brody's Good Food Book*

3. Mami let go our hands and ran under the roof overhang, where water fell in a thick stream. She gave each of us a turn at being massaged by the torrent, which banged against our skinny bodies and bounced off in silver fans onto the ground.

   ESMERALDA SANTIAGO, *When I Was Puerto Rican*

Authorspeak

Some writers can't let well enough alone. They keep nipping at your heels, specifying every connection between ideas, heading off the most improbable misunderstandings, tugging at your feelings:

> **When considering first time marriage or remarriage at an advanced age, we must remember among other often unexpected consequences for the persons involved that** the combined income of the new couple may **unfortunately** put **one or both of** them over the limit for escaping taxation, **as we all would like to do,** on **social security and/or other** benefits.

The message? "When old people marry, previously untaxed benefits sometimes become taxable." But the writer doesn't trust you to grasp this by yourself. The language in boldface keeps trying to dictate your reactions. Some consequences of marrying when you are old are **unexpected** and **unfortunate**. The marriages in question could be **first time marriages or remarriages**; the benefits to be taxed could be **social security and/or other**. Surely we'd rather see these old delinquents escape taxes **as we all would like to do.** These are facts we should **remember** on those occasions **when we consider marriage at an advanced age**. It's difficult to get away from the helicoptering author long enough to see what is being said.

This leads to further categories of deadwood to weed out.

Intensifying Nudges. If surprise and strong feelings are not aroused by your subject, it won't help to say they are.

> The ~~heartbroken~~ dowager never recovered from the ~~tragic~~ curtailment of her intangibles tax exemption.
> ~~In an achingly poignant passage,~~ the author ~~stoically~~ recalls the death of his ~~cherished~~ rubber tree.

Backpedaling. Some writers feel it is poor taste to make an unqualified statement.

> ~~In a sense,~~ her figures ~~may~~ seem ~~at least somewhat~~ suspect to the auditors.
> ~~It could be argued that~~ assault rifles have no sporting use ~~by many definitions~~.

Unneeded Transitions. This is a ticklish subject. Beginning writers often fail to supply *enough* transitions:

> Many people feel guns in the home are dangerous. Most murders are committed by persons who have a history of violence (NRA, 1996). People don't just go "psycho" all of a sudden. Accidents are not all that common. Only 27 children met accidental deaths from firearms in 1991, many fewer than died from car wrecks (3,087) or fire (1,104) (Barnes, 1996).

These writers need to post more signs to guard readers against getting lost:

> **While** many people feel guns in the home are especially dangerous, most murders are committed by persons who have a history of violence (NRA, 1996). **Even in the home**, people don't just go "psycho" all of a sudden, **so in most houses guns do not provoke extra violence. Fears that guns in the home will kill or maim children seem equally exaggerated**. Only 27 children met accidental deaths from firearms in 1991, many fewer than died from car wrecks (3,087) or fire (1,104) (Barnes, 1996).

But it is also entirely possible to swing to the opposite extreme—transition overkill:

> **While** many people feel guns in the home are dangerous, **however**, most murders, **as a matter of fact**, are committed by persons who have a history of violence (NRA, 1996). **Even in the home, in other words**, people don't just go "psycho" all of a sudden, **so, to put the matter plainly, in most houses guns do not provoke extra violence per se. In like fashion, fears that guns in the home will kill or maim children seem equally exaggerated. For instance**, only 27 children met accidental deaths from firearms in 1991, **or, to put this statistic in context**, many fewer than died from car wrecks (3,087) or fire (1,104) (Barnes, 1996).

What you need is a happy medium, easier to recognize than to describe. As you edit ask yourself whether phrases like the following are really necessary. If they are, keep them; but you may discover many you can do without. Most readers can find their way through your arguments without constant prodding. Trust them.

~~In addition to voice coils~~, speakers need a mechanism to generate sound waves.
~~In conclusion it should be sufficient to note that~~ binge drinking is a growing problem even at high school ages.

As I've noted, some transitions, emotional intensifiers, and qualifications are necessary to prevent misunderstanding. If you really don't know whether guns in homes deter crime, it's best to say so: "It's at least possible that guns in homes deter crime." Be careful, too, about removing contrastive transitions like *but, however, on the other hand,* and *nevertheless.* These signal sharp breaks in your line of thought and are usually helpful to readers. See what happens when you leave out a needed *however*: "English setters weigh around sixty pounds; ~~however~~ English setters used in field trials average only thirty-five."

Still, few experienced writers need all the transitions, intensifiers, and qualifications they put in first drafts. When you edit, cut the suspect ones out.

EXERCISE 5

Rewrite the following passages, removing unnecessary transitions, intensifiers, and qualifications. How do your revisions change the writer's voice? You'll find a sample answer on the *Understanding Style* website.

1. We conclude, then, that lettuce, interestingly enough, is scandalously devoid of nutrients, at least according to many studies.

2. Many observers have thought that earthworms are vital to maintaining a healthy, fertile soil, as I have shown earlier.

3. According to the others in the plane, it was side-splittingly comical to see Harris try to delay his jump.

EXERCISE 6

Rewrite the following passages, adding unnecessary transitions, intensifiers, and qualifications. How do your revisions change the writer's voice? You'll find a sample answer on the *Understanding Style* website.

1. We are all strong enough to bear the misfortunes of others.

   LA ROCHEFOUCAULD, *Maximes*

2. Easy writing's vile hard reading.

   R.B. SHERIDAN, *Clio's Protest*

3. The mass of men lead lives of quiet desperation.

   THOREAU, *Walden*

Overexplaining

Overexplaining also generates deadwood. The writer fails to take into account what readers know and belabors common points in numbing detail.

> A crucial feature of conventional bicycles is the sprocket or toothed wheel that advances the chain or, in the case of the rear sprocket, is advanced by it and in turn advances the rear wheel, which is driven by the force of the rider's legs as he or she pedals, driving around the front sprocket to advance the chain, which in turn drives the rear sprocket and wheel, propelling the bicycle forward.

There's no easy way to avoid overexplaining. You simply have to work your way through whatever you write keeping your intended readers in mind. Ask yourself, *"Do they need to know this?" "Don't they already know it?"*

The answers will vary with your readers. Writing for chemical engineers, you wouldn't have to spell out the formula for salt or explain the Periodic Table. Writing for lawyers or accountants, you might.

EXERCISE 7

Rewrite the following passages, removing unnecessary set phrases, transitions, intensifiers, and qualifications. Eliminate any repeated information or overexplanation. Change the sentence structure if you like, but include all the major ideas of the original. How many words did you save? How do your revisions change the writer's voice? You'll find a sample answer on the *Understanding Style* website.

1. For general readers:

   In order to define a neutron star it is necessary to state that it is a small star, but in spite of its small size it is very dense; in fact, amazing as it may seem, most neutron stars are comparable to our sun in mass, or gross weight. But although neutron stars are as heavy as our sun, however, it is important to realize that they are much smaller. In other words, these dense stars are only a few miles in radius, whereas the radius of the sun is about 700,000 miles. (93 words)

2. For medical professionals:

   SIDS or sudden infant death syndrome or crib death accounts for a whopping 10% of all deaths of apparently healthy infants under one year old, the second-leading cause of death for this cuddly group after accidents, which, unlike SIDS can be prevented. Or can this wanton killer be placed under control after all? On the likely theory that the fatal breath stoppage of SIDS may be prefigured by other episodes of apnea—temporary breath stoppage—some cribs are outfitted with alarms set to go off whenever Baby's breathing becomes ragged or abnormal. (92 words)

3. For meteorologists:

   Last Sunday's warm, rainy weather was perfect for staying in and watching the NBA quarterfinals on TV until violent storms in the afternoon cut the power off. Electrical workers were thankful for the bright cool weather Monday, but then the low pressure front backed up, returning to the area, colliding with the cool high pressure air, and generating another round of scary thunderstorms. Wouldn't you know it? Blam! Out went the lights again! (73 words)

A Caution against Underwriting

Children tend to write one simple sentence after another, generally sticking to the same sentence type, or to string a series of ideas together with *and*'s:

It was Friday. We got a dog. She is black and white. She is a cocker spaniel.

It was Friday, *and* we got a dog, *and* she is black and white, *and* she is a cocker spaniel.

Unfortunately, even after they've grown up and developed more complex ideas and vocabularies, some writers are afraid to venture much beyond these childish constructions:

Some people don't like affirmative action programs. They say they have good reasons. They say affirmative action is unfair. But no one cared when colleges promoted geographical diversity. No one cared when a kid from Montana got preferential treatment. No one cared when children of former students and donors got moved up the admissions list. They only cared when the people being admitted were black.

Neanderthals had a problem, *and* it was the way they had adapted to glacial conditions *and* developed heavy bodies and specialized respiratory systems *and* these seemed out of place in new conditions. Natural selection worked against those traits *and* so did intermarriage, if there was intermarriage, between archaic humans and modern, *and* even today I have a special respect for the uncommonly burly stranger passing me in the crowd. He or she just might carry traces of the Neanderthal lineage, *and* his or her ancestors might have hunted mammoth, horse, and reindeer within sight of the ice fronts and enshrined the cave bear, *and* we may need those genes again.

While there's nothing grammatically wrong with these passages, their monotonous, repetitive structure makes them sound simple-minded and hard to follow, leaving readers to discover connections between the ideas for themselves. Here's what two professional writers made of the same material:

The opponents of affirmative actions programs say they are opposing the rank unfairness of preferential treatment. But there was no great hue and cry when colleges were candid about wanting to have geographic diversity, perhaps giving the kid from Montana an edge. There has been no national outcry when legacy applicants whose transcripts were supplemented by Dad's alumni status—and cash contributions to the college— were admitted over more qualified comers. We somehow only discovered that life was not fair when the beneficiaries happened to be black.

ANNA QUINDLEN, *The Great White Myth*

Their main problem, I gather, was that they had adapted so well to glacial conditions that their heavy bodies and specialized respiratory systems seemed out of place when those conditions changed. Natural selection worked increasingly against those traits, with the helping hand of intermarriage, if intermarriage there was, between archaic humans and modern. Today I have special respect for the uncommonly burly stranger passing me in the crowd. He or she just might carry traces of the lineage that once hunted mammoth, horse, and reindeer within sight of the ice fronts and enshrined the cave bear. We may need those genes again.

WILLIAM H. MACLEISH, *The Day before America*

By combining what might have been seven sentences into four, Quindlen makes her point about affirmative action lively and coherent. Specific connections like "so well...that," "when," and "the lineage that," allow MacLeish not only to explain his point about the passing of the Neanderthals but to convey his sense of wonder that some of their genes may still survive among us today.

Even writers who ordinarily write well developed sentences sometimes find themselves caught up in a series of blunt, disjointed ones in need of combining. Chapter 11, "Grammatical Variety," is full of advice and exercises on how to build complex and interesting sentences. Refer to it now if you think you need help forming a more mature style. In the meantime, remember to avoid underwriting as well as overwriting. Don't get so involved in cutting away deadwood that you leave your writing over-simplified and structurally impoverished.

EXERCISE 8

Rewrite the following passages, combining simple, repetitious constructions into a more coherent mix of sentence lengths and types. Include all the major ideas of the original. Refer to Chapter 11 if you need help. How do your revisions change the writer's voice? You'll find a sample answer on the *Understanding Style* website.

1. There is a shortage of entry-level workers. This threatens employers. The threatened employers include fast food restaurants. Other minimum-wage jobs are also affected. These include messenger services. Workers may be available. Disadvantaged and minority youths may fill these jobs. These youths will need training.

2. The Patent Office grants many patents, and some are on engineered genes, and many people think genetic engineering is immoral. But biotechnology companies have large research and development costs, and they can't recover these costs without patents to protect their profits, and the seventeen-year term of patent protections doesn't seem like too much to ask.

3. Tornadoes are measured on the Fujita-Pearson "F" scale. It goes from F1 to F5. The 73–112 mph winds of an F1 tornado can overturn mobile homes and shove moving cars off the road, and F5 tornadoes carry cars and houses hundreds of feet through the air. F5 tornadoes have winds of 261–318 mph.

MAKEOVER 1

Rewrite the following passage, intended for a general audience, removing unnecessary set phrases, transitions, intensifiers, and qualifications. Eliminate any repeated information or overexplanation. Change the sentence structure if you like, but include all the major ideas of the original. Reduce the passage by half or more. How do your revisions change the writer's voice?

In conclusion I feel it necessary to state that our current welfare system for distributing benefits to the poor is none other than ineffective, not because it supports that proportion of the people who may find themselves in need but because of the way in which benefits are administered, or misadministered, even as we speak. Imposing demeaning need requirements (requirements that must be met before a person is acknowledged to be in need of welfare benefits) and regulations based on someone else's arbitrary moral beliefs, however they arose, on downtrodden welfare recipients is shameful and counterproductive. In words of one syllable, why not just provide every man, woman, and child whose income is under a certain figure to be determined by policymakers in light of current fiscal realities with enough money to bring them up to the threshold figure so defined and let those persons spend the money in any way or fashion they feel inclined to spend it? Present figures indicate that on average it costs twenty thousand dollars a year to provide an average amount of benefits to a family of three—usually a father, a mother, and a child or a mother and two children, though other configurations are of course possible. About half that money goes to cover administrative costs, which include enforcement costs brought on by regulatory red tape or needlessly complicated regulations. If we just gave those funds to the families in question to use as they wished, no strings attached, they would be better off than under the current system, which provides less support (because much of the money goes into administrative costs or overhead) and keeps them under the thumb of the government by making them conform to unnecessary and intrusive regulations.

MAKEOVER 2

Rewrite the following passage, intended for a general audience. Correct its over-simple sentence structure by combining ideas and clarifying logical connections. If you need help, refer to Chapter 11, "Grammatical Variety." Change the sentence structure as you like but include all the major ideas of the original. How do your revisions change the writer's voice?

Many marketers put customers to work. This represents a saving. The work used to be done by employees, and they had to be paid. Customers carry merchandise home themselves. They use their own cars and pick up appliances and furniture and even building supplies, and these things used to be delivered. Customers serve themselves in groceries and restaurants. They are their own tellers in banks. They assemble toys and pump gas. Many items are now sold by mail. More every year are sold over the Internet. This saves merchandisers even more. Customers serve themselves in these transactions. They supply their own sales pitch. They fill in their own order forms. They provide their own store settings. They pay for delivery. The merchandiser's role is reduced. The merchandiser merely links customers and suppliers.

Your Writing

Without much reflection on style, write two pages on something you learned during the past year. This should represent your base-line style, the way you tend naturally to write. Go over the piece carefully, highlighting deadwood in one color and choppy sentences that should be combined in another. This will give you a sense of the amount of over- or underwriting revision your first drafts are likely to require.

◇◇

POINTS TO REMEMBER

1. Make a habit of eliminating as much deadwood as possible from your writing. Keep an edited piece on hand to remind yourself how much you should expect to cut from a typical draft.

2. Make sure verbal filler phrases, "authorspeak," and explanatory details are justified. Will the readers you have in mind really need them? If not, cut them out.

3. Notice the texture of your sentences. If they seem too simple and disjointed, try combining several. See Chapter 11, "Grammatical Variety," for techniques.

◇◇

PART TWO

Accurate, Effective Word Choice

CHAPTER 4

Finding the Right Words
What's in a Name?

Crack open a word and you find something like the hidden life in a drop of pond water: teeming levels of association, family resemblances, and history that determine its meaning and where it can be used. No two words mean exactly the same. As Katherine Anne Porter put it, "There is no such thing as an exact synonym."

At first glance, the word *pagan* seems unremarkable. But no word really is. *Pagan* derives from Late Latin *paganus*, meaning a country dweller. *Peasant*, an agricultural laborer, comes from the same source. How did *paganus* become *pagan*? As Christianity first spread through the cities of the Roman Empire, the countryside remained largely unconverted, peopled with backward *pagans*. The word's history reflects the urban roots of early Christianity and also the age-old opposition between town and country. To see how the same process of association worked in a word of Germanic ancestry, look up *heathen.*

A World of Words

Words grow out of life and history. Some knock around for centuries, changing as the world changes. *Sepia* was once a kind of ink obtained from cuttlefish, then a brownish color resembling this ink, then a brownish print produced by an early photographic process. Decades later the word became the title of a popular magazine for African Americans. S*ilo* (from Latin *sirus*, drawn from an earlier Greek word) meant an underground pit for storing grain and fodder until above-ground silos became common at the end of the progressive nineteenth century. But when people needed a name for underground storage cylinders for guided missiles, *silo* won out, regaining some of its subterranean resonance. Other words, just as interesting and often more lively, seem to have been invented yesterday. A *fuzzy elevator* is run by a computer that guesses how many people are waiting on a given floor. A *cross functional* employee's job has been stretched to cover for a colleague laid off in a spasm of corporate *rightsizing*.

The monumental *Oxford English Dictionary* lists nearly half a million words, an ocean of language that is deep as well as wide. It's nice to know that *lady*, a word often considered prissy, derives from a homely Old English term for "kneader of bread." *Woman*, the term many prefer, is Old English too, but hardly politically correct: it means "wife-man," the kind of man who becomes someone's wife. *Female*, originally Latin, came to English by way of French. Like many **Latinate** borrowings, *female* sounds almost clinical beside its Old English-descended equivalents, *woman* or *lady*. Incidentally, *female* was at first spelled *femel* in keeping with French *femelle*. The word was given its present ending to make it more like English *male*. If this seems unfair to women, look up the etymology of *virtue*.

Many English words echo thousands of years of human history. They range from *mother* (still close to prehistoric Sanskrit *matr*) to *smackdown*, offering writers endless shades of meaning and color. Do your companions *dawdle* (English), *dally* (Anglo-French) *delay* (Middle French), *lag* (Scandinavian), *loiter* (Dutch), or *procrastinate* (Latin)? Does it matter which one you choose? You bet. Believe Mark Twain: "The difference between the right word and the almost-right word is the difference between lightning and a lightning bug."

The more you know about the history, weight, and meaning of words the more words you'll get right. Study the sample entries in the front matter of the next dictionary you pick up. It's amazing how much information is crammed into each entry. Then look up a few words and note their pronunciation, grammatical codes, primary and secondary definitions, etymologies, and cross references. For some words you may also find usage guides, synonyms with several shades of meaning, and attestation dates. Dictionaries are addictive. Once you've got the bug, you will never again look up *front matter* (all material in a book that precedes the text proper) without pausing at *forb*, *francolin*, and *fricassee*.

Of course you can find much of this information online, often with audio files to let you hear how words are pronounced. Merriam-Webster

Online (merriam-webster.com) and Oxford (askoxford.com) are great places to look. But online searches may whisk you past the lucky discoveries you make as you thumb through a physical book. An honorable exception is the *Online Etymology Dictionary* (etymonline.com), which offers two modes of browsing. You can flip through the alphabet, seeing all the words that start with the same letters, just as you would with a printed dictionary; or you can enter a single word and get a page with your term and an extended family of its relatives. Searching *Etymonline* this way is serious fun. Look up *sweet*, for example, and you get your word; but you also see other entries (67 in all) that contain the term. The entry for *sweet* yields synonyms like *dulcet*, but also strangely and wonderfully related words like *twee* (a childish mispronunciation of sweet), *assuage* (based on an Old French verb meaning "to sweeten"), and *scrotum*, simply because James Joyce once called the sea "a grey sweet mother. The snotgreen sea. The scrotum-tightening sea." You could spend weeks exploring *Etymonline*.

Serious word freaks go further. Like golf and cooking, language has a large, rewarding literature. Libraries offer whole shelves of language books. Try Robert McNeil's *Story of English* (video tapes available) or any number of enthusiasts' books about words and word histories. A good start would be John Ciardi's cantankerous *Browser's Dictionaries* (sample: "*bikini*: the minimal two-string, three-cup (all demitasses) bathing suit"). Also notable and fun is Elizabeth Webber and Mike Feinsilber's *Grand Allusion* series. The authors explain terms and phrases like "Mau-Mau" and "Parkinson's Law," allusions you see everywhere but may not fully understand. A perfect allusion, like just the right word, can light up a page. A mistaken one can swallow your credibility like a Florida sinkhole.

EXERCISE 1

Study the information online or in your college dictionary on these words. (The *Online Etymology Dictionary* will be the most entertaining.) Look up the meaning of notations and abbreviations you don't understand in the front matter.

address	genius	same
buxom	hell	salad
congregation	lie (verb)	temple
cross	moraine	ukulele
draw	multiplex	voice
frisk	pin	wince

Other Word Books

Every writer needs a few basic reference books. First get a good desk dictionary—the *American Heritage, Merriam-Webster*, and *Random House* college dictionaries are all first rate. Merriam-Webster offers a free online counterpart that also includes sound files, a thesaurus and other tools. No doubt your computer checks spelling, but you need a dictionary to dig down into the meanings and histories of words. If your grammatical skills are shaky, a handbook of the sort used in college writing classes is indispensable. Any English teacher can recommend one or you can find one online. The *Understanding Style* website provides links to handbooks and other online writing aids. If you'll be writing college papers, make sure the reference you choose has sample research essays and guides to the latest Modern Language Association (MLA) and American Psychological Association (APA) documentation styles. You'll find these reference styles described and illustrated at the Purdue Online Writing Lab (owl.english.purdue.edu). Be sure you know which documentation system you're supposed to use. Many humanities departments and journals still prefer the *Chicago Manual of Style* and its derivative, the Turabian manual, while other disciplines or even academic departments may have stylesheets of their own.

Get a Roget's thesaurus in dictionary form so you can look up words alphabetically. Roget will give you more synonyms for your word than you can shake (*agitate, brandish, flourish, jiggle, joggle, jolt, jounce,* or *wiggle*) a stick at. As William Zinsser put it, a thesaurus helps you "find the word that's right on the tip of your tongue, where it doesn't do you any good." But use it with caution. Each synonym expresses a different shade of meaning and level of formality. No matter what Roget says, don't use a word unless you're dead sure it's right for the place you want to put it. It was an uncritical thesaurus user who wrote, "The president employed a mess of data and tables to pooh-pooh the proposal from Congress concerning tax cuts."

A dictionary of synonyms (more detailed than a thesaurus, but usually offering fewer words) not only gives *peaceable, peaceful, irenic, pacifist,* and *pacifistic* as synonyms for *pacific* but may spend half a page explaining how and when each should be used, with examples.

On the other hand, usage guides (alphabetical lists of words frequently misused, like *lay and lie*) can be cranky and unreliable. Henry Watson Fowler set the tone in his still-cited *Dictionary of Modern English Usage* (the original 1926 edition, not more recent, milder versions). Fowler was often wrong even for his own time. He indignantly rejects *stomach* as a "genteelism" for *belly*, and calls *chiropodist* an ignorantly puffed-up name for a *corn-cutter*. More up-to-date and temperate usage guides like Mager and Mager's *Encyclopedic Dictionary of English Usage*, the *Harper Dictionary of Contemporary Usage,* or Margaret Bryant's *Current American Usage* are more helpful, as are the usage labels in standard dictionaries. *The American Heritage Dictionary* is especially proud of its usage notes. Be warned; opinions on usage differ widely. Authorities often disagree. There's more on usage in Chapter 5, and Appendix A at the back of the book lists and explains some common usage problems.

EXERCISE 2

Look up the following words in a thesaurus and a dictionary of synonyms. How many of the choices listed in the thesaurus are really interchangeable?

artistic	injure	physique
blame (noun)	joke (verb)	poor
contest (noun)	laugh	remainder
dull (adjective)	maim	save
evidence (noun)	new	sour (adjective)
fame	pale	thin (adjective)

EXERCISE 3

Look up the following words and phrases in a usage dictionary. If the book you consult doesn't discuss certain items, just look up the others. How clear and accurate are the writer's opinions?

aggravate	heinous
between you and I	split infinitive
could care less	kind of
should of	nauseated/nauseous
disinterested/uninterested	OK
divorcee	real/really
equally as	slang
fulsome	that/which

Types of Diction

Your **diction**, the exact words you choose and the settings in which you use them, means a great deal to the success of your writing. While your language should be appropriate to the situation, there is generally still room for variety. Skillful writers mix general and particular, abstract and concrete, long and short, learned and commonplace, connotative and neutral words to administer a series of small but telling surprises. Readers stay interested because they don't know what's coming next.

Formal and Informal Words

English offers a huge range of language choices suited to various audiences and subjects. At its stuffiest, **Formal English** features elevated diction for special purposes such as convention speeches, commencement addresses, and liturgical solemnities. In formal English, opponents are *dastardly*; "goodbye" may be *godspeed*; and church services are *liturgical solemnities*. But formal English can also sound exactly the right note in serious circumstances. Consider Franklin Roosevelt's characterization of the bombing of Pearl Harbor as "a date which will live in infamy," not ordinary language, but perfect as a measured response to the onset of war. **Informal** or **Colloquial English** is the diction of everyday speech. Contractions are OK, as are shortened forms like TV and LA for Los Angeles. People get *hitched*; lovers get *ditched* because somebody *snitched*. Still more informal are slang and dialect words like *into* in "She's into Yoga" (slang) and regionalisms like *you'ns* (dialect).

Between formal and informal English, with some overlap on both sides, is **Standard English**, the language of good popular writing, clear proposals, effective memos and letters, and most good books. Written standard English is flexible enough to adapt to almost any situation. For instance, contractions, abbreviations, and borderline informal words like *hassle* that would be out of place in an official report do perfectly well in more intimate communications like popular essays and books or letters to friends.

EXERCISE 4

Choose the most appropriate word in each case. How would the wrong choice change the writer's voice?

1. Generating convincing computer images of fire has proven difficult compared to constructing fractal images of trees and landscapes, which experts regard as [elementary/no brainers].

2. Deer living near airplane runways are systematically [eliminated/offed] by airport personnel.

3. [Vestiges/traces] of the all-girl band fad [lasted/tarried] until the mid-fifties.

4. "Carlos," [expostulated/said] Darla, "You're [treading/stepping] on my bunion."

5. Water, water, everywhere, nor any drop to [imbibe/drink].

General and Particular Words

General words, like *wine*, name a large class of things. Specific words, like *red wine*, name items or subsets within the class. Making a general word more particular in a series of steps quickly carries you from hugely inclusive to very specific meanings:

Material entity/living thing/mammal/human/judge/John G. Roberts, Jr.

Of course *general* and *particular* are relative terms. *Red wine* is more specific than *wine* but general itself compared to *pinot noir*, which is general in comparison to *2007 Sebastiani pinot noir*.

Particularity isn't limited to nouns. *Slouch* is more particular than *sit*. *Weighing* someone's words is more particular than *listening* to them. *Ice blue* is more particular than *blue*. *Nauseated* is more particular than *sick*. In each case, the set/subset relationship holds good. Being *nauseated* is a kind of being *sick*. If you care to go a step further, *projectile vomiting* is a more particular form of being *nauseated*.

If you choose particular words when possible, your writing will seem more lively and clear:

Not

The judge likes his wine

But

Judge Roberts likes his pinot noir. (You heard it here first.)

But don't overdo it. You might find yourself enmeshed in the **creative genius** style of overwriting:

The judge's reaction to the 2007 Sebastiani pinot noir was immediate: nauseated, he slumped forward, his lips and forehead ice blue.

EXERCISE 5

Go through this passage choosing the more general terms in each case; then the more specific. Specific terms will name subsets of the general ones. How do your choices change the writer's voice?

Pneumatic [devices/tubes] are making a comeback. Once considered [old fashioned/obsolete] these [expedients/devices] are now often the [technique/solution] of choice for [moving/transporting] physical items [of use/needed] in health care and [business/industry], such as [body fluids/blood or urine samples], [machine components/aircraft parts] and [hazardous/toxic] materials. The [advanced/high tech] tubes used for these purposes have come a long way from the [earlier/primitive] pneumatic systems once used to [transport/deliver] [money/bills and change] in [businesses/department stores]. Those systems were considered [remarkable/modern] in their day. They replaced [humans/young children] previously [employed/exploited] for the job.

Abstract and Concrete Words

An abstract word names something that cannot be seen, heard, touched, tasted, or smelled; a concrete word names something that can. *Courage* is abstract. *Potato* is concrete. Verbs and adjectives can be concrete or abstract also. *Appreciate* is an abstract verb; *snuffle* more concrete. *Intriguing* is an abstract adjective; *lumpy* is concrete.

Like particulars, concrete terms enliven your style. They help readers *sense* what you're talking about, not just apprehend it mentally. Here's a passage with concrete word choices highlighted.

[Tree peonies] are, as everyone familiar with their images in **Oriental paintings**, **silks** and **porcelains** knows, among the world's loveliest **flowers**, at once sumptuous and subtle in their **golds** and **moonlight pinks** and **snowy whites**; their **finely cut foliage** makes that of the common, herbaceous peonies look **coarse**.

ELEANOR PERÉNYI, *Green Thoughts*

See what happens when most of the concrete information is removed:

Tree peonies are, as everyone familiar with their images knows, among the world's loveliest things, and quite subtle compared with the common, herbaceous variety.

The difference between the two versions is like the difference between tree peonies and tree stumps.

Like particularity, concreteness can be overdone, but including a reasonable number of details is a fine way to strengthen your style.

EXERCISE 6

Compare the following relatively concrete and abstract passages. What effect does omitting details have on the writer's voice?

1A. A false start of a garden has yielded a few pale tomato plants dwarfed in a grove of weeds before the house. The barnyard—staging area for all on-farm action—is in a state of barely controlled chaos. A long hog house whose cement block walls have cracked sits off at the east end of the yard.... Weeds ring every building. An old grain bin has been split into two half-cylinders and both halves lie near the house, garaging machinery and trucks.

MARK KRAMER, *Three Farms*

1B. A false start of a garden has yielded a few plants in a grove of other plants before the house. The barnyard—staging area for all on-farm action—is in a state of barely controlled chaos. A damaged structure is in the yard. There are plants around each building. Halves of a disused grain bin house machinery near another building.

2A. Daisy. The common wild flower. [OE *daeges_age*, day's eye; compounded of *daeges*, genitive form of *daeg*, of day; with *eage*, eye; and by later contraction *daisy*. This root image is a charmingly typical act of the English folk imagination and does not occur in any other language in the name of this flower].

JOHN CIARDI, *A Browser's Dictionary*

2B. Daisy. A common plant. [The term is old and originally meant "day's eye." This underlying image represents the imagination of a particular group of people. Other groups never made the same association].

3A. Luddites. Bands of craftsmen in industrial England, 1811–16, who smashed textile machines that were displacing them from their jobs. They were named after their semi-mythical leader, Ned Ludd.

ELIZABETH WEBBER AND MIKE FEINSILBER,
Grand Allusions

3B. Luddites. Groups of workers who damaged machines that threatened their livelihoods. They were named after a fellow worker about whom little is known.

Long and Short Words

This is a simple but important distinction. Short words are stronger than long ones. They are usually more particular, more concrete, more emphatic. They shrink the distance between writer and reader. Multisyllabic words generally appear softer, because they are often general and abstract and because the rhythms they form are less rousing. Long words widen the gap between writer and reader, sometimes, as in the **official style,** in order to build the writer up at the reader's expense.

Not convinced? Compare "Short words are stronger than long ones" (syllable/word ratio, 1.14/1) with "Multisyllabic words generally appear softer" (syllable/word ratio, 2.8/1). Read the two statements aloud. If you're like most people, the first will seem punchy and direct, the second quieter and far less emphatic.

How many long and short words should there be in your writing? It depends. Writing in a formal situation or on a technical topic where professional terms add to the syllable count might come in at over two syllables per word and still be effective. Really dramatic utterances ("Keep your hands on the wheel!") benefit by being as monosyllabic as you can make them. For most other writing, you could hardly do better than to imitate two American luminaries, Thomas Jefferson and Abraham Lincoln. The first paragraph of the Declaration of Independence measures 1.5 syllables per word. The first hundred words of the Gettysburg Address go 1.4/1. Analyze a few hundred-word samples of your writing. Your syllable/word ratio should come out somewhere in that neighborhood. Then analyze the prose of two or three writers you admire. Their ratios will probably fall in or near that range as well. It's the home range of good writing.

A final point about short words: they are especially effective at the end of a sentence where they receive major emphasis as the last significant word in the sentence (see **sentence nucleus** and Chapter 9). Compare these examples:

I no longer have much use of my left **HAND**. Now my right side is weakening as **WELL**. I still have the blurred spot in my right **EYE**. Overall, though, I've been lucky so **FAR**.

NANCY MAIRS, *On Being a Cripple*

I no longer have much left hand dex**TER**ity. Now my right side is weakening in ad**DI**tion. I still have the blurred spot in my right **VI**sion. Overall, though, I've been lucky to the **PRES**ent.

Mairs' version sounds more emphatic because of those strong mono-syllables she put in the sentence nucleus position.

EXERCISE 7

Rewrite the following passages with longer words, aiming for a syllable/word ratio above 2:1. What do your revisions do to the writer's voice? You'll find a sample answer on the *Understanding Style* website.

1. When in the course of human events, it becomes necessary for one people to dissolve the political bands which have connected them with another, and to assume among the powers of the earth, the separate and equal station to which the Laws of Nature and of Nature's God entitle them, a decent respect to the opinions of mankind requires that they should declare the causes which impel them to the separation. (1.5 syllables/word)

2. Four score and seven years ago our fathers brought forth on this continent, a new nation, conceived in Liberty, and dedicated to the proposition that all men are created equal.
    Now we are engaged in a great civil war; testing whether that nation, or any other nation so conceived and so dedicated, can long endure. We are met on a great battlefield of that war. We have come to dedicate a portion of that field as a final resting-place for those who here gave their lives that that nation might live. It is altogether fitting and proper that we should do this. (1.4 syllables/word)

3. Time is but the stream I go a-fishing in. I drink at it; but while I drink I see the sandy bottom and detect how shallow it is. Its thin current slides away, but eternity remains. (1.3 syllables/word)
                                                            THOREAU, *Walden*

Learned and Commonplace Words

Another useful way of thinking about words is to classify them loosely as learned or commonplace. A good style makes room for both:

There is one quality which unites all great and perdurable writ-ers, you don't NEED schools and colleges to keep 'em alive. Put them out of the curriculum, lay them in the dust of libraries, and once in every so often a chance reader, unsubsidized and unbribed, will dig them up again, put them in the light again, without asking favors.

EZRA POUND, A B C of Reading

The ten-dollar words here—*perdurable, curriculum, unsubsidized*—work because they're played off against plain words and idioms like *put out, once in every so often,* and the **colloquial** *'em.* Pound's comments would lose force if his diction were all of one kind:

> There is one quality which unites all great and perdurable writers; schools and colleges are unnecessary to guarantee their survival. Omit them from the curriculum, immure them in libraries, and yet a random reader, unsubsidized and selflessly motivated, will unearth them again, make them current again, without requesting rewards.

Many learned **Latinate** words, words borrowed from Latin or sometimes (illogically) from Greek, have native synonyms descended from Germanic roots. *Female/woman* is one pair, along with thousands of others, like *commodity/goods, contiguous/near,* or *corpulent/fat.* Writing with a high percentage of native words sounds unvarnished and strong. But big words can be wonderfully effective too. Just make sure the setting is right. If you've got a stunner like *perdurable* in your pocket, don't let it get lost among a lot of other learned terms. Put it in a setting of ordinary words, where it can glitter (or *coruscate*).

EXERCISE 8

Go through the following passage choosing the more learned terms in each case; then the more commonplace. Experiment with a mix of both groups. How do your choices change the writer's voice?

> A rare [problem/disorder] called [life-long overall hairiness/congenital generalized hypertrichosis] appears to be [linked/attributable] to a [throwback gene/avatistic mutation]. People [with/experiencing] this condition are [really hairy/singularly hirsute], with [thick fur/impenetrable hisipity] everywhere except the palms of their hands and [bottoms/soles] of their feet. These [poor people/unfortunate individuals] may be [behind/responsible for] widespread legends concerning werewolves.

Connotative and Neutral Words

In addition to their dictionary meanings (**denotations**), words often carry an unofficial but telling emotional charge or **connotation**. A person who won't do what you want is *stubborn, obstinate, intransigent, head-strong, bullheaded.* All these words have negative connotations. You, on the other hand, refuse to bend because you are *determined, resolute, ada-mant, uncompromising,* and *tough.* These words make you look good. They have positive connotations. To be objective, you'd have to break away from emotion-laden terms and find an unslanted way of talking about the disagreement: you might say the two of you had reached an *impasse* or *deadlock.* These words are neutral. They don't imply anyone is to blame.

Connotative words are indispensable in their place. You need them when you want to convey not just a meaning but your feelings about it. Would someone's proposal *compromise* or *gut* a program you care about? How much damage would it do, and how much do you care? You shouldn't say *gut* where *compromise* is called for—you'd be overreacting. But you shouldn't say *compromise* either if *gut* is what you really mean—that might amount to giving up without a fight.

EXERCISE 9

Reverse the emotional charge of the following passages by supplying language with connotations opposite to those of the italicized words: for example *saunter* (positive) might become *trudge* (negative). You may have to change meanings slightly on occasion. Then supply another set of language choices (like *walk*) that are neutral. What do these changes do to the writer's voice? You'll find a sample answer on the *Understanding Style* website.

1. Marvin's *autocratic* boss *terrorizes* the office staff, *inflexibly* insisting that everything be done a certain way. She's *fanatical* about deadlines. She's *absurdly* demanding about quality work. She *browbeats* everyone to live up to her *finicky* requirements and then *whines* that they haven't succeeded.

2. The Justice Department *investigation exonerated* any *government peacekeepers* of wrongdoing in the Branch Davidian *enforcement event* at Waco.

3. *Ignoring* the evidence of Kanzi, a pygmy chimpanzee who uses *over fifty* symbols and syntactical rules *to compose* sentences,

many linguists *pigheadedly* refuse to *admit* that some animals
can master language.

MAKEOVER 1

Rewrite the following passage to provide an effective mix of formal and
informal, general and particular, abstract and concrete words for a general audience.

About a jillion years ago earth's only natural satellite impacted
our planet and rebounded into shallow space where it was captured in an orbital trajectory. There it remains at the present
time. This conclusion is based on analysis of the composition
of the satellite in question, which turns out to be greatly at variance with the makeup of mother earth. Data from the lunar
research satellite *Clementine* substantiate hunches that the
moon and earth are of separate origin and tend to refute notions
that the lunar orb might have broken away from the earth while
both were hotter than hell, in fact in a molten state. Other theoretical wild hairs, like the idea that the moon and earth formed
at the same time or that the moon was sucked into the earth's
gravitational clutches and captured in orbit without a collision
to take the steam off its speed, just don't hold water.

MAKEOVER 2

Rewrite the following passage to provide an effective mix of long and
short, learned and commonplace, connotative and neutral words for a
general audience.

Lewis Thomas characterizes cumbersome medical technology
such as the now little-used iron lung, clanking artificial hearts,
and various disgusting and invasive treatments we have devised
for cancer as "halfway technology." A key feature of these
abominable expedients is that they are based on medicine's
abject failure to understand underlying disease mechanisms
and minister directly to the root cause of the problem. When
root causes are ultimately comprehended, treatment becomes
blessedly economical and efficient. Arduous nursing and surgical intervention to mitigate the symptoms of typhoid fever used
to extend for long, weary months as the disease ran its course.
Now the sinister illness may be vanquished in a day or two using
the comparatively inexpensive nostrum chloramphenicol.

Your Writing

Write a one-page report on a current news event and include at least one word each from six of the following categories: formal, informal, general, particular, abstract, concrete, long, short, learned, commonplace, connotative, and neutral. Highlight your six special words and consider their effect on the piece. What audience, if any, would it be appropriate for as written? What sorts of words would you want to include more or less of in different situations, say writing for an employer or for a close friend?

◇◇◇

POINTS TO REMEMBER

1. Gather a small library of writer's references including a desk dictionary, a writer's handbook, a usage guide, and a thesaurus. Consult these frequently to increase your feel for written English and its conventions. But don't let the the thesaurus mislead you into using words you don't really know just for effect.
2. Explore the word tools offered on the Internet, especially online dictionaries like Merriam-Webster's and browsable sites like *Etymonline*.
3. Within the limits of what's appropriate for your writing situation, try for a mixture of word choices that will keep readers interested in your diction as well as your content.

◇◇◇

CHAPTER 5

Finding Fresh Words
Clichés, Usage, Quoting, Figurative Language

The last chapter talked about issues that come up whenever you choose a word. This one concerns particular cases: avoiding clichés, dodging a number of usage demons, handling quotations, and using imaginative comparisons or figurative language.

Clichés Beat a Hasty Retreat: A Learning Experience

Clichés are weed-like phrases that sprout up in everyone's writing. You know them by heart. "Fit as a what?" "Innocent as a what?" "There's more here than meets the what?" Anyone who grew up speaking English knows the answers. Many clichés started life as trenchant phrases. It was an anonymous poet with a truly bizarre imagination who first noted that something was "finer than frog hair." Shakespeare is a fount of clichés, including "The wheel is come full circle" (*King Lear*), "I have not slept one wink" (*Cymbeline*), "Frailty, thy name is woman" (*Hamlet*), and hundreds more. These notable sayings would still *bowl us over* if they hadn't become *common as ditch water*. But they have. And you need to give the more shopworn ones *a wide berth*.

On the other hand, as handy phrases that are immediately intelligible, clichés have their uses. A quick survey of a 600-word news article on sheep cloning unearthed these clichés and cliché-like phrases: *lost in the hoopla, quiet enthusiasm, host of applications, untrammeled growth, potential boon, reach out and touch* (concerning genetic switches), *run amok, whole gamut,* and *life-support system.* Although this sounds like a lot of canned language for a brief article, the piece itself does not sound especially hackneyed. In fact, because these familiar phrases communicate so effortlessly they may be more efficient here, where subject matter is uppermost, than more original language would be. Think, for example, of the phrase "quiet enthusiasm." How many words would it take to explain this concept as if for the first time? And would the effort be worthwhile in an article where the "quiet enthusiasm" of scientists is only a passing concern? In spite of all the diatribes published against clichés, good writers continue to find uses for them, especially when discussing tangential matters where more original language might draw attention away from the real subject.

This is not a blanket endorsement of clichés. Many are so overused that it's hard to imagine an acceptable place for them in anyone's writing. Suppose the author of the cloning article had announced that the development he was describing *"takes the cake."* Worse, imagine that after explaining several objections to cloning he could do no better for a dramatic conclusion to the whole article than to say cloning is *"not everyone's cup of tea."* The more central the ideas you are discussing are to your purpose, the closer you come to summing up your chief point, the fresher your language should be.

Clichés can cause other problems. Because many started life as **figurative language** they lend themselves to surprising and sometimes wildly illogical **mixed metaphors**. Take a moment to savor this picture:

> He's nothing but a *snake in the grass gnawing at the roots* of the *ship of state.*

But most clichés are simply dull, though you can occasionally bring one back to life by twisting it a bit or by taking it literally. Explaining how World War II bestsellers shied away from direct descriptions of men and women making love, Anthony Lane wrote, "Whenever sex reared its head, it had to keep its hat on." The poet Knute Skinner ended a somber poem about winter rain and watching someone he loved being buried in a dismal Irish cemetery with these lines: "down at Healy's cross/the Killaspuglonane graveyard/is *wet to the bone.*"

Another class of clichés is made up of nonfigurative but somehow catchy phrases that infiltrate nearly everyone's writing. Formulaic expressions like *in the final analysis* or *it goes without saying* or *this day and age,* are as hackneyed as *bite the dust* (a vivid image when it first appeared in Homer's *Iliad*) and equally numbing.

In a manner of speaking it was a meaningful experience to see how *painfully obvious to all intents and purposes* was the *viable alternative* she offered in her *youthful enthusiasm.*

A complete roster of clichés, if there could be such a thing, would run to thousands of items, but this list shows you the kind of phrase to avoid. Think how the more colorful clichés must have dazzled the first people who heard them.

acid test	over and above
against the tide	painfully obvious
astronomical sum	point with pride
bolt from the blue	proud possessor
bottom line	rude awakening
brain trust	salt mines
by the same token	short and sweet
come to grips	shot in the arm
cool as a cucumber	slow but sure
cut and dried	smell a rat
down and out	sneaking suspicion
each and every	spread like wildfire
eager beaver	stack the deck
face the music	straight and narrow
fatal flaw	tangled web
fine-toothed comb	tender mercies
fly in the ointment	the call of duty
garbage in, garbage out	the nose on your face
hands-on	thick and thin
hasty retreat	thin ice
in a very real sense	this day and age
in a nutshell	tiger by the tail
it goes without saying	time-honored
last but not least	tip of the iceberg
learning experience	to all intents and purposes
make a long story short	too little too late
meaningful experience	tried and true
midnight oil	twist in the wind
more than meets the eye	up in arms
nail on the head	viable alternative
needle in a haystack	wildest dreams
no sooner said than done	wry humor
off the beaten path	yes man
on the brink	zero hour

EXERCISE 1

Rewrite following sentences with fresher language. If you feel adventurous, replace clichés based on comparisons ("the ball's in your court") with original comparisons of your own ("the snake's under your chair"; "dig your own peanuts"). You'll find sample answers to the first three on the *Understanding Style* website.

1. Latisha is just a true believer caught in a web of circumstances.

2. I worked like a dog only to get cut off at the knees when the chips were down.

3. Her Yankee ingenuity was too little too late to stem the tide.

4. Francesca was walking tall on the fast track when the unthinkable happened.

5. They beat the drum for a broad array of software solutions.

6. It is worth noting that venturing off the beaten path can lead to untold riches and leave you on top of the world.

7. My natural inclination is to take a pot shot at any rotten apple who crosses my path!

8. With a sheepish grin the old fox made a play for the whole enchilada.

9. The method in her madness shows she's just green with envy.

10. With a murmur of approval the many-headed monster of the pit greeted the pivotal figure in this unfolding drama.

Usage Cranks and Usage Demons

It's frustrating to writing teachers when language fetishists (a more numerous tribe than you'd imagine) start moaning about English being murdered. Writers use contractions and the first-person pronouns *I* and *me*! They write fragments, end sentences with prepositions, or start them with *and* or *but*! What's the world coming to?

Actually, there's nothing necessarily wrong with any of these practices, but that's not what the moaners want to hear. They want to be agreed with—and petted. They learned not to write *I* and *me* back in seventh grade and still think this is the height of language sophistication. In extreme cases they have stopped looking for anything but their pet writing peeves in whatever they read. Heaven help the underling who sends them a memo with a split infinitive!

Some years ago a researcher sent a list of usage questions to a group of language experts. Should you end a sentence with a preposition? Should you distinguish between *fewer* (with count nouns like *lions*) and *less* (with mass nouns like *floor wax*)? Should you say *different from* or *different than*? Should you say *you*? And so on. She also asked the experts to rate their feelings on each question, from mildly concerned to incensed, and left room for comments.

When the results were in, she found not only that her experts seldom agreed completely but that there was no correlation between the degree of agreement and the strength of their feelings. An item that made Expert A's blood bubble ("*Utilize* is **NEVER** an acceptable substitute for *use!*") commonly left Expert B unruffled or mystified ("What's wrong with *utilize?*"). And vice versa.

This doesn't mean that usage issues don't matter, just that the area is (to mix one last metaphor) a minefield of sacred cows. I've served on committees that tossed out job letters because the applicants used *media* as a singular noun (for example, "Radio is a media making a comeback," where they should have said *medium*). If you have to deal with bosses or teachers or application committees you suspect have crochets like these, it will pay you to write very carefully. Appendix A at the back of the book lists usage problems and solutions that most writers and readers regard as valid. (In other words, usage problems and solutions that seem valid to me.) Look over the list and make a note of any items that seem strange or arbitrary. These are the ones you need to eliminate from your Sunday-best writing.

EXERCISE 2

Pick the best usage choice in each of the following cases. For doubtful cases, consult Appendix A.

1. Except for fitful bouts of guilt, the students here are (all together, altogether) (immoral, amoral).

2. (Every day, Ever day, Everyday) a person should oblige someone (who, whom) asks for help.

3. Jill and (myself, me, I) went several miles (farther, further).

4. (A lot, Alot) of (your, you're) energy is spent on keeping warm.

5. Between you and (I, me) (whomever, whoever) comes (shall, will) be welcome.

6. You'll regret missing this opportunity when (it's, its) (past, passed).

7. I agreed to pay only for your food, room, (cloths, clothes) (etc., and etc.).

8. What kind of (complement, compliment) is it to tell me I'm just (all right, alright)?

9. (Between, Among) the two of us, I'd like to (lay, lie) down for an hour or so.

10. Mother is under the (allusion, illusion) her (capital, capitol) is safe in the bank.

Some Notes on Quoting

At times the best words you can use are someone else's. Don't hesitate to use quotations when you're sure they will strengthen your presentation by giving an authority's exact words or by making a point better than you could yourself. No one could beat Milton's reference to "necessity, the tyrant's plea," or Flannery O'Connor's assessment of college writing programs: "Everywhere I go I'm asked if I think the university stifles writers. My opinion is that they don't stifle enough of them."

This writer uses quotations effectively to let a pair of eccentric botanists characterize themselves through their own words:

[Linnaeus's] decision to classify plants according to their sexual parts provoked considerable comment in his day. Professor Dillenius, the Oxford Professor of Botany, wrote to Linnaeus in 1837: "I consider sexual differences altogether useless, superfluous, even misleading, for establishing the character of a plant. What is the point of it all? It is puerile; and it is quite enough that one botanist—Vaillant—should have had his head turned by them." But Linnaeus clung to his sexual system and even, rather tactlessly, emphasized its metaphorical possibilities. Thus he glossed the Monandria as "one husband in a marriage," the Diandria as "two husbands in the same marriage," and the exciting Polyandria as "twenty males or more in the same bed with the female."

LYNN BARBER, *The Heyday of Natural History*

Handling Quotations. Notice how clearly Barber identifies her sources and how smoothly she integrates quoted material into her own writing. The complete sentences from Dillenius are introduced with a colon. They can stand on their own. Linnaeus's racy definitions of the Monandria, Diandria, and Polyandria are all introduced by *as* and linked in a **parallel series** supported by the grammar of Barber's sentence. Try to arrange quotations, as Barber does here, so that it would be hard to tell what was quoted and what was not if a passage containing quotations were read aloud.

Not

Concerning the Polyandria, Linnaeus stated: "twenty males or more in the same bed with the female." [Here the wording and punctuation imply the quotation is a complete thought when it isn't.]

But

Linnaeus characterized the Polyandria as "twenty males or more in the same bed with the female."

In most writing it is enough to identify the person you quote by name as Barber did. Include the title of the piece if you think it will be useful to the reader. Scholarly articles and research papers have much stricter rules on documenting sources, but the formulas vary from field to field and sometimes even within fields. Find out what system is required and consult a current stylesheet or handbook.

EXERCISE 3

Write three paragraphs of your own around two quotations from each of the following passages. Be careful to identify the source clearly and smoothly integrate the quoted material into the grammar of your sentences. You'll find a sample answer on the *Understanding Style* website.

1. Where we need protection [from lightning] is overhead, not on the ground. Closed vehicles act as Faraday cages—named after Michael Faraday, the nineteenth-century British physicist and chemist, who specialized in electromagnetism—and are a good choice for cover, because the metal that encases them channels the charge into the ground. As it descends to earth, lightning current is drawn to isolated objects, anything taller than others in its field. This might be a lone tree, a skyscraper, a mound of granite in a riverbed, or you in your small craft on open water. Farmers are vulnerable because of where they are when they're out in their fields— the tallest object in an open space, plowing or haying as the summer day heats up.

   JILL FRAYNE, *Struck by Lightning*

2. But canine fabrication is not a new idea. There weren't any trendy "designer" hybrids like puggles or schnoodles on Noah's ark, nor even any certified purebreds like Boston terriers or French bulldogs. As their not-exactly-biblical names suggest, these dogs are modern inventions, painstakingly crafted by uncompromising artisans following detailed blueprints, a.k.a. "breed standards," drafted by 19th-century canine eugenicists.

   GREG BEATO, *Man's Best Friend Forever*

3. In January 1991, Gina Grant pleaded no contest to her mother's killing. She served approximately eight months in detention. Three years later, in the fall of 1994, she applied for admission to next September's freshman class at Harvard. Nearly eighteen thousand students applied for places in the Harvard Class of 1999, and just over two thousand were

admitted. Gina Grant was one of them. It was a remarkable turn-around.

JANE MAYER, Rejecting Gina

Figurative Language

Discussing red shift, which allows astronomers to determine the velocity of galaxies from their color, K.C. Cole, a science writer with the Los Angeles *Times,* explains that "the spectra of colors emitted by stars stretch like taffy along with the expansion of space." "Like taffy" is a **simile**, a figure of speech comparing stretched taffy, something familiar, with light waves bending toward the red end of the spectrum, something Cole wants us to understand.

Not all comparisons are figures of speech—only those built on logically unequal relationships. "Melissa looks like her mother" is not a figure of speech. It's probably quite true and quite unremarkable. Figures of speech wake up your imagination. "Melissa looks like a bulldog chewing a wasp" or "starlight stretches like taffy" do this; "that bird looks like a cedar waxwing" doesn't. Imaginative comparisons in most general writing are often only moderately engaging, small indications that the writer is aware of readers and wants to keep them entertained. But used brilliantly they can carry meanings impossible to express any other way. Trumbull Stickney created this simile to explain how he felt to be dying from cancer of the brain:

> Within me 'tis as if
> The green and climbing eyesight of a cat
> Crawled near my mind's poor birds.

Mary Crow Dog and Richard Erdoes used another simile to describe her grandfather's 1890 experience at Wounded Knee, where federal soldiers massacred about 300 unarmed Indians. The Lakota victims heard "rifle fire, salvos making a noise like the ripping apart of a giant blanket."

Similes are upfront comparisons. Stickney's brain cancer makes it seem *as if* a cat were stalking his unprotected consciousness. Crow Dog's federal rifles make a noise *like* a ripping blanket. **Metaphors** dispense with *as* and *like*. They say instead that something *is* something it isn't, occasionally by using only a few words in unexpected ways. Traveling through the West, William Least Heat Moon climbed a hill above the Pecos River:

> From the top, the rubbled land below—*veined* with the highway and arroyos, topographical relief *absorbed* in the dusk—looked like a roadmap.
>
> *Blue Highways*

Veined doesn't say the highway and gullies were like veins. It says they *were* veins. *Absorbed* doesn't say the action of the dusk was like the process of absorption. It says it *was* absorption. It's not until the end of the passage that an overt comparison appears. "Like a roadmap" is a simile.

Other figures of speech are more specialized, but all of them stretch your imagination by using words in unexpected ways.

Personification (treating something that isn't human as if it were)

> England expects that every man will do his duty.
>
> LORD NELSON

Apostrophe (talking to someone or something that cannot hear you as if it could)

> Milton! Thou shouldst be living at this hour.
>
> WILLIAM WORDSWORTH

Hyperbole (deliberate exaggeration)

> Earth's crammed with heaven,
> And every common bush afire with God.
>
> ELIZABETH BARRETT BROWNING

Understatement (giving something less emphasis than it normally deserves)

> Guns aren't lawful;
> Nooses give;
> Gas smells awful;
> You might as well live.
>
> DOROTHY PARKER

Metonomy (using the name of one thing to indicate something associated with it)

> Keep the home fires burning.
>
> Lena Guilbert Ford

Synedoche (using part of something to stand for the thing itself)

> Set thine house in order.
>
> II Kings, 20:1

Paradox (a seeming contradiction that must be solved by an imaginative leap)

> Nobody does it better
> Makes me feel bad so good.
>
> Carly Simon

Except where they have lapsed into clichés, figures of speech call attention to themselves. Their job is to do things everyday English doesn't. That's why they seem at home in poetry. While similes and metaphors are common in popular and informal writing and in the full-blown rhetoric of sermons and campaign oratory, they are less frequent in professional communications. The other figures are fairly rare, but can light up an occasional passage. Barbara Ehrenreich combines personification (the "pushy" world), metonomy ("dress-for-success" as a name for the upward mobility ethos), and metaphors (the commonplace "thick and thin" and more original "skidding as well as climbing," for bad luck and good luck) to explain why she thinks best friendships between women are on the wane:

> But in the pushy new dress-for-success world, there's less room than ever for best friendships that last through thick and thin, through skidding as well as climbing.
>
> *In Praise of 'Best' Friends*

Everyone who's tried to invent effective figures of speech knows that sometimes they remain just out of reach. The new software will make record-keeping as easy as...what? "Pie?" No, a cliché, and imprecise. "A six-inch putt?" Wrong audience. "Stealing pens from the supply cabinet?" Dangerous associations. "Picking your teeth?" Ugh! Sometimes the right image just won't come. But when the Force is with you, use figures to describe the indescribable, as William H. MacLeish does, noting how the continents "*creep* about on their crustal plates." Or use them to trap a difficult idea, as Lewis Thomas did, comparing the living sky to "the world's biggest membrane." Or use them to entertain. Michael D. Lemonick, a writer for *Time*, once explained how discovering a new species of bird or insect has become commonplace, "a little like finding a new use for duct tape."

EXERCISE 4

To get a taste of what it's like to make up figures of speech, try sorting out these fourteenth-century sayings. Match one item from the first column with one from the second. More than one combination may be possible. Try reading straight across, as in "naked as a saddle on a sow." Picture the combinations. Have fun.

A. naked as a	1. saddle on a sow
B. welcome as a	2. small boat
C. cheap meat never makes a	3. barrel of fishhooks
D. like shoveling smoke with a	4. crate of finches
E. fits like a	5. needle
F. happy as a	6. cat drinking vinegar
G. looks like a	7. fire at sea
H. crooked as a	8. squirrel
I. like feeding salt to a	9. twig
J. never dance on a	10. good soup

EXERCISE 5

Identify figures of speech in the following passages. There are only one or two per passage, probably as many as most writers would want. Remember that not all comparisons or details are figurative, only those that require you to use your imagination to get past their initial lack of logic. Rewrite each passage without the figurative language. How does this change the writer's voice? You'll find a sample answer on the *Understanding Style* website.

1. The clouds were low enough that I couldn't see the lip of the canyon, only where the red cliffs, now more of an

antique rust color, dissolved. The rocks were wet and shiny, with rainwater running over them, sometimes in flat sheets, sometimes in little eroding streams that you could somehow hear above the noise of the rain and the river. The stream itself made the usual slurping sound of current with overtones of the rain sizzling on its surface. Now and then a rock would come loose and fall with a clacking sound. All this had the effect of silence.

JOHN GIERACH, *Sex, Death and Flyfishing*

2. A staggering seventy-six million babies were born in the United States between 1946 and 1964. The bulge. These baby boomers are traveling through American society like a pig moving through a python—visibly changing our culture as they get older.

HELEN E. FISHER, *Anatomy of Love*

3. Over the continent, the ice had spread southward about as evenly as spilled milk, and there is a great irregularity in its line of maximum advance. South of Buffalo, it failed to reach Pennsylvania, but it plunged deep into Ohio, Indiana, and Illinois. The ice sheets set up and started Niagara Falls. They moved the Ohio River. They dug the Great Lakes.

JOHN MCPHEE, *In Suspect Terrain*

MAKEOVER

Rewrite the following passage to eliminate clichés and usage problems, correct quoting technique, and supply at least two original figures of speech. For usage problems, consult Appendix A. What effect do your changes have upon the writer's voice?

Warehouse shopping clubs jump up and down about they're prices, the lowest available on more household goods, appliances, and hardware then you could shake a stick at. These prices are real, not just an allusion. To make a long story short, warehouse store savings come from low cost marketing and militantly plane stores stripped as bare as a baby's bottom where customers wonder up and down on there own. The clubs advertise once in a blue moon and offer as few frills as possible, usually sitting paletted goods straight off the boat from manu-facturers on cold steel shelves and selling them with almost no personnel service. As a result expenses average a vanishingly small 8 percent of sales as opposed to 22 percent at grocery stores, which are themselves slick operators compared to other retailers. Club markups are lower than a snake's belly. *Consumer Reports* sites warehouse clubs' 10 percent margin, far below those at other stores, stating "less than half the 20 to 24 percent average markup of items sold in supermarkets...even higher at department stores, which typically sell items at 40 to 50 percent above their cost."

Your Writing

Read an article on a subject that interests you from a newsmagazine like *Newsweek* or *U.S. News and World Report* and write a short account of it. Allow yourself a mild cliché or two in discussing a secondary point (e.g. "The author starts by recounting last week's *furious rally* in the bond market") or in a transitional passage (e.g. "Next, she gets to *the heart of the matter*"). But work at least one fresh figure of speech and one quotation of language you find especially effective into your account of the main point. Make sure the quotation fits neatly into the grammar of your own sentences. Highlight all clichés, figures of speech, and quotations so you'll remember what the exercise was sup-posed to show.

◇◇

POINTS TO REMEMBER

1. Generally avoid clichés, but don't be fanatical about it. Allow an occasional cliché to stand if rewriting it would not be worthwhile under the circumstances. But put your most important ideas in the freshest language you can find or invent.
2. Be somewhat broad-minded also about many usage questions, but if you have reason to think an important reader may strongly

object to a particular usage, avoid it or be ready to face the consequences.

3. When appropriate, enliven important points with effective quotations or figures of speech.

PART THREE

Clear Subjects and Lively Verbs

CHAPTER 6

Subjects and Predicates

So, he's going to talk grammar after all! Well, not too much grammar, and the most important part of it is pretty simple. You need to know how to recognize **subjects** and **predicates**, especially the subjects and predicates of the independent clauses that make up the most emphatic part of what you say. This skill is the key to finding your way around the basic structure of sentences, and you'll need it to make the most of Chapters 7 and 11, "Naming Definite Actors and Actions" and "Grammatical Variety." The good news is that you already know how to recognize subjects and predicates. If you didn't, you wouldn't be able to speak English. But bringing that knowledge up into the light, where you can do things with it, isn't always so easy.

Subjects

The subject of a sentence is sometimes called its actor—the person, place, or thing the sentence describes as *doing* or *being* something:

> *Bruno* hit Sylvie.
> *Hal and I* saddled the horses.
> *Opposable thumbs* allow humans to grasp tools.
> *The economic situation* looks grim.

Isolated subjects like *Bruno* are hard to miss. Who hit Sylvie? *Bruno.* Nothing changes when subjects are doubled or tripled. Who saddled the horses? *Hal and I.* Subjects embedded in phrases can be broken down a bit further. What allows humans to grasp tools? *Opposable thumbs.* What kind of thumbs? *Opposable* ones. What looks grim? Some *situation.* What kind of situation? *The economic* situation. In these two examples *thumb* and *situation* are the one-word, **simple subjects.** *Opposable* and *the economic* are modifiers that tell us what kind of thumb or situation the writer means. Simple subjects give you the most basic answer to the question, "Who or what is the actor in this sentence?" Add modifiers and you have a **complete subject,** that is, the simple subject and all the words that go with it:

> The **farmer** in the dell raises artichokes.
> Rising **prices** for everything from food to heating oil ate up our income.
> **One** of the most striking differences between them is their economic views.

As you see, complete subjects can grow long, but there is a simple subject at the heart of each one. A quick and dirty way to chip complicated subjects down to size is to cross out any **prepositional phrases** (phrases made up of prepositions—words *like in, of, around, between, over,* and so on—followed by **nominals**):

> The **farmer** ~~in the dell~~ raises artichokes.
> Rising **prices** ~~for everything from food to heating oil~~ ate up our income.
> **One** ~~of the most striking differences between them~~ is their economic views.

Another signal is that simple subjects are essential. You can't leave them out without opening a gaping hole in the grammar of the sentence.

> The _____ in the dell raises artichokes.
> Rising _____ for everything related to the cost of oil ate up our income.
> _____ of the most striking differences between them is their economic views.

EXERCISE 1

Underline complete subjects and highlight the simple subjects in the following sentences. Prepositional phrases will not be part of the simple subject. You'll find answers to the first three items on the *Understanding Style* website.

1. The distracting sound of heavy machinery echoed through the building.

2. The soft center of a guava tastes a bit like a strawberry.

3. Plumage is highly variable in this polymorphic species.

4. A false start of a garden has yielded a few pale tomato plants dwarfed in a grove of weeds before the house.

5. A long hog house whose cement block walls have cracked sits off at the east end of the yard.

6. Time is but the stream I go a-fishing in.

7. A chance reader, unsubsidized and unbribed, will dig them up.

8. Home plate don't move.

SATCHEL PAIGE

Standard Sentence Order and "You-Understood"

In most English sentences the subject comes first. But some (like the one you just read) start with an introductory element like "in most English sentences." Though these introducers add to the meaning of the sentence, they are not grammatically essential. Leave them out and you still have a sentence left. In the case of "In most English sentences the subject comes first," that sentence would be "The subject comes first." However drawn out they become, introductory elements can always be omitted:

~~Later~~ **we** slipped out to sit by the pool.
~~After the second-to-last presentation on new depreciation rules,~~ **we** slipped out to sit by the pool.

Sentences starting with "there is" or "there are" also change the standard sentence order:

There is a **mouse** in the feed bin.
There are plenty of **reasons** to prefer flash memory.

In these examples, *there* is just a place filler, a device to turn the sentence structure around so that the main emphasis falls where it normally wouldn't—on the real subjects, MOUSE and REAsons. You'll find more on this sort of construction in Chapter 9, "Assigning Emphasis."

Finally, some sentences involving requests or orders may seem to have no subjects at all:

Step lively!
Just think of all those calories.

In both these cases the subject is "you-understood," the unnamed person to whom the order is directed.

EXERCISE 2

Underline complete subjects and highlight simple subjects in the following sentences. Add "you-understood" subjects in brackets. You'll find answers to the first three items on the *Understanding Style* website.

1. There should be a final decision on the Patterson proposal tomorrow morning.

2. After pruning, rake up and burn the clippings.

3. Even at the polls on election day many voters had not made their final choices.

4. Dented and encrusted with marine growth, the gold cup weighed over a pound.

5. According to an agency official who spoke at the meeting, the FTC has started investigations into deceptive marketing of genetic tests.

6. At the meeting of the East and the Hudson rivers, there is an underwater canyon left over from the runoff of the Continental Glacier.

7. There is certainly a lot of research on computer-based education.

8. According to brokerage surveys cited in *National Real Estate Investor*, the average office space per worker in the United States dropped from 250 square feet in 2000 to 190 square feet in 2005.

DAVID FRANZ, *The Moral Life of Cubicles*

Subjects in Dependent Clauses

A **clause** is a group of words containing a subject and verb. While all sentences contain subjects and verbs, some have more than one set. Look at this example:

You can't get spoiled if you do your own ironing.

MERYL STREEP

"You" and *"can[n't] get"* are the subject and verb of the **independent clause** *You can't get spoiled*, the part that could stand by itself as a complete sentence. But *"if you do your own ironing"* has a subject and verb too. *You* is the subject, and *do* is the verb. *"If you do your own ironing"* is a **dependent clause**—meaning it does not stand by itself, but plays a supporting role, adding a telling condition to *"You can't get spoiled."* Independent clauses usually carry the most important content of what you are saying. In fact, Chapter 11, "Grammatical Variety" suggests you deliberately shift less important ideas into dependent constructions. But as Chapters 7 and 8 point out, the subjects of dependent clauses matter too, so it pays to be aware of them.

Types of Dependent Clauses

Dependent clauses do the work of **nouns**, **adjectives**, or **adverbs** in other clauses. In the Meryl Streep sentence, *"If you do your own ironing"* is **adverbial**. It tells *why* or *when* you can't get spoiled, an adverb function. Noun and adjective clauses? Here's a sentence with one of each:

> A marriage is always made up of two people who swear that only the other one snores.
>
> TERRY PRATCHETT

"A marriage is always made up of two people" is the independent clause; *"who swear that only the other one snores"* tells us more about those two people, as an adjective would, and *that only the other one snores* acts as a noun. It's the object of the verb *swear*. What do those people swear? *That only the other one snores.*

Here are some hallmarks of adjectival, nominal, and adverbial clauses.

ADJECTIVAL CLAUSES

- These clauses answer the questions *"Which one?"* or *"What kind?"* about a noun.

- They start with one of the relative pronouns—*who* (or *whom*), *that*, or *which*—and contain a predicate. The pronoun may be left out if it is not the subject of its clause. But if it is present, it always comes first.

    The girl **whom** *they mentioned* is my sister.
    The girl *they mentioned* is my sister.

The girl ***that*** *they gave the contract to* is my sister.
The girl *they gave the contract to* is my sister.

- They follow the nouns they modify and can be omitted without wrecking the underlying grammar of the sentence: in the examples above, that underlying sentence would be *The girl is my sister*.

NOMINAL CLAUSES

- Nominal clauses answer the question "*Who?*" or "*What?*" with regard to the rest of the clause.

- They start with *that* or the interrogatives (*who, whose, whoever, whom, which, what, where, when,* or *how*) or with *if* or *whether*. (Caution: *if* and *whether* can also introduce adverbial clauses.)

  What they said is still a mystery to me.
  We gave *whoever asked* our opinion.
  I noticed *that they ate their share.*
  How they got in has not been determined.
  Whether they got in at all is still unknown.

- They always name a *something* or *someone*. Try substituting one of these words for the clause: "*Something* is still a mystery to me"; "We gave *someone* our opinion."

- They generally *cannot* be omitted without destroying the grammar of the sentence in which they appear.

ADVERBIAL CLAUSES

- Adverbial clauses answer the questions "*How?*" "*When?*" "*Where?*" "*How often?*" or "*Why?*" about the main clause.

  We're still going, *unless she changed her mind.*
  As we drove east, they came west to meet us.
  Where the road ended, Sandra shouldered her pack and walked on.
  They would make small changes *whenever we complained.*
  Because she was late, we put off the starting time.

- They start with a subordinating conjunction. Typical examples:

after	provided (that)
although	seeing (that)
as	since
as far as	so (that)
as if	such that
as long as	supposing (that)
as though	than
because	that
before	though
considering (that)	till
even if	unless
except (that)	until
if	when
in order that	whenever
in that	where
now (that)	wherever
on condition (that)	while
once	whether

- They can be omitted without destroying the grammar of the sentence in which they appear.

EXERCISE 3

Underline the complete subjects and highlight the simple subjects in the following sentences. Each sentence contains more than one clause. Look for subject and verb combinations. Each set you find signals a new clause. If you get confused, try crossing out prepositional phrases. You'll find answers to the first three items on the *Understanding Style* website.

1. Liberty doesn't work as well in practice as it does in speeches.

WILL ROGERS

2. When I was born, I was so surprised I didn't talk for a year and a half.

GRACIE ALLEN

3. The first principle is that you must not fool yourself.

RICHARD FEYNMAN

4. When I read about the evils of drinking, I gave up reading.

HENNY YOUNGMAN

5. People always call it luck when you've acted more sensibly than they have.

ANNE TYLER

6. If your mother gives you away, you think everybody who comes into your life is going to give you away.

EARTHA KITT

7. This is a night when kings in golden mail ride their elephants over the mountains.

JOHN CHEEVER

8. I'll make him an offer he can't refuse.

MARIO PUZO

Coordinate Clauses

Coordinate clauses are simply clauses combined into a series, usually by one of the coordinating conjunctions (*and, but, or, nor, for, so, yet*):

He huffed and *he puffed* and *he blew the house down.* (Three independent clauses)
After we got there but *before you came in*, we had a talk with Mother. (Two dependent adverbial clauses followed by an independent clause)
I told her to keep quiet, but *she wouldn't because she was shocked* and *she wanted to know why.* (Two independent clauses and two dependent adverbial clauses. Notice that the *because* applies to both dependent clauses: *because she was shocked* and [*because*] *she wanted to know why.*)

Remember that what makes these constructions clauses is that each one has a subject and a verb. Whenever you see that combination, you're looking at a clause.

EXERCISE 4

Underline the complete subjects and highlight the simple subjects in the following sentences. Each sentence contains more than one clause.

Look for subject and verb combinations. Each set you find signals a new clause. Be ready to say whether the clauses you find are dependent or independent. You'll find answers to the first three items on the *Understanding Style* website.

1. When you are logged in to your meeting room and an attendee uses the URL to access it, you are notified immediately.

2. Because its "recipe" of 25 main and trace elements varies from one deposit to the next, pumice, which was widely used as an abrasive in ancient cultures, can usually be traced to a specific volcanic eruption.

3. Whether you think you can or you think you can't, you're right.

HENRY FORD

4. Faith is taking the first step even when you don't see the whole staircase.

MARTIN LUTHER KING, JR.

5. *The Wall Street Journal* reported that Google's first android release was pushed back to 2008, but that was what Google intended all along.

6. Because the average person walks thousands of miles in a lifetime, the 26 bones, 33 joints and 100-plus tendons, ligaments and muscles in each foot must absorb enormous strain.

7. The good we secure for ourselves is precarious and uncertain until it is secured for all of us and incorporated into our common life.

JANE ADDAMS

8. We act as though comfort and luxury were the chief requirements of life, when all that we need to make us happy is something to be enthusiastic about.

ALBERT EINSTEIN

Predicates

The subject is the someone or something a sentence or clause concerns. The **predicate** is the comment made about it. The subject is the someone or something that does or is X. That X is the predicate.

Just as the complete subject includes the simple subject and the words attached to it, the predicate consists of the verb and all the words that go with it. Dividing your sentences and clauses into these two basic units is a powerful first step toward increasing their effectiveness and coherence.

> The **subject** / **is** the someone or something [that] a **sentence** or **clause** / **concerns**.
> The **predicate** / **is** the comment made about it.
> The **subject** / **is** the someone or something
> **that** / **does** X or **is** X.
> That **X** / **is** the predicate.

Hmmm. *Is, concerns, is, is, does, is, is*—a pretty dispirited collection of verbs, though *to be* verbs always crowd into passages geared to definition. Let's try a more typical passage.

> People of the same trade seldom meet together, even for merriment and diversion, but the conversation ends in a conspiracy against the public, or in some contrivance to raise prices.
> ADAM SMITH

> **People** of the same trade / seldom **meet** together, even for merriment and diversion, but the **conversation** / **ends** in a conspiracy against the public, or in some contrivance to raise prices.

Meet and *ends* are the verbs in the Adam Smith quotation. The predicates are those verbs and all the words that explain or complete them. Tradespersons meet when? *Seldom.* Meet how? *Together.* Meet why? *For merriment and diversion.* Conversations end how? *In a conspiracy against the public*, and so on.

Why should you care about all this? Two reasons: liveliness and coherence. Much of the force of your writing comes from its verbs. As Chapter 7 argues, strong and lively verbs make for strong and lively writing. Knowing where your verbs are is an essential first step toward keeping them forceful.

Then too, subjects and predicates play quite different roles in sentences and paragraphs. Glance back over the last few sets of example sentences. As you see, most clauses are unevenly balanced.

Grammatical subjects tend to briefly name what a clause is about, while the meat of the remark, the new information, comes in the predicate. Chapter 8 tells you how to use these traits to keep your sentences linked together, but the process starts with recognizing subjects and predicates.

EXERCISE 5

Put a slash between the complete subjects and predicates in the following sentences. The sentences may contain more than one clause. Look for subject and verb combinations. Each set you find signals a new clause. You'll find answers to the first three items on the *Understanding Style* website.

1. I wonder if other dogs think poodles belong to some weird religious cult.

   RITA RUDNER

2. Wireless USB looked like a good bet at first, but the technology never caught on.

3. When the Phoenix Mars Lander became unable to recharge its batteries, it had to be reprogrammed every day because it lost its memory each night.

4. While capitalism is the exploitation of man by man, communism is the exact opposite.

   BEN LEWIS, *Hammer and Tickle*

5. Root cellars could keep potatoes and winter squash from harvest to February or March and onions even longer.

6. Since insurance rarely covers cosmetic surgery, doctors often offer two-for-the-price-of-one specials and even zero-percent financing.

7. I like to fly on an airline right after they've had a crash because it improves your odds.

   GEORGE CARLIN

8. She said he swept her off her feet, but then he wouldn't help her up again.

Multiple Predicates and Predicates in Dependent Clauses

Just as subjects can be doubled or tripled, so can predicates:

> (*Hal and I*) / saddled the horses. (Two subjects; one predicate)
> (Hal) / *saddled* the horses, / *adjusted* their bridles, / and *led* them out of the barn. (One subject, three predicates)

Multiple predicates don't change the nature of a sentence, but they do influence it. One key to effective writing is using strong verbs. It helps to know where all of them are.

Of course, every dependent clause has its predicate, too, and each of these predicates has a verb. But the basic principle doesn't change: every subject-verb combination signals a new clause, and every new clause can be divided into a complete subject and a predicate.

EXERCISE 6

Put a slash between the complete subjects and predicates in the following sentences. Highlight the simple subjects and verb. The sentences may contain more than one clause, and clauses may contain more than one subject or verb. You'll find answers to the first items three on the *Understanding Style* website.

1. Homer held the rooster by its feet as it flapped wildly and craned its neck, trying to peck him.

2. My cousin Lela is by far the prettiest, but Martha and Corinne are more athletic.

3. Because of the letter I wrote, the mayor made me grounds supervisor.

4. I come from Des Moines; somebody had to.

   BILL BRYSON

5. The coffee there always tastes stale, and I swear they microwave their fried eggs.

6. My sister works out every day after she comes in from school.

7. I bowed deeply and handed my mother the DVD she was so eager to watch.

8. The Romans massed in the Forum near the Tiber while their enemies held the heights.

Your Writing

Choose a passage of at least a hundred words written in your usual style. Highlight the simple subjects and verbs, perhaps in different colors. Keep this marked-up paper to analyze after you've completed Chapters 7 and 8. Ask yourself at that point whether you named definite actors and actions and whether your passage uses clustered subjects to make your ideas cohere. Then rewrite the passage to see if you can improve its liveliness and coherence.

◇◇

POINTS TO REMEMBER

1. The subject of a sentence or clause is sometimes called its actor—the person, place, or thing the clause describes as *doing* or *being* something.
2. Subjects often appear as phrases—complete subjects—in which one word—the simple subject—is the focal point. The simple subject will be the one word or group of words you couldn't leave out.
3. Predicates consist of the verb and any words that go with it. The verb will be the heart of this phrase, the word or words you couldn't leave out.
4. Whether dependent or independent, every clause has a subject and predicate.
5. Striking out prepositional phrases is a good way to uncover the basic structure of a sentence or clause.

◇◇

CHAPTER 7

Naming Definite Actors and Actions

The most important relationship in a **sentence** or **clause** is the one between the **subject** and the **verb**, the actor and the action being performed. Each subject and verb combination makes a new statement about some person or thing doing something or being something. In good sentences, subjects name clear and appropriate actors, and verbs name definite and expressive actions. For a review on identifying subjects and verbs see Chapter 6 and the headings for those words in the Glossary at the end of the book.

Naming Definite Actors

The chief rule for writing clear and effective sentences is keeping readers aware of who is doing what, or as Richard Lanham once put it, "Who's kicking who?" Here is a clear and effective sentence:

> By 1967, when tens of thousands of young protesters were marching on the Pentagon against the Vietnam War and General William C. Westmoreland was demanding the deployment of another two hundred thousand men, Lyndon Johnson believed that Robert McNamara, his Secretary of Defense, was going mad.
> SIDNEY BLUMENTHAL, *McNamara's Peace*

Consider the actors and actions named in this statement. Who were marching? Thousands of young protesters. Who was demanding more troops? General William C. Westmoreland. Who believed something? Lyndon Johnson. Who might have been going mad? Robert McNamara. The sentence works as well as it does because these actors and their actions are made unmistakably clear.

Avoiding Indefinite Actors

Look what happens when you remove the distinct actors listed above and replace them with **abstractions** as subjects:

> By 1967, when protest marches on the Pentagon against the Vietnam War were occurring and military demands were being made for the deployment of another two hundred thousand men, a belief arose in the White House that a mental disturbance threatened a high official.

"Marches...were occurring; demands...were being made; belief...arose; disturbance...threatened." The cast of human characters disappears, and in their place we see only disembodied protest marches, military demands, beliefs, and mental disturbances. Because these actors are harder to picture, their actions seem equally fuzzy. Although the sentence says much the same as before, the force and color have been drained out of it.

Subjects don't always have to be people to work well, but they should represent the clearest, most definite way you can think of to say what you mean. Prefer "General William C. Westmoreland" to "a high ranking officer." Instead of "a successful niche software firm" say "Adobe." Don't write "The study established" when you could write "Doctor Marie Farnsworth found."

> Buying into a firm that manages mutual funds sounds unsexy, but PIMCO Advisors Limited Partnership (stock symbol: PA; recent price: $18) has plenty of charm.
>
> JACK EGAN, A Lode of Undiscovered Nuggets

The chief subjects here, "buying into a firm..." and "PIMCO," are certainly not persons, but they express precisely what the writer has in mind. To see how effective these words are as subjects consider what Egan might have written instead:

> Sounding unsexy could be an objection raised to the idea of buying into a firm that manages mutual funds, but the charm

of PIMCO Advisors Limited Partnership (stock symbol: PA; recent price: $18) is notable.

EXERCISE 1

Highlight the subjects and verbs in the following passages. Which one from each pair has a more definite cast of actors? What effect do the differences have on the writer's voice? You'll find a sample answer on the *Understanding Style* website.

1. As Selma, Alabama's first black school superintendent, [Dr. Norward Rousell] couldn't help but notice that "gifted and talented" tracks were nearly lily white in a district that was 70 percent black. When he looked for answers in the files of high school students, he discovered that a surprising number of low track minority kids had actually scored higher than their white top track counterparts.

PATRICIA KEAN, *Blowing up the Tracks*

Observation by Selma, Alabama's newly establish black school leadership established that "gifted and talented" tracks were nearly lily white in a district that was 70 percent black. Investigation of files of high school students showed that a surprising number of scores for low track minority kids were actually higher than those of their white top track counterparts.

2. At 15,000 feet, its best operating height, the Kittyhawk IA could fly at a maximum speed of only 354 mph and climb to that height in 8.3 minutes, a longer time than the AGM2 Zero took to reach 20,000 feet.

JOHN VADER, *Pacific Hawk*

Maximum speed of the Kittyhawk IA at 15,000 feet, its best operating height, was only 354 mph. Climb rate to that altitude was 8.3 minutes. Climb rate for the AGM2 Zero to 20,000 feet was shorter than this.

3. Mario Livio, of the Space Telescope Science Institute in Baltimore, was reviewing what he called "observational evidence of the actual existence of black holes in the sky." He displayed a Hubble image of the center of the galaxy NGC

4261. It showed a glowing doughnut of gas and dust with a
hellish-looking funnel of white-hot material jetting out of its
center—exactly what one would expect if, as the theorists
predicted long ago, there were a massive black hole there.

TIMOTHY FERRIS, Minds and Matter

A review of "observational evidence of the actual existence of black holes in the sky" was being conducted by an
astronomer from the Space Telescope Science Institute in
Baltimore. A display associated with this review pictured a
Hubble image of the center of the galaxy NGC 4261. Shown
in this display was a glowing doughnut of gas and dust with a
hellish-looking funnel of white-hot material jetting out of its
center. Longstanding theoretical expectations of a massive
black hole in this location were confirmed by this review.

The Problem of Nominalizations

Nominalizations—nouns formed from other parts of speech, especially
verbs—darken many a sunless sentence. Here is a straightforward statement with clearly defined actors and actions (verbs in bold type):

The defendant categorically **denied** he **knew** about the stock split
before it **was** officially **announced**.

Look what happens when you start replacing the verbs with
corresponding noun forms:

The **denial** by the defendant that he knew about the stock split
before it was officially announced was categorical.

The **denial** by the defendant of **knowledge** about the stock split
before it was officially announced was categorical.

The **denial** by the defendant of **knowledge** about the stock split
before its official **announcement** was categorical.

By the time you get to the third version, the life of the sentence,
its actors and actions, has been extinguished. The writing has entered
the gray underworld of **official style**, the bloodless language of on-duty
bureaucrats and lawyers.

Reversing the nominalization process—replacing nominalizations
with verb forms and actors—can reanimate a passage that has stiffened
into official style:

The **solution** to the problems of **evaluation** of medical care
providers has the **appearance** of difficulty.

Solution, evaluation, and *appearance* are all derived from verbs—*solve, evaluate,* and *appear.* Switch them back to verb forms and the sentence instantly grows more natural and clear:

Solving the problems of **evaluating** medical care providers **appears** difficult.

Of course nominalizations have their uses. If they didn't, they wouldn't be in the language, let alone be as common as they are. Sometimes the nominalized version of a verb is the most familiar and clearest name for the concept it expresses. No one would suggest you replace *Industrial Revolution* with "that time when manufacturing moved forward from handwork to machines" or do without staples like *profession, exploration, convention, attention,* and many others. But if nominalizations are clogging your style, replace them with more definite actors and actions. The response of your readers will be appreciation. That is, they'll appreciate it.

EXERCISE 2

Replace nominalizations in the following sentences with actors and actions. Change the sentence structure however you like, but include all the major ideas of the original. How do your revisions change the writer's voice? You'll find a sample answer on the *Understanding Style* website.

1. The coroner's determination that the victim died of smoke inhalation was the key to the jury's decision in favor of the defendant's conviction.

2. Mozart's reaction to Haydn's innovations in the construction of string quartets was a reevaluation and amendment of his own practices.

3. The company's performance in the third quarter is expected to show improvement following the curtailment of its customer base erosion.

Naming Definite Actions

Avoiding Weak Verbs: *to be*

Not all verbs were created equal. Some—like *hit, shove,* or *masticate*—name physical actions. Some—like *hope, resemble* or *ponder*—name abstract mental operations or relationships. Others do not name much of anything at all. They're vague enough to fit in almost anywhere, pre-cisely because they are limp and unexpressive. Writing overladen with vague, weak verbs is—you guessed it—vague and weak.

Far and away the weakest verb in English is *to be* in one of its many forms: *am, is, are, was, were, shall be, will be, have been, has been, had been, will have been being*, etc. *To be* says little on its own. It usually works like an equal sign to connect subjects and **complements**, adjective or noun phrases that rename the subject:

The plumber *has been* ill with a stomach virus.
Zenda *is* an energetic German Shorthair.

To be is also the most frequently used verb in English, and under-standably so. After all, most communication requires defining subjects or giving their attributes. If Zenda really *is* an energetic German Shorthair, what else can you say?

Plenty. Some writers have been warned off *to be* so effectively they keep any form of the word out of their sentences. That's going too far. But if you feel you depend more heavily than you should on *to be*, it's usually possible to rewrite every second occurrence or so to allow for another verb:

The plumber *has come down with* a stomach virus.
Zenda, the German Shorthair, *quivers* with energy.

Another way to cut down on *to be* and other weak verbs is to change your sentence structure (see Chapter 11 for ways of doing this). Here's a problem passage:

The European birthrate *is* low and *is* now in the danger zone. The rate in much of Europe *is* down to about 1.3 children per couple, and that *is* far below the 2.1 "replacement" rate that *is* what it *takes* to keep populations level. Forty years ago 12.5 percent of the world's population *was* European. Now the fig-ure *is* 7 percent. In forty more years at the present rate it *will be* 5 percent.

Eight of the nine verbs here are some form of *to be*. Reshaping and com-bining sentences can enliven the style and eliminate words at the same time:

A birthrate of about 1.3 children per couple—far below the 2.1 "replacement" ratio—*has plunged* Europe into the danger zone for population loss. Forty years ago 12.5 percent of the world *lived* in Europe. Now only 7 percent *does*, and in forty more years at the present rate that number *will drop* to 5 percent.

EXERCISE 3

Locate the *to be* verbs in the following passages. Rewrite to replace or eliminate most of them. How do your revisions change the writer's voice? You'll find a sample answer on the *Understanding Style* website.

1. Maple is a dense wood that is light-colored. It is often nearly free of grain. Because it is hard, maple is often used for countertops and chopping boards. But the wood has been used for furniture as well. Maple furniture was popular during the later 1950s.

2. The presumed ugliness that makes women buy makeup and push-up bras is analogous to the male sex organ, which is an object of shame. The meaning of many cultural messages is that what women really are is better hidden.

BASED ON DEAN MACCANNELL AND JULIET
FLOWER MACCANNELL, *The Beauty System*

3. According to cosmologists, the estimated age of the universe is between 10 and 20 billion years, and its major component is dark matter, which is transparent because it is incapable of reflecting light and is unable to cast a shadow.

Other Weak Verbs

Below is a very incomplete list of weak verbs besides *to be*. Many sound finicky, like *pertain*, or trendy, like *mandate*. All are at their weakest when they name some vaguely imagined action or relationship—especially, as often happens, when the effect is compounded by abstract or nominalized subjects:

Financing needs will be **determined** and an operational plan **developed**.

As the example shows, these verbs are all mainstays of the official style at its stuffiest.

acknowledge	contribute	exist	provide
assist	determine	expand	put forth
attempt	develop	find	receive
cause	do	have	require
change	employ	help	respond
complete	erode	make	result
concern	establish	mandate	seek
conduct	examine	occur	seem
consider	exhibit	pertain	transform

If verbs like these dominate your sentences, think about replacing them with more expressive action words:

Not

We will **attempt** to **establish** why the valve failure **occurred**.

But

We will **learn** why the valve **failed**.

Unnecessary Auxiliaries

Another sort of weakness results when verbs are combined with a string of waffling auxiliaries like *should, would, might, may, could, can* and *help*. These words should be reserved for cases of genuine uncertainty:

If Saturn's rings were not seen edge-on for about a half hour every 15 years, 13 of the planet's 18 moons **might** have remained hidden.

They shouldn't be used to tiptoe around a straightforward situation:

Students **would** be well advised to keep a journal, for this **can help** them consolidate what they **may** have learned.

Although the extra verbs here blunt the statement, they don't fool anyone. The writer meant, and should have said:

Students, keep a journal to consolidate what you learn.

EXERCISE 4

Locate weak verbs and waffling auxiliaries in the following sentences, and replace them with more expressive choices. How do your revisions change the writer's voice? You'll find a sample answer on the *Understanding Style* website.

1. To assist with historical research, America Online has established a database which should provide information on the 59,196 men and women whose names are exhibited on the Vietnam Veteran's Memorial in Washington, D.C.

2. Critics acknowledge that Piet Mondrian's tree pictures, completed around 1908, might have contributed to the artist's development by transforming his style.

3. A female reticulated python at the National Zoo had developed a length of 25 feet and a weight of 300 pounds when last exhibited; the reptile employed a hundred teeth in six rows to help hold prey for ingestion.

Unnecessary Passive Verbs

Most verbs you meet with are in the **active voice**. The subject *does* something, even if it is something vague. With verbs in the **passive voice** something is *done to* the subject. Instead of "Malcolm *visited* Pensacola," you get "Pensacola *was visited* by Malcolm," or just "Pensacola *was visited*." Asking whether the subject is doing something or having something done to it is the classic way to recognize passive verbs, but other clues also help. All passives contain some form of *to be* as an auxiliary verb. Look carefully at these passive verbs. Passive forms of other verbs are very similar:

Passive Present Tense

The life *is lived*. The essay *is written*.

Passive Past Tense

The life *was lived*. The essay *was written*.

Passive Future Tense

The life *will be lived*. The essay *will be written*.

Passive Present Perfect Tense

The life *has been lived*. The essay *has been written*.

Passive Past Perfect Tense

The life *had been lived*. The essay *had been written*.

Passive constructions refocus attention in a sentence by moving the **sentence nucleus** or major stress. You'll find more on sentence nuclei in Chapter 9. In place of an active sentence like "In 1906 Dr. Cherry founded the uni**VER**sity," passives produce constructions like "The university was founded in 1906 by Dr **CHER**ry," or "The university was founded in 1906." In the right circumstances either of these restructured sentences could be effective: the first if you wanted to emphasize the founder's name, the second if you wished to focus on the date of the founding, regardless of who carried it out.

But passive constructions have drawbacks. They are generally longer and less natural-sounding than their active counterparts, and they can obscure the **actor-action relationship** at the heart of a sentence. The most objectionable passive verbs are those that hide the actors in a sentence in order to save the writer from taking a stand. Passives weaken this passage, making it sound as if no one in particular were answerable for the opinions it sets out:

> Gore Vidal **has been said** to be a great contemporary novelist. He **is credited** with a gift for style and characterization. His books **are** widely **read** and **appreciated**. His *1876*, a historical novel, **has been called** a fine achievement.

Are these the opinions of specific critics? Who are they, and how reliable are their views? Or do the opinions belong to the writer? If so, he or she should make that clear:

> I **think** Gore Vidal **is** one of our best contemporary novelists. Like other fans, I **enjoy** all his work. I especially **appreciate** his gift for style and characterization, which **shows** clearly in his historical novel *1876*.

Use passives when you want to emphasize actions whose actors are not important:

> Dogs should not be fed chocolate.

> The facade was decorated with colored lights.

Use passives to emphasize important words:

> The baby was kept alive by an **IN**cubator.

> We were carried to the top by an inclined **RAIL**way.

But don't use passives to dodge making a definite statement or to keep actors hidden:

> Not

> Japanese art is considered sophisticated and delicate.

But

Japanese art is sophisticated and delicate.

Not

The investments were unwisely chosen.

But

Your broker has lost your money.

EXERCISE 5

Make the italicized active verbs in the following sentences passive. Under what circumstances, if any, would the passive versions work better than the originals? You'll find a sample answer on the *Understanding Style* website.

1. Some genetically altered potatoes *manufacture* a natural toxin capable of killing Colorado Potato Beetles, the number one potato pest.

2. Music publishers *should bind* music books so that they will stay open on a stand.

3. When Hans Kung *criticized* papal authority, the Catholic Church stripped Kung of his right to teach as a Catholic theologian.

4. When Hans Kung criticized papal authority, the Catholic Church *stripped* Kung of his right to teach as a Catholic theologian.

5. Pomologists continually *develop* new varieties of apples.

EXERCISE 6

Make the italicized passive verbs in the following sentences active. Under what circumstances, if any, would the passive versions work better than the originals? You'll find a sample answer on the *Understanding Style* website.

1. While mistakes *were made* by the grant administrators, criminal intent *has* not *been demonstrated*.

2. In general the greatest economic rewards *are reserved* for services society regards most highly.

3. In general society reserves the greatest economic rewards for services which *are regarded* most highly.

4. It *is* widely *thought* that many animal habitats *are threatened* by logging.

5. The timetable for the evolution of today's birds *has* recently *been shortened* by millions of years by paleontologists.

Keeping Actors and Actions Together

Even clearly named actors and definite actions can get lost if the structure of a sentence obscures the relationship between them. Most sentences start with a subject and its modifiers (see Chapter 6) and move on to a **predicate**, the verb and the words that go with it. As we saw earlier, the verb names what is done in a sentence. We can think of the verb as a single action word or—along with its modifiers, objects, and complements—as a comment about the subject:

The European Parliament has rejected a proposal for patenting life forms.

All the words up to *has rejected*, the verb, center on *Parliament*. *Parliament* is the subject; "The European Parliament" is the complete subject. *Has rejected* is the verb. "Has rejected a proposal for patenting life forms" is the expanded verb, or predicate. What's the sentence about? The European Parliament. What about the European Parliament? It has rejected a proposal for patenting life forms. This action is predicated of the European Parliament.

If you want to make your writing easy to understand, think twice before letting long sentence elements come between subject and predicate. Consider this sentence:

The European Parliament in a surprise victory for the Green Party, which has long opposed genetic manipulation for economic gain, has rejected a permissive ruling in favor of patenting life forms.

Parliament is clearly the subject of the sentence, but a reader has to wade through another eighteen words for the verb *has rejected* to appear, along with the rest of the predicate that completes the thought.

Because objects and complements are part of the essential meaning of a sentence, separating these from the verb with a long interrupter can be equally awkward and confusing:

The European Parliament has rejected by a substantial margin that must have been gratifying to the Green Party, which opposes genetic manipulation for economic gain, a permissive ruling in favor of patenting life forms.

To improve sentences like these, pull subject, verb, and complement closer together. Move interrupting material to the beginning or end of your new sentence, or give it a sentence of its own.

In a move that must have been gratifying to the Green Party, which opposes genetic manipulation for economic gain, the European Parliament has rejected a permissive ruling in favor of patenting life forms.

The European Parliament has rejected a permissive ruling in favor of patenting life forms, a move that must have been gratifying to the Green Party, which opposes genetic manipulation for economic gain.

The European Parliament has rejected a permissive ruling in favor of patenting life forms. This move must have been gratifying to the Green Party, which opposes genetic manipulation for economic gain.

EXERCISE 7

Rewrite the following sentences to bring subjects, verbs, objects, and complements closer together. Move interrupting material to the beginning or end of the sentence or recast it as an independent sentence or sentences. What effect do your revisions have on the writer's voice? You'll find a sample answer on the *Understanding Style* website.

1. A low power holographic radar scanner that can image a body beneath clothes with enough accuracy to spot non-metallic weapons and explosives and also distinguish male and female anatomy easily may be used at security-check stations in the future in spite of the risks it poses to personal modesty.

2. Barbed bone fish-spear points eighty to ninety thousand years old which were discovered in Africa alongside bones of a

catfish that would have been six feet long in life have radically pushed back the age of this technology.

3. Four mile long Hampton Roads, the sheltered estuary through which three rivers empty into Chesapeake Bay and an uncommonly fine natural harbor, accommodates the largest naval complex in the world.

MAKEOVER

Use a combination of techniques—naming definite actors, avoiding unnecessary abstractions and nominalizations as subjects, supplying strong verbs, eliminating unnecessary passives, removing interruptions between major sentence elements—to strengthen the following passage. Change the sentence structure however you like, but keep all the major ideas of the original. How do your revisions change the writer's voice?

Public funding and preferential legislation that favor improvement in the fuel economy of private automobiles and trucks ought to be opposed by popular opinion. The cost/load ratio of automobiles and other gas powered private conveyances such as trucks and vans might be vastly improved upon by mass transit options, whose efficiency as people transporters can be up to hundreds of times greater. Lower maintenance costs and pollution per passenger mile, traffic reduction, and increased safety can also be gained from mass transit systems such as busses and trolleys. Freight can be handled more economically and with less environmental damage by railroads and airlines than by trucks. Excessive amounts of fuel, even allowing for continuing improvements in economy, are burned by trucks, and expensive roadways and interstate highways are increasingly damaged by their overabundant use. In an era when fuel reserves are threatened, traffic is constantly rising in volume and danger, and infrastructure damage is increasingly common and expensive to repair, use of automobiles and trucks should be curtailed. Mass transit systems and more efficient ways of moving freight should be encouraged instead by decision-makers.

Your Writing

Write two versions of a letter to a friend on some recent happening that concerns you both. Write first version in the voice you would normally use—pretty much the same words and constructions you would use in speaking to him or her. In the second, replace personal actors with impersonal actors, strong verbs with weak verbs and passives, and add nominalizations. For example, "If this proposal goes through we won't be able to put up siding or storm windows unless some bureaucrat okays it first" might become "Prior permission will be a requirement for home improvements ranging from storm window utilization to installation of siding." For more examples, review exercises in this chapter. How do your changes affect the written voice of your letters?

◇◇◇

POINTS TO REMEMBER

1. Choose definite actors as the subjects of your sentences. Be especially wary of using nominalized verbs as subjects: for instance, saying "Adequate maturation for job related self motivation is required of candidates" instead of "Candidates must have matured enough to motivate themselves on the job."
2. Choose definite actions as the verbs of your sentences. When you have a choice, prefer strong, active verbs to weak verbs and passives.
3. Think twice about placing interrupting elements between subjects and verbs.

◇◇◇

PART FOUR

Making Connections: Coherence and Emphasis

CHAPTER **8**

Coherence: Making Sentences Connect

Maintaining Related Grammatical Subjects

Except in textbooks, sentences rarely stand alone. Most interact with other statements around them to form connected discourse, which must be *coherent* if it is to reflect the forward sweep of your thinking. Each sentence should join with the others to help readers follow your developing thoughts. Fortunately, most techniques for keeping your sentences connected are not hard to use once you are aware of them. Consider this workmanlike if unappetizing discussion:

> No matter how unpretentious and simple or how fancifully adorned, terrines, pâtés, and galantines are basically composed of a forcemeat cooked in some sort of wrapping. Forcemeat, called *farce* in French, is finely or coarsely chopped, ground, or pureed meat, poultry, or fish, seasoned and bound with egg, cream, bread, or a combination of the three. It may be layered with strips or pieces of meat, livers, sweetbreads, fat, vegetables, or truffle to vary color, texture, and taste. The wrapping may be caul fat, fatback, bacon strips, salt pork, pastry crust, fish fillets, grape leaves, or, as sometimes in the case of galantines, the skin of the animal.
>
> VICTORIA WISE, *American Charcuterie*

You begin this passage with little idea of what to expect, but that's no problem: as a reader you are used to finding your bearings at the start of a new topic. That's why the first sentence of each paragraph in a piece of writing is often a **topic sentence** that clearly announces the next point the writer plans to take up.

But the moment you learn what the new subject will be, your attitude changes. You expect the writer's sentences to twine around this acknowledged topic until a new subject is announced and a new cluster of sentences begins, often but not always after a paragraph break. Most writing moves from one **sentence cluster** to the next, each cluster unfolding a little more of what the author has to say.

How does this interlacing work? Much of the effect depends on grammatical and formal connections between sentences. Notice how *forcemeat*, the new topic proclaimed in the passage above, becomes the grammatical **subject** of the second sentence. *It*, the subject of the third sentence, refers to *forcemeat* too, so the second and third sentences of the passage grammatically center on the announced topic of the first. True, sentence number four introduces a new grammatical subject—*wrapping*—but wrappings were mentioned back in the opening statement also, so listing the forcemeat artist's wrapping options here seems wholly appropriate. Terrines, pâtés, and gallatines are made up of some sort of forcemeat wrapped in something else, and the subjects of each sentence in the passage keep you inescapably focused on this central fact: in order, they include (1) "terrines, pâtés, and galantines," (2) "Forcemeat," (3) "It" [forcemeat], and (4) "wrapping." As Wise's sentences show, a classic way to make writing hold together is to make the subject of each new sentence something already announced in a previous one. It's hard to believe a simple trick like this can do so much to improve the coherence of your writing until you try it.

Maybe you're unconvinced. See how this revision of the forcemeat passage strikes you:

No matter how unpretentious and simple or how fancifully adorned, terrines, pâtés, and galantines are basically composed of a forcemeat cooked in some sort of wrapping. The French finely or coarsely chop, grind, or puree meat, poultry, or fish—seasoning and binding it with egg, cream, bread, or a combination of the three into a mixture they call *farce*. Strips or pieces of meat, livers, sweetbreads, fat, vegetables, or truffle may be layered with the forcemeat to vary color, texture, and taste. Caul fat, fatback, bacon strips, salt pork, pastry crust, fish fillets, grape leaves, or, as sometimes in the case of galantines, the skin of the animal may form the wrapping.

Although this passage says almost exactly what the first version did, chances are you found it harder to follow. What are "the French" doing in the subject slot of sentence two? Is sentence three really about "Strips or pieces of meat"? The ideas in the passage are as closely related as ever, but the second version doesn't help you see that. The way it jumps from previously unannounced subject to previously unannounced subject leaves you to uncover the connections for yourself. Multiply this impression over a whole series of sentence clusters and you have a common but fairly subtle problem. A great deal of writing that appears disjointed and pointless, whether it really is or not, seems that way because the writer chose the wrong grammatical subjects. Chapter 11 explains in detail how sentences can be combined and reconfigured to make their grammatical subjects whatever you choose. For maximum coherence, it's usually best to make them refer to something already announced in the sentence cluster you're working on.

EXERCISE 1

Rewrite the following passages so that each sentence has a word or concept mentioned in the opening sentence for its subject. Pronoun subjects that refer to a word in the first sentence will be fine. If you need help with the rewriting, read ahead in Chapter 11. How do your revisions affect the coherence of each passage? You'll find a sample answer on the *Understanding Style* website.

1. Logical positivists formed a school of modern philosophy led by the Vienna Circle of the 1920s. Mathematical precision was their model for philosophical thinking. Moral and value statements were considered nonsensical. Analysis of language rather than things provided their mode of operation.

2. Antarctica is home to a strange body of fresh water. Researchers there have found an unfrozen cache of fresh water the size of Lake Ontario. The Russian base Vostok is directly over the lake, which is trapped under 2 ½ miles of ice. Measurements show the lake is 124 miles long and averages 400 feet deep. Scientists believe it may harbor ancient life forms but are reluctant to try to tap the water. Contamination is one problem they fear. The tremendous pressure caused by the lake's icy overburden is another.

3. Longer wash cycles are a feature of front loading washing machines. But front loaders are still more efficient than top loaders. Comparisons of energy use reveal that. You save on

water and detergent as well. Cleaning, though, is the bottom line. The newer model top loaders are poorly rated for cleaning. Government regulations have reduced the amount of energy they consume, lessening their performance. "Agitation," which top loaders use, is also less effective than tumbling. And front loaders are easier on your clothes.

EXERCISE 2

Rewrite the following passages so that each sentence has a new word or concept for its subject (current subjects shown in boldface). One way to do this is to select a new subject from the words and ideas in second part of the sentence. For instance, "Western **lakes** are ringed with the king-sized nests of bald eagles" could become "Bald **eagles** build king-sized nests along the shores of Western lakes." How do your revisions affect the coherence of each passage? You'll find a sample answer on the *Understanding Style* website.

1. Roman **artists** often used "clarifying perspective" in inventive ways. A **muralist** from Pompeii painted a riot in an amphitheater to show events taking place inside and outside the arena at the same time. Another **painter** showed the beginning and end of the fall of Icarus at the top and bottom of the same picture. The **artist** of the famous *Nile Mosaic* presented the whole course of the river from the Sudan to the delta in four contiguous panels, one on top of the other within the same frame.

2. Saint **Laurence** has long been the most popular of the Roman martyrs. According to traditional stories, when **he** was commanded by the prefect Valerian to hand over church treasures to the state by a certain day, **he** sold the treasures instead and gave the money to poor Christians. Called to account for this, **Laurence** presented the poor people **he** had helped to Valerian. "**These**," **he** proclaimed, "are the treasures of the church!"

3. **People** who scraped out a living in forests and on untilled common lands long nourished democratic sentiments in England. Forest **outlaws** became egalitarian heroes in the Robin Hood stories, and poor **tradespeople and outcasts** with no place in towns or on established estates provided support for various movements of social unrest. These **groups** made up a significant population. According to the seventeenth century commentator Richard Baxter, "the **woods and commons** are planted with

nailers, scythe-smiths and other iron labourers, like a continued village."

BASED ON CHRISTOPHER HILL,
The World Turned Upside Down

Patterns of Old and New Information

As Chapter 9 explains, a key feature of the English stress system is that the chief stress in a sentence, or **sentence nucleus,** typically falls on the stressed syllable of last significant word.

Palmetto hearts are not only edible but de**LI**cious.

Swimming snakes undulate from side to **SIDE**.

Our word *farce* comes from the French term for **FORCE**meat.

This trait arises from the fairly strict word order observed in English sentences, where in the great majority of cases the **subject** comes first and is followed by a **predicate**, or comment about the subject. Palmetto hearts [subject] are edible and delicious [predicate]. Swimming snakes [subject] undulate from side to side [predicate]. *Farce* [subject] means forcemeat [predicate]. You'll find a good deal more about recognizing subjects and predicates in Chapter 6.

The reason predicates typically get more emphasis than subjects in English sentences is that in normal coherent discourse most subjects look back to already established information, while the predicates present some new thought or detail. As we saw at the beginning of this chapter, subjects hold passages together by referring to things already known. Predicates keep the thought rolling forward by introducing new ideas. Here a series of subjects maintains unwavering focus on a topic announced in the first sentence:

By middle age, **the lonely** are less likely to exercise and more likely to eat a high-fat diet, and **they** report experiencing a greater number of stressful events. **Loneliness** correlates with an increased risk of Alzheimer's. During a four-year study, **lonely senior citizens** were more likely to end up in nursing homes; during a nine-year study, **people with fewer social ties** were two to three times more likely to die.

CALEB CRAIN, *Lonely Together*

All Crain's subjects name lonely people or the loneliness they experience. Meanwhile, the predicates pile on new details in support of the central idea, that these people face special risks in life. Each sentence anchors itself through its subject in the previously known—the passage is about loneliness—before launching into the accumulating evidence that gives the argument its weight.

Although most writing is less intensely focused than Crain's passage, alternation between familiar topics in the subject slots of your sentences and new material in the predicates is still the most important secret of writing coherently. For instance, in this apparently relaxed discussion of oranges, John McPhee allows himself much greater latitude than Crain in choosing grammatical subjects, but with one telling exception he still makes sure each subject refers to something already established or "known" from earlier statements:

> The **Valencia** has emerged in this century as something close to a universal orange. **It** is more widely and extensively planted than any other. From Florida and California and Central and South America to South Africa and Australia, **Valencias** grow in abundance in nearly all the orange centers of the world except Valencia. Having given the world the most remunerative orange yet known, **Spain** now specializes in its celebrated strains of bloods and navels. Only two **percent** of the Spanish crop are Valencias, and perhaps only **half** of that comes from the groves of Valencia itself; **much** of the remainder grows in old, untended groves near Seville, where **cattle** wander through and munch oranges on the trees, on either bank of the Guadalquivir.
>
> JOHN McPHEE, *Oranges*

McPhee's first three grammatical subjects—*Valencia, it, Valencias*—name the same thing, the variety of orange he is writing about. *Spain*, the fourth subject, ventures a little farther afield, but not much. Valencia is located in Spain, after all, and this fact plus the way the word chimes with McPhee's earlier geographical references—Florida, California, Central and South America, and so on—qualifies it as a "known" concept, the sort of thing you've been led to expect this passage will discuss. The same can be said for "two percent," "half," and "much," the next group of subjects. The beginning of the passage established that McPhee is interested in the number of Valencia oranges grown throughout the world, so his focus on quantities here comes as no surprise.

At first glance *cattle*, the subject of McPhee's final clause, seems a major exception. Maybe at second glance, too. McPhee runs some risk injecting this subject at the end of his passage, but it is tucked away in a subordinate clause modifying "orange groves," surely a "known" concept by this point, and the image neatly rounds off a key idea: Valencia oranges are big business everywhere *except* in Valencia. McPhee finds this surprising and uses the cattle image, which comes as a surprise to us, to drive his point home. Think how much flatter the end of the passage would sound if he'd structured his final sentence for maximum coherence:

> Only two **percent** of the Spanish crop are Valencias, and perhaps only **half** of that comes from the groves of Valencia itself; **much** of the remainder grows in old, untended groves near Seville, where **oranges** are used as cattle fodder along either bank of the Guadalquivir.

Still, writing in a formal situation where objective, businesslike communication is the order of the day, you'd be wise not only to drop *cattle* as a subject but to edit out other details that lend color to McPhee's oranges:

> Only two **percent** of the Spanish crop are Valencias, and perhaps only **half** of that comes from the groves of Valencia itself; **much** of the remainder grows near Seville, where **oranges** are used as cattle fodder.

EXERCISE 3

Examine the following passages for coherence problems caused by too great a gap between the subject of a new sentence and the known material that has gone before. Rewrite the passages to close the gaps. Rearrange the sentences if you like, but make sure your revision contains all the ideas of the original. You'll find a sample answer on the *Understanding Style* website.

1. The natives of Benin in Africa created superb bronze plaques. Armor, guns, feathered hats, and dogs are beautifully rendered in their portraits of Portuguese explorers in the region. Ancient Greece and Rome never produced better metalwork than these plaques. Through a process of independent discovery, these

isolated natives must have learned the lost wax technique of
casting bronze and brought it to near perfection on their own.

    BASED ON SANCHE DE GRAMONT, *The Strong Brown God*

2. Somehow English archers at Agincourt must have been given
a signal to "fire" simultaneously. The distance between them
and the French had to be conveyed somehow also. Their targets
would have been invisible to archers standing behind the first
ranks. After rising over one hundred feet in the air, their arrows
fell at a steep angle on the enemy troops 250 yards away. Steel
armor with cleverly designed glancing surfaces insured that not
many of the French troops were injured.

    BASED ON JOHN KEEGAN, *The Face of Battle*

3. On one side of Mount Rainer, a scooped-out crater overlooks
southern Puget Sound. The Sunset Amphitheater, the name
by which this crater is known, is a mark left by a great event.
A huge avalanche, the Oceola Mudflow, thundered down the
mountain about 5,000 years ago. The grip of the upper 2,000
feet of the peak on the mountain had been loosened by an earth-
quake or a volcanic convulsion. Parts of Seattle and Tacoma
are built on the debris that filled the plain between Rainier and
Puget Sound. Scientists worry that a new mudflow could crush
this area.

    BASED ON JON KRAKAUER, *Geologists Worry
    About Dangers of Living 'Under the Volcano'*

Reinforcing Coherence with Transitional Devices

Chapter 3 warned against unnecessary transitional words and phrases
as a form of stylistic deadwood, but not all **transitions** are unnecessary. Consider these comments on the cerebellum, a part of the brain
whose role in higher order thinking was first suggested by Henrietta
Leiner:

Neurologist Robert Dow of Good Samaritan Medical Center
in Portland, Oregon, **was the first to provide some clinical**

support for Leiner's ideas, in 1986. He tested a patient with cerebellar damage and found—to his surprise—problems in subtle cognitive functions, such as planning. **Since that finding, several other studies have implicated the cerebellum in nonmotor skills.** **Among the first** was a report of cerebellar activity in word-selection tasks; it was **followed** by a report of poor performance on similar tasks by a patient with cerebellar damage. **In yet another study**, researchers asked a normal subject to put rings of different sizes on a pole. If the subject slipped the rings on randomly, the cerebellum showed normal activity. **But** when the subject had to put the rings on in order from small to large, the cerebellum's activity increased.

SARA RICHARDSON, *Tarzan's Little Brain*

The transitional devices in bold type include everything from a full sentence, *Since that finding, several other studies have implicated the cerebellum in nonmotor skills*, to the one-word conjunction *but*. What makes them transitional devices is the way they all serve to link new details about the cerebellum to each other and to the material that went before in Richardson's essay. Her subject is complicated enough to demand this careful handling. Look what happens when you knock away its transitional scaffolding:

Neurologist Robert Dow of Good Samaritan Medical Center in Portland, Oregon, tested a patient with cerebellar damage and found—to his surprise—problems in subtle cognitive functions, such as planning. A report of cerebellar activity in word-selection tasks was made; a report of poor performance on similar tasks by a patient with cerebellar damage was published. Researchers asked a normal subject to put rings of different sizes on a pole. If the subject slipped the rings on randomly, the cerebellum showed normal activity. If the subject had to put the rings on in order from small to large, the cerebellum's activity increased.

Without the author's transitions, her presentation is much harder to follow. It's not even clear how many separate experimental findings she is talking about.

Deciding whether or not to include a transition in a given passage requires judgment. Ask yourself if unclear relationships between your ideas are likely to trip up a reader unless you explain them. If they are, smooth the way with one or a combination of these devices:

Transitional Sentences

Early prototypes of these fasteners were much more primitive.

But there is much more to learn from Queen Elizabeth's successes.

Transitional Clauses

While much can be said for the Big Bang theory, . .

Although Carver's main point is valid, . .

After this hot steam process has rendered the wood flexible, . .

Transitional Phrases

On the other hand, at the same time, in the opposite fashion, etc.

Coordinating Conjunctions:

And, but, or, nor, for, so, yet.

Conjunctive Adverbs

However, therefore, moreover, in fact, for instance, etc.

Transitional Words

First, second, third, later, before, other, another, additional, etc.

EXERCISE 4

Add transitional devices to guide readers through the following passages. Supply connections only where you think they're really needed and try to include several classes of transitions—sentences, clauses, phrases, and so on. How do your additions affect the coherence of each passage? You'll find a sample answer on the *Understanding Style* website.

1. Utopias always aim to present a society without tensions. Everyone knows his or her place. No one wants major changes. A utopian society is stable. Stability can be a problem. A society in which everyone is happy may not be able to develop. Ant hills and beehives are stable. Worker ants and bees are not models for people to follow.

2. Huxley had no automatic reason to reject personal immortality. The conservation of force contradicted appearances. The indestructibility of matter seemed unlikely on the face of it. He accepted those beliefs. Scientific evidence made him accept them. He had no evidence souls were immortal. He refused to believe it. The death of his son did not cause him to change his mind.

3. Surgical operations in which the patients' body temperature was kept normal produced half as many post-operative infections as procedures where body temperatures fell below 95 degrees. Cold reduces blood flow to the wound site. The immune system needs the blood's oxygen to fight infections. Immune cells break molecular oxygen into separate atoms. Atomic oxygen kills bacteria.

Reinforcing Coherence with Coordinate Structures

Striking patterns of repetition can sound a little oratorical ("Ask not what your country can do for you—ask what you can do for your country.") but writers sometimes use them to good effect, especially in messages laden with feeling, like these comments on the nature of art:

> What is always needed in the appreciation of art, or life, is the larger perspective. Connections made, or at least attempted, where none existed before, the straining to encompass in one's glance at the varied world the common thread, the unifying theme through immense diversity, a fearlessness of growth, of search, of looking that enlarges the private and the public world.
>
> ALICE WALKER, *In Search of Our Mothers' Gardens*

Walker wants her prose to demonstrate her theme. She wants to sound as if she must struggle herself to explain the imaginative boldness she is calling for. Art and the world need more "Connections...straining...fearlessness..." This parallel series of **nominals** defines "the larger perspective" Walker wants to see. The artist's glance should encompass "the common thread, the unifying theme..." Art should proceed with "a fearlessness of growth, of search, of looking." Throughout the passage Walker doubles and triples sentence structures in her effort to convey the full scope of what she means.

More workaday uses of repetition include passages like this one on a trendy restaurant outside London:

> Nobody goes to Heston Blumenthal's restaurant because they are feeling a bit peckish (though it happens that a visit to the Fat Duck will sate your hunger). Likewise, no one should open *The Big Fat Duck Cookbook* because they are looking for something to cook for supper (though it does contain recipes). You go to the Fat Duck for theatre; for intriguing flavor combinations and cooking techniques that will screw with your head and make you think about the relationship between the way we feed ourselves and our emotions. You go for green tea and vodka palate-cleansers "cooked" in liquid nitrogen, or snail porridge the color of grass clippings, for sardine on toast ice cream.
>
> JAY RAYNER, *First, take your snails*
> *and your porridge…*

Rayner's passage is bound together by coordination and repetition: "Nobody goes…no one should open"; "though it happens….though it does"; "you go for…you go for"; "green tea and vodka palate-cleansers…snail porridge…sardine on toast ice cream." Why don't you go to Heston Blumenthal's restaurant? Why do you go? What do you find when you get there? Rayner uses coordination to separate these levels of content from each other and keep the relationships between them plain.

EXERCISE 5

Identify structural parallels that promote coherence in each of the following passages. Would it improve the passages to add transitional words, phrases, and clauses as well? You'll find a sample answer on the *Understanding Style* website.

1. It's sometimes argued that there's no real progress; that a civilization that kills multitudes in mass warfare, that pollutes the land and oceans with ever larger quantities of debris, that destroys the dignity of individuals by subjecting them to a

forced mechanized existence, can hardly be called an advance
over prehistoric times.

ROBERT PIRSIG, *Zen and the Art of
Motorcycle Maintenance*

2. So the question is not whether we will be extremists, but what
kind of extremists we will be. Will we be extremists for hate or
love? Will we be extremists for the preservation of injustice or
the extension of justice?

MARTIN LUTHER KING, JR.,
Letter from a Birmingham Jail

3. At thirteen, in a Dominican convent, [Georgia O'Keeffe] was
mortified when the sister corrected her drawing. At Chatham
Episcopal Institute in Virginia, she painted lilacs and sneaked
time alone to walk out to where she could see the line of the
Blue Ridge Mountains on the horizon. At the Art Institute in
Chicago she was shocked by the presence of live models and
wanted to abandon anatomy lessons.

JOAN DIDION, *The White Album*

EXERCISE 6

Combine these ideas using parallel structures. For an overview of possible
methods, consult "Vary Sentence Structure with Parallel Constructions"
in Chapter 11. You'll find a sample answer on the *Understanding Style*
website.

1. The last glacial period had a great effect on today's vegetation.
Topsoil was scoured from some areas. Only certain plants
can live there now. It deposited soil elsewhere. New drainage
patterns were created. It created new lakes.

2. In Europe, east-west running mountains cut off the retreat of
plants that could not tolerate cold conditions. In the Americas,
lines of retreat were left open by the north-south running
mountain chains.

3. North America has a greater diversity of trees than Europe. A
similar number of cold-tolerant species exists in each place. We

have species like the hickories that cannot stand extreme cold. Europe once had these. They died out during the last glacial age.

Reinforcing Coherence with Subordinate Structures

Chapter 11 on sentence variety lists many options for reducing separate ideas to **nominal, adjectival, and adverbial** elements attached to an **independent clause**. Because they knit ideas closely together by using grammar to stress logical relationships, sentences with subordinate elements promote coherence too. Here is a technical passage from an essay on the author's psoriasis:

> In the 1970s, dermatologists at Massachusetts General Hospital developed PUVA, a controlled light treatment: florescent tubes radiate long-wave ultraviolet (UV-A) onto skin sensitized by an internal dose of methoxsalen, a psoralen (the "P" of the acronym) derived from a weed, *Ammi majus*, which grows along the river Nile and whose sun-sensitizing qualities were known to the ancient Egyptians.
>
> JOHN UPDIKE, *Self-Consciousness*

There are only two independent clauses here. "Dermatologists developed PUVA" is the first. Updike added **prepositional phrases**— "In the 1970s," "at Massachusetts General Hospital"—to tell when and where this took place, and an appositive, "a controlled light treatment," to define PUVA. His second independent clause, "flourescent tubes radiate long-wave ultraviolet," is developed more elaborately. The appositive "UV-A" renames long-wave ultraviolet; "*onto* skin sensitized *by* an internal dose *of* methoxsalen" is a chain of prepositional phrases giving the where and how of the radiation; "a psoralen" is another appositive— and so on. The sentence ends with two **adjectival** clauses that supply more information about the weed *Ammi majus*—"which grows along the river Nile and whose sun-sensitizing qualities were known to the ancient Egyptians."

Grammatical orchestration like this would be out of place dealing with a simple topic, but subordinate elements in moderation help lash your ideas together. And nothing beats subordination when it comes to explaining complicated material in as few words as possible.

EXERCISE 7

Use subordinating techniques like those explained in Chapter 11 to connect the following groups of ideas. Do certain groups or ideas lend themselves more to this subordinating approach than others? Why? You'll find a sample answer on the *Understanding Style* website.

1. Alexander the Great loved his horse Bucephalus. That name means "ox-head." Bull-like determination may have given Bucephalus his name. Perhaps it was because there was a bull on Alexander's flag. Bucephalus died before Alexander did. A town was named in his honor by his grieving owner.

2. The largest of the ancient flying reptiles was *Quetzalcoatlus*. Its body was nearly twenty feet long. Forty feet was the measurement of its wing span. It may have lived in colonies like some modern seabirds. Fish were almost certainly its diet. On the ground, it may have humped along on legs and wings like a prodigious bat.

3. Vermeer clearly worked mostly in the same studio with the same props. A yellow satin jacket appears in six of his paintings. It has ermine trim. An identifiable Turkish carpet figures in nine pictures. The same wooden chairs can be seen in eleven. Carved lion heads decorate these chairs.

MAKEOVER

Revise the following passage to improve its coherence. Be sure to use each of the techniques described in this chapter—making grammatical subjects name "known" concepts, adding transitional devices, and creating parallel and subordinate sentence structures. Think about which technique works best in each case.

Human beings' desire to have everything their own way was remarked on by Freud. Darwin has light to shed on this trait. Gluttony, lust, greed, and anger could help early humans survive. More food might help a person survive and reproduce. The tendency to hoard food for oneself and one's relatives would be encouraged by natural selection. Whether the food was gained honestly would not matter. Natural selection might favor those willing to fight. They could cow others. They could monopolize resources. They could attract mates. Now guns and knives make it easy to do more damage to others. The old impulses still survive. Infidelity is adaptive. Males spread their genes around. Protection and access to more providers are benefits for females. Creatures strive for evolutionary advantage. Passing your genes to as many of the next generation as possible is evolutionary advantage. Early humans lived in tougher times. Altruistic behavior is something we can afford. They could not. Many of the traits of the evolutionary winners have been passed to us. Saint Augustine knew a lot in the 5th century. He didn't have a Darwinian explanation. Our corrupt nature was "already present in the seed from which we were to spring." This was said by Augustine.

BASED ON ROBERT WRIGHT, *Science and Original Sin*

Your Writing

Write a one-page account of some process you are familiar with—making silk flowers or wiring an attic, for instance—in which you self-consciously group sentences into sentence clusters with

1) related, "known" subjects
2) new material in the predicates
3) transitional devices
4) coordinate structures
5) subordinate constructions

Highlight these devices in your passage and code them using the numbers supplied here. What effect do they have on your writer's voice?

POINTS TO REMEMBER

1. Clusters of related sentences hold together best if they have the same or closely related subjects, with new information introduced in the predicates.
2. Transitional devices also help promote coherence.
3. Grouping similar material in coordinate constructions helps readers see the similarities.
4. Subordinate structures clarify which ideas are most important and how they are related to each other.

CHAPTER 9

Assigning Emphasis

A good sentence is clear because the words are well chosen and it fits clearly into its context, but also because it emphasizes the right ideas by placing them in positions where they receive special **stress** or by giving them extra **grammatical bulk**. Chapter 11 discusses another type of **grammatical emphasis** that can be used along with these to make important words and ideas stand out.

Nuclear Emphasis

Spoken or written English moves along in a series of **breath units**, each one containing a separate bit of information. Within each breath unit a distinctly stressed syllable or **nucleus** highlights a certain word. Although sentences (like this one, for instance) can contain more than one breath unit and therefore more than one nucleus, a **sentence nucleus** generally receives the greatest degree of emphasis in the sentence as a whole.

Here are some sentences to read aloud. As you say each one, you should hear stress differences produced by moving the nucleus to a different word. Pronounce the sentences as you normally would in light of the explanation given after each version, letting the nuclear stress arise from the meaning. In each case the syllable you emphasize—the one you pronounce most forcefully and clearly—is the nucleus, printed here in boldface capitals.

Bill should **DRIVE**. *A neutral observation, the usual form.*
BILL should drive. *Bill should, not you.*
Bill **SHOULD** drive. *Deny it if you can.*
Kara said it was supposed to **RAIN**. *Usual form.*
Kara said it was sup**POS**ed to rain. *But it didn't.*
Kara said it **WAS** supposed to rain. *It isn't any longer.*
Kara **SAID** it was supposed to rain. *Who believes Kara?*
KARA said it was supposed to rain. *Kara, not Becky.*
Horace has been bleaching his **HAIR**. *Usual form.*
Horace has been **BLEACH**ing his hair. *Not dyeing it.*
Horace has **BEEN** bleaching his hair. *He didn't start yesterday.*
Horace **HAS** been bleaching his hair. *Yes, he has.*
HORace has been bleaching his hair. *Horace, not Lionel.*

As these examples show, English speakers routinely move the nucleus of spoken sentences by pronouncing them differently to produce different meanings. We learn this system as preschoolers and use it with great precision, even though most of us would be at a loss to explain how it works. Compare a normal question form like "Was that MaDONna?" with "**WAS** that Madonna?" The second question actually means "I didn't think so at first, but I'll take your word for it." English encourages speakers to fine tune meaning in all sorts of ways simply by emphasizing different words in the same sentence.

Written sentences are less flexible. With no speaker to juggle the emphasis for them, **subvocalizing** readers tend to stress sentences the same way, placing the main stress in its most common or default position, on the last highly significant word.[1] As Chapter 8 explained, sentence endings are also where readers are conditioned to look for important new information, so in written English this part of the sentence becomes a real communications hot spot. Our tendency to put new and emphatic material at the end of a construction is called **end focus**. End focus causes the nuclear stress, or greatest emphasis, in a written sentence to fall on a word at or near the end.

---

[1] Or more exactly, on the accented syllable of the last highly significant word in the breath unit or sentence. In most multisyllabic words, one syllable is accented, or spoken with more emphasis than the others. When such a word appears in a stressed position it is the accented syllable that receives the stress. Accented syllables are indicated in dictionary entries.

The Anisazi beans over there are beautifully **COL**ored.

Chop shops reduce stolen cars to resellable com**PO**nents.

Ginger always tastes **SOAP**y to me.

What does this mean to you as a writer? Constructing sentences so that stress falls just where you want it to is a potent secret of effective writing. Here are the last three sentences rephrased to emphasize a different word. The comments in each case describe a situation in which the restructured version might suit the writer's intentions better than the first:

> Over there are beautifully colored Ani**SA**zi beans. (The writer is distinguishing between Anisazi and other kinds of beans.)
>
> Stolen cars are reduced to resellable components by **CHOP** shops. (The writer is discussing various ways crooks convert stolen goods into cash.)
>
> I always associate a soapy taste with **GIN**ger. (The writer is talking about how to identify various spices.)

As these examples show, emphasis should arise from the purpose of your writing. You've undoubtedly toyed from time to time with several ways of writing the same sentence. Which one is best? Often, it's the one emphasizing a word that reinforces the point you're trying to make.

EXERCISE 1

Restructure the following sentences using the principle of end focus to emphasize the specified words. Change the sentence structure however you like to reposition the chosen word at the end of its sentence, where it will receive an extra degree of stress. For instance, "Electric guitars convert sonic vibrations into electrical **IM**pulses" could be rewritten to emphasize *guitars* or *vibrations*: "Sonic vibrations are converted into electrical impulses by electric gui**TARS**"; "Electric guitars create electrical impulses from sonic vi**BRA**tions." Under what circumstances would each of the restructured versions you write work better than the original? You'll find a sample answer on the *Understanding Style* website.

1. Northern New Mexico is swarming with craftspersons and **ART**ists.
   Restructure to emphasize **CRAFTS**persons.
   Restructure to emphasize Northern New **MEX**ico.

2. Huge landfills generate large amounts of methane **GAS**.
Restructure to emphasize **LAND**fills.
Restructure to emphasize a**MOUNTS**.

3. In my neighborhood everyone has a backyard **GRILL**.
Restructure to emphasize back**YARD**.
Restructure to emphasize **NEIGH**borhood.

Coming to a Good End

Because the chief stress in most sentences comes at the end, the final words in a sentence are particularly important. They should reinforce the ideas you want to leave in the reader's mind. Compare these versions of a sentence from a letter appointing someone to a committee:

Your efforts will be much appreciated as we go about this crucial **TASK**.

As we go about this crucial task your efforts will be much ap**PRE**ciated.

The nucleus of the first sentence falls on **TASK**, making the job sound grim. This sentence could frighten off potential committee members. The second version is better. Its nucleus is a**PRE**ciated, a more inviting key word. Later, after the task force has piddled for weeks and accomplished nothing, they may need to be goaded into action. In that case you would not want to say

While time is growing short to complete this crucial task, be assured we appreciate your unremitting **EF**fort.

Emphasizing **EF**fort makes it sound as if they've done all they can and may now rest on their oars. What you mean is more like this:

While we appreciate your unremitting effort, please be aware that time is growing short to complete this crucial **TASK**.

This sentence nods toward the committee's efforts, but then makes it clear they've fallen short. They still need to complete the **TASK**.

EXERCISE 2

Restructure the following sentences so that the nuclear stress falls on a word appropriate for the circumstances. Change the sentence structure however you like. How do the revisions affect the writer's voice? You'll find a sample answer on the *Understanding Style* website.

1. Believe me, Mr. Korn, I offer my deepest sympathy on the death of your little dog **LUCK**y.

    Restructure to highlight **SYM**pathy

2. It is outrageous for you to charge $75 for simply resetting a **CIR**cuit breaker.

    Restructure to highlight out**RA**geous

3. Nine stitches could be saved by one that comes in **TIME**.

    Restructure to highlight **NINE**

While only you can say which words or ideas you want to stand out in a given situation, each word that carries nuclear stress should deserve the extra weight it gets. Be careful to keep your sentences from trailing away in unimportant phrases instead of ending with a more significant word you would really rather emphasize:

Chimpanzees and other apes have a strong enough sense of self to recognize themselves in a mirror, something that lower animals never do, according to **RE**searchers.

My favorite hideaway was the old hay barn beside Snake Creek across the tractor trail from the **WOOD**lot.

Anticlimactic elements like the phrases at the end of these sentences are usually **adverbials** telling where, when or why the sentence happened or explaining how readers should take what it says. This information is commonly less important to what the writer is trying to accomplish than some key word in the main **clause**. When sentences with weak endings like these appear in your writing, consider turning them around to provide a stronger climax:

According to researchers, unlike lower animals, chimpanzees and other apes have a strong enough sense of self to recognize themselves in a **MIR**ror.

Beside Snake Creek across the tractor trail from the woodlot stood an old hay barn, my favorite **HIDE**away.

Or simply to trim away some or all of the extra phrases:

Chimpanzees and other apes have a strong enough sense of self to recognize themselves in a **MIR**ror.

Beside Snake Creek stood an old hay barn, my favorite **HIDE**away.

EXERCISE 3

Bring the following sentences to a more effective end by eliminating or moving anticlimactic phrases. Make the sentence nucleus in your revised versions fall on the word indicated. You'll find a sample answer on the *Understanding Style* website.

1. Plastic surgeons are using leeches to encourage blood circulation in reattached body parts according to published **NEWS** stories. Emphasize *LEECHES*

2. Kudzu lacks environmental checks in this country so it spreads over everything, covering structures and other plants with a dense mass of **VINES**. Emphasize *CHECKS*

3. The cost of food is soaring out of sight, except for eggs, which have remained a bargain for **YEARS**. Emphasize *SIGHT*

Nuclear Stress in Lesser Breath Units

Up to now we've dealt with sentence nuclei, but there's a nucleus in every lesser breath unit of a complicated sentence also. It's just less heavily emphasized. In the following examples, the sentence nucleus is capitalized and printed in boldface type, lesser ones capitalized only. Notice how these stresses and the pauses between the breath units associated with them affect the sound of the sentences, creating multiple rhythms and centers of emphasis.

If the student senses that to parrot these technical vocabularies would do violence to something withIN,❙ and senses this so strongly that he or she can't or won't LEARN the stuff—|that student **FAILS**.

MICHAEL VENTURA, *Talkin' American 2*

One of the artists told me that his PAINTings,| which included African and Afro-American mythological symbols and IMagery,| were hanging in the local McDONald's restaurant.

ISHMAEL REED, *Writin' Is Fightin'*

To slide from the sublime to the riDICulous,|you can also make moLASses,| BEER,| and VINegar| from perSIMmons.

EUELL GIBBONS, *Stalking the Wild Asparagus*

One reason sentences are often more effective with internal pauses than without is that nuclei in minor breath units allow you to emphasize selected ideas—like Gibbons' "moLASses,| BEER,| and VINegar|"—in addition to the sentence nucleus, which still gets the major stress. Here's a sentence in crying need of additional nuclear emphases, which would also improve its **rhythm**:

Her work with the public relations office at Carthage College during the past year has added valuable opportunities to help her make use of her academic studies as well as helping her to develop social skills.

Restructuring could allow the writer to highlight *public relations*, *academic studies*, and *social skills*:

She has worked for a year in the Carthage College office of public reLAtions,|where she had valuable opportunities to use her academic STUDies.| The job also developed her SOCial skills.

As you see here, one way to inject more stresses and pauses into a passage is to create more sentences. Within sentences, provide more breath units by adding 1) introductory or concluding **dependent clauses** and **phrases**, 2) parenthetical elements, or 3) **coordinate series** of three or more grammatical items. These same strategies are also useful for adding structural variety to your writing (see Chapter 11).

Parenthetical Elements

YES,❘ VirGINia,❘ there is a SANta Claus.

My UNcle,❘ in OTHer words,❘ was disPLEASED.

COModore,❘ boxed in along the RAIL,❘ was unable to make a RUN.

Coordinate Series

Their colors are GREEN,❘ BLUE,❘ and WHITE.

CHAMber music,❘ COOKing,❘ and CARpentry❘ are her chief enTHUsiasms.

The room was filled with SMOOTH,❘ SMILing,❘ soPHISti-cated TALKers.

Dependent Clauses

Even though it is a small COUNtry,❘ Jordan is divided into three PARTS.

John D. Rockefeller first established Standard Oil in OHIO,❘ where he lived at the TIME.

Introductory and Concluding Phrases

With regard to your BUSiness plan,❘ we feel more attention should go to MARketing.

Beast fables have been popular for CENturies,❘ appearing in all human CULtures.

Notice that not all introductory and concluding clauses and phrases are set off by pauses. Introductory elements are likely to be set off if they are (1) more than ten or so words long or (2) based on verb forms used to modify the subject that follows: "*To conclude* the program,❘ Richard played a cello sonata"; "*Sliding* into third base,❘ Mazie skinned her hip."

Phrases and clauses at the end of a sentence are set off only if they are **nonrestrictive**—that is, if they supply additional information that the sentence could do without. For example, in "The archangel Gabriel is often thought of as a Christian figure,❘ even though he also appears in the *Koran*," the first part of the sentence would be true and accurate without the second. "Even though he also appears in the *Koran*" supplies additional, nonessential information and so is set off. Compare "Computer networks cause incredible problems when they crash." Here it is only "when they crash" that computer networks cause incredible problems. "When they crash" is essential to the meaning and so is not set off.

Although this distinction between restrictive and nonrestrictive elements can be tricky, most people have good enough linguistic instincts to get it right most of the time by saying sentences aloud. If this doesn't work for you, it might be worthwhile to get a grammar handbook or look online for some intensive practice on the subject. Google "restrictive and nonrestrictive." There's more on these terms in the Glossary at the end of the book.

A Note on Punctuation

As you've undoubtedly guessed, breath units and pauses are related to punctuation. In general, punctuation marks the pauses between breath units—that is, pauses between **independent clauses** and elements in a **coordinate series**, pauses before and after **parenthetical elements**, and pauses that set off the kinds of introductory and concluding modifiers discussed in the previous section. Expert writers may even use punctuation to make readers pause where they ordinarily wouldn't. A good example is John Jerome in the "Gallery of Voices" from Chapter 1. When Jerome wrote, "The slowly moving water on the inside of the curve can no longer carry as much sediment, and drops its particulate load," he added the comma after "sediment" knowing it would make most readers pause. The comma isn't necessary because the "and" connects only two **predicates** that would ordinarily not require punctuation—"can no longer carry as much sediment" and "drops its particulate load." Jerome must have felt he needed a pause at that point whether or not the grammar called for it. Without the pause, his readers would have had to deal with a 33-syllable breath unit, too long to read gracefully. With the pause inserted, they need to negotiate only two more manageable breath units of 25 and 8 syllables apiece. For more on punctuation, see the alphabetical guide in Appendix B.

EXERCISE 4

Combine each set of simple sentences into a longer sentence with parenthetical elements, coordinate series, dependent clauses, and/or introductory or concluding phrases. Mark each pause and nucleus in the new sentences you create. Look for more on combining sentences in Chapter 11. You'll find a sample answer on the *Understanding Style* website.

1. The first mausoleum was a white marble tomb.

   It was built for King Mausolus.

   He lived at Halicarnassus.

   Halicarnassus was a town in Asia Minor.

2. Duluth is on the western end of Lake Superior.

   It is the Great Lakes' second-largest port.

   It ships grain.

   It ships iron ore.

   It ships machinery.

   It ships other cargo all over the world.

3. Porcupines are rodents.

   They have quills.

   The quills are actually modified hairs.

   The quills have barbs.

   The quills are loosely attached.

   The quills can be erected.

   Porcupines weigh up to 60 pounds.

Patterns of Emphasis

While dwelling on isolated sentences helps show how the nuclear stress system works in general, it's also important to see how stressed syllables can work together over several sentences to reinforce a dominant message or theme. Consider this passage, especially the words that receive the main stress in each breath unit and sentence:

Neanderthals seem to have enjoyed **MU**sic. A length of cave bear thigh bone clearly pierced with finger holes was unearthed in an ancient Neanderthal shelter in SloVENia. According to the wondering archaeologists who have SEEN it, the object must have served a musical FUNCtion. That it is a primitive flute is their conSENsus.

The writing here is intelligible, but the words that receive emphasis—*music, Slovenia, seen, function, consensus*—have almost nothing in common. They certainly don't reinforce a central idea. If the writer wanted to impress us with the strangeness of Neanderthal music makers, it would have been better to write

Neanderthals seem to have enjoyed MUsic. A length of cave bear thigh bone unearthed in an ancient Neanderthal shelter in Slovenia is clearly pierced with FINger holes. Wondering archaeologists have identified it as a primitive FLUTE.

Here the emphasized ideas—*music, finger holes, flute*—work together to keep the theme of caveman musicality in the forefront. These sentences use nuclear stress to strengthen the writer's message.

EXERCISE 5

Mark sentence and breath unit nuclei in the following sentences. Remember that emphasis will fall on a particular syllable, not necessarily a whole word. Do the words stressed reinforce what the writers are saying? How? You'll find a sample answer on the *Understanding Style* website.

1. Despite all the marvelous things that computers can do today, they simply lack many of the qualities that are present in human intelligence—they don't even have common sense.
   GINA KOLATA, *How Can Computers Get Common Sense*

2. That night in my rented room, while letting the hot water run over my can of pork and beans in the sink, I opened *A Book of Prefaces*.
   RICHARD WRIGHT, *Black Boy*

3. Jordan's first game in Chicago came five days later, against the Orlando Magic, a first-place team featuring two of the best young talents in the sport: Shaquille O'Neal, a Goliath with grace, and Anfernee (Penny) Hardaway, a silky guard who,

with his preternatural sense for the flow of the game, reminds everyone of Earvin (Magic) Johnson.

DAVID REMNICK, *Back in Play*

Although controlling stresses over passages several sentences long will never be an exact science, it is an important element of style. If your writing seems dull and vague, with important ideas buried beneath lesser ones, try restructuring selected sentences so that the most relevant words are highlighted by nuclear stress. Be especially careful to make the sentence nucleus or chief stress of each sentence coincide with a word you have reason to emphasize.

EXERCISE 6

Rewrite the following passages so that the words receiving nuclear stress are more closely related to each other and to the writer's main idea. Keep the number of sentences the same, but restructure using the principle of end focus to emphasize the specified words. How do your changes affect the writer's voice? You'll find a sample answer on the *Understanding Style* website.

1. That words are just symbols is well known to the **WISE**. Changing the names things are called doesn't make them react **VI**olently. The underlying thing remains the same, and they **KNOW** that. The only people taken in by name-calling are **FOOLS**.

   Restructure to emphasize **SYM**bols, **NAMES**, **SAME**, and **NAME**-calling.

2. An ecotour is a guided trip to an ecologically sensitive lo**CA**tion. The Amazon is one frequent ecotour desti**NA**tion. Tourists can see exotic birds along the **RIV**er. Native villages are also explored by the **TOUR**ists.

   Restructure to emphasize Ecotours, **AM**azon, **BIRDS**, and **VIL**lages.

3. Conservatives praise decentralized welfare programs for turning over control to the **STATES**. But there's only a degree of decentralization in **THAT**. Why not directly mail recipients their **PAY**ments? A real breakthrough in decentralization could be achieved **THAT** way.

Restructure to emphasize **STATES**, decentrali**ZA**tion, di**RECT**ly, and decentrali**ZA**tion.

Using Grammatical Transformations to Shift Emphasis

The relationship between emphasis and meaning is so fundamental to English that the language has developed a number of standard restructuring techniques, called **transformations**, to pinpoint emphasis on words that would usually not receive it, or to move words from unemphatic positions at the beginning of a sentence to emphatic positions at the end.

Untransformed Sentence: Several telephone poles leaned dangerously over the **ROAD**.

There Transformation

There were several **TEL**ephone poles leaning dangerously over the ROAD.

[*In this sentence the word* there *does not indicate a specific location as it would in "There are my socks." Instead, its only function is to relocate stress, displacing the subject "***TEL***ephone poles" so that it appears after the verb* to be *and becomes the sentence nucleus, though as the last significant word ROAD still receives stress as well.*]

Untransformed Sentence: Connie sold a lithograph to get her **MO**torcycle repaired.

What Transformation

What Connie sold to get her motorcycle repaired was a **LITH**ograph.

[Emphasizes **LITH**ograph *by moving it to the end of the sentence]*

It Transformations

It was to get her **MO**torcycle repaired that Connie sold a LITHograph.

*[Putting a sentence in the form "It was (something) that…"
or "It was (someone) who…," automatically assigns nuclear
stress to the word in the "something" or "someone" slot. This
transformation can be used to highlight almost any idea in a
sentence.]*

It was **CON**nie who sold a lithograph to get her **MO**torcycle
repaired. *[Emphasizes **CON**nie.]*

It was a **LITH**ograph that Connie sold to get her **MO**torcycle
repaired. *[Emphasizes **LITH**ograph.]*

Passive Transformation

Untransformed Sentence: Swans bully Canada **GEESE**.

Canada geese are bullied by **SWANS**. *[Emphasizes **SWANS** by
moving the word to the end of the sentence.]*

Because these transformation techniques disrupt customary English
word order and usually add words as well, you should use them sparingly. *There* transformations and passives have a particularly bad reputation. Some writing teachers condemn them out of hand. But all these
constructions allow you to place the emphasis in a sentence with great
precision. For instance, the *it* transformation sentence emphasizing
Connie might fit perfectly into a passage concerning Connie's feelings
on the value of art: evidently she values her motorcycle above her lithograph. The passive transformation might find a home in a discussion
of hierarchies of aquatic abuse: "Fish are chased away from food by
DUCKS. Ducks are dominated by Canada **GEESE**. Canada geese are
bullied by **SWANS**." For more on uses and misuses of passive sentences,
see Chapter 7 on actors and actions.

EXERCISE 7

Transform these sentences so that the emphasis falls on a new word
or concept. You'll find a sample answer on the *Understanding Style*
website.

1. Salt provides extra surfaces for gas to collect on and form
    bubbles so that beer foams vigorously when salted peanuts are
    added.

It transformation to emphasize *salt*
It transformation to emphasize *gas*
What transformation to emphasize *extra surfaces*

2. Twain castigated Cooper for sloppy writing.

   Passive transformation to emphasize *Twain*
   *Wha*t transformation to emphasize *sloppy writing*
   It transformation to emphasize *Cooper*

3. New therapies offer some relief from the symptoms of
   Parkinson's Disease.

   There transformation to emphasize *therapies*
   What transformation to emphasize *symptoms*
   Passive transformation to emphasize *therapies*

Emphasis Through Grammatical Bulk

Placing emphasis by manipulating stress is a subtle writing technique.
The finished sentence looks natural as sea oats. The work you put into
it doesn't show.

Transformed sentences call more attention to themselves and need
to be used with caution.

More obvious still are strategies for adding grammatical bulk to
selected concepts. Although you may use this approach occasionally, a
little goes a long way.

Consider this unexceptional sentence:

Several 100-foot waves formed in the North Atlantic during the
early 1990s.

You could emphasize the waves by adding modifiers of various
shapes and sizes:

Several **monstrous** 100-foot waves formed in the North Atlantic
during the early 1990s.

Several **monstrous, awe-inspiring** 100-foot waves, **the highest ever recorded in the North Atlantic**, formed during the
early 1990s.

Several **monstrous, awe-inspiring** 100-foot waves, **which were by far the highest ever recorded in the history of the stormy North Atlantic**, formed during the early 1990s.

Several **monstrous, awe-inspiring** 100-foot waves (**These waves were by a long way the highest ever recorded in the eventful history of the stormy North Atlantic**.) formed during the early 1990s.

You see the problem. This sort of emphasis-by-the-pound quickly gets out of hand. After a certain point it starts sounding like a Fat Blaster infomercial. A more effective way of using grammar to emphasize selected ideas is discussed in Chapter 11.

EXERCISE 8
Add grammatical bulk for emphasis in the following sentences. Write two new versions of each sentence: one with a moderate and acceptable amount of emphasis, and one where the added emphasis is excessive. You'll find a sample answer on the *Understanding Style* website.

1. A company offers to dry a sample of your DNA and store it indefinitely in a glass capsule.

   [Emphasize *company*. The company is in Seattle, it's called Third Millennium Research, it's a recent start-up, it's the inspiration of microbiologist Dr. James Bicknell, and so far there are few takers.]

2. An engineering student pointed out that the Citi-corp Center might not be adequately braced against quartering winds.

   [Emphasize *Citi-corp Center*. The center is in Manhattan. It was completed in 1977. The building's steel structural members weigh 25,000 tons. It is the world's seventh-tallest building.]

3. A good handbag suits your body shape.

   [Handbags should contrast with your body shape. If you are tall and thin, you should get a round, puffy handbag. If you are round yourself, get a square or rectangular one. Look at yourself wearing the bag in a mirror. If you are little, don't get a big bag. If you are tall, don't get a small one.]

MAKEOVER

Use a combination of techniques—nuclear stress, transformations, and grammatical bulk (in moderation)—to correct emphasis problems in this passage. Change the sentence structure however you like, but keep all the major ideas of the original. How do your revisions change the writer's voice?

Objections to the elaborate packaging that has become a feature of American grocery marketing are partly right and partly wrong, experts say. Much waste is avoided by this packaging. For instance, American producers get a larger percentage of available foodstuffs to market than producers do in China, mostly because our packaging is still more effective than packaging in China. The well-known problem of landfills heaped with discarded packaging is probably balanced out by savings in this area. But marketing purposes are also served by packaging. Not retarding waste but these other purposes are its real function, according to critics. Deceptive packaging can make consumers think they're getting more of a product than they really are. Emotional appeal is another aspect to consider. Buyers used to interact with salespersons in the old days. Producers might even supply their food to them directly. Now shoppers wander up and down aisles filled with reassuring familiar faces—on packages. The logo on Tyson chicken or Campbell's chicken-noodle soup is comforting to people who have never seen a chicken factory and do not know a butcher personally. Their trust makes them buy.

Your Writing

Write at least a page explaining to someone in authority why you want to do something. For instance, you could be an employee justifying a new computer to her boss or a husband trying to convince his wife he needs a bandsaw. Go through the first draft highlighting the emphasized syllables (look for one in each breath unit). Now write another draft in which a greater percentage of persuasive words receive emphasis. (For example, "With a bandsaw I could rip wood for home improvements to the right **SIZE**" might become "With a new bandsaw I could rip wood to the right size for home im**PROVE**ments.") Highlight the emphasized syllables in the new version as well. Which version would be more likely to win over the reader?

POINTS TO REMEMBER

1. Make a habit of subvocalizing your own sentences, especially sentences that don't sound right, to see where the nuclear stress falls.
2. Try to adjust your writing so that the emphasis falls on syllables in words relevant to the point you are making.
3. Selectively use *there, what,* and *it* transformations and passive constructions to place emphasis where you want it to fall.

PART FIVE

Changing the Pace: Rhythmic and Grammatical Variety

CHAPTER 10

Controlling Rhythm

No matter how brilliant your insights are, they'll put readers to sleep unless you present them with a lively and attractive voice. Rhythmic variety is one key to liveliness. Writing that lacks interesting, changing **rhythms** seems to come from a machine. Consider this mind-numbing passage on Chicano life in the barrio of Sacramento:

> We had only one institution. This gave the *colonia* an image. It was the *Comisión Honorífica*. This was a committee to organize celebrations. One celebration took place on the *Cinco de Mayo*. The other was on the Sixteenth of September. One commemorated the battle of Puebla. The other commemorated the Mexican War of Independence. The *Comisión* was picked by the Mexican Consul. He lived in San Francisco. The celebrations stirred everyone in the *barrio*. Everyone liked celebrating the heroes of Mexico. Everyone liked feeling we were still Mexicans ourselves. Following speeches and a concert we had a dance. We elected queens to preside over the celebrations.

Imagine several pages of this Dick-and-Jane style. Here's what Ernesto Galarza made of the same material:

> The one institution we had that gave the *colonia* some kind of image was the *Comisión Honorífica*, a committee picked by the Mexican consul in San Francisco to organize the celebration of the *Cinco de Mayo* and the Sixteenth of September,

the anniversaries of the battle of Puebla and the beginning of our War of Independence. These were the two events which stirred everyone in the *barrio*, for what we were celebrating was not only the heroes of Mexico but also the feeling that we were still Mexicans ourselves. On these occasions there was a dance preceded by speeches and a concert. For both the *cinco* and the sixteenth queens were elected to preside over the ceremonies.

BARRIO BOY

Compared to the first version, Galarza's paragraph takes us on a pleasant ride through changing scenery. His voice speeds up and slows down. He varies the sentence structure to provide a mix of longer and shorter **breath units**. This is a voice you could live with for a good, long while.

Sentence Rhythms

Three factors control the rhythm of sentences: the length of **breath units**, the position of the **nuclear stresses**, and the length of the words. Generally speaking, you want to vary all three. Breath units are simply the words that come between pauses in a sentence and are spoken all in one breath. Nuclear stress, the emphasis that highlights a certain word in each breath unit, was discussed in Chapter 9. Add variations in word length—slow, heavy monosyllables like *stone* versus quicker, lighter polysyllabic words like *malachite*—and you are dealing with a system capable of great variety of musical effects. Say the following sentences to yourself, listening for the breath units, nuclear stresses, and speed of each one. Sentence nuclei are printed in bold capitals, nuclei of other breath units in regular capitals.

Long Breath Units, Short Words:

These were the two days that stirred us most as we hailed the heroes of our **RACE.**|

Long Breath Units, Long Words:

These exciting celebrations energized the community in an all-consuming commemoration of Mexican **HE**roes.|

Short Breath Units, Short Words:

For two days we re**JOICED**.| We hailed the heroes of our **RACE**.|

Short Breath Units, Long Words:

These celebrations energized the comm**UN**ity.| We eagerly commemorated Mexican **HE**roes.|

Mixed Forms:

These celebrations stirred the community to pay tribute to Mexican HEroes,| the idols of our **RACE**.|

For two days each year we reJOICED,| launching our all-consuming celebration of Mexican HEroes,| the idols of our **RACE**.|

Aside from slight alterations in meaning brought on by changing the words, the differences between these variations on the same theme arise from their rhythms. Both versions with short words move with a steady, deliberate tread. They sound stripped down and serious, maybe too much so. Short words are powerful. You expect writers to save them for content more remarkable than this. The versions with long words sound more rushed and less deeply felt, especially the one with long words and short breath units, which will sound disjointed to most readers.

Because they match the mixture of long and short words and breath units in the language at large, the last two versions sound neutral, neither too grave or too flustered for the circumstances. In most writing situations mixed forms like these would be your best choice.

EXERCISE 1

Rewrite the following sentences with two extreme stylistic combinations: short breath units with short words and long breath units with long words. What effect do your revisions have on the writer's voice? Next try a mixture of long and short breath units and words. Is that better? You'll find a sample answer on the *Understanding Style* website.

1. Chaos seems to be everywhere. A rising column of cigarette smoke breaks into wild swirls. A flag snaps back and forth in the wind.

   JAMES GLEICK, *Chaos*

2. At a meeting run by black women domestics who had formed a job cooperative in Alabama, a white housewife asked me about the consciousness-raising sessions or "rap groups" that are often an organic path to feminism.

GLORIA STEINEM, Sisterhood

3. It is a characteristic irony that while the learning of languages can be an expensive business, nearly all those people in the world who grow up bilingual do so because their mother tongue or dialect has associations with poverty which make it likely to be thought inappropriate for education and some kinds of employment.

JANE MILLER, How Do You
Spell Gujarati, Sir?

Types of Breath Units

Each pause in a sentence defines a breath unit. While readers and speakers don't always pause in exactly the same spots, certain principles generally hold, especially in writing. Not only is each full sentence followed by a strong pause, but other pauses occur within sentences, usually at places like the following, where internal punctuation is required:

Between Independent Clauses

The hurricane is moving this way,| and the town must be evacuated.

Tintoretto was a master of color,| but he wasn't history's greatest draftsman.

Many cobras can spit venom with great accuracy;| in fact, people have been blinded by spitting cobras.

Before Independent Clauses to Set Off

Sentence Modifiers

All things considered,| this job has been a bust.

Long Introductory Phrases and Clauses

Because we graduated from the university and help support it with our contributions,❚ we feel entitled to free tickets.

Introductory Verbal Phrases

To love,❚ one must understand.

Satisfied,❚ Sula leaned back against the railing.

Sighing with boredom,❚ Max toyed with his pen.

After Independent Clauses to Set Off

Nonessential Dependent Clauses

Now he will be unwelcome,❚ even if he does come.

Trailing Sentence Modifiers, Questions, and Contrasts

Babs was always a strong student,❚ especially in algebra.

You have my number,❚ haven't you?

We are interested in quantity,❚ not quality.

Trailing Appositives or Summaries

Helmut did not invent much,❚ just the drop-down menu.

Maria is an impressive woman,❚ poised and intelligent.

Within Independent Clauses to Set Off

Nonrestrictive Modifiers

Chicago,❚ which was settled about the same time,❚ monopolized shipping.

Coach Gravel,❚ excited by the play,❚ bit through his cigar.

Other Parenthetical Elements

Your boombox,❚ Charles,❚ is making my head throb.

Two lines that are parallel,❚ in other words,❚ will never meet.

Louisville's chief attraction,❚ the Kentucky Derby,❚ is actually growing in popularity.

EXERCISE 2

Use any combination of the sentence structures illustrated above to vary the rhythms of this passage. Combine sentences to add pauses between, after, and within independent clauses. See Chapter 11 for advice on how to do this. What effect do your changes have on the writer's voice? You'll find a sample answer on the *Understanding Style* website.

> Science and Humanities majors are different. Science majors value precision. Every move they make has a purpose. They rarely act on impulse. Humanities majors trust their feelings. They make decisions on intuition. They often seem inconsistent. Sometimes they seem downright spacey. Humanities and Science majors can get along. It's not because they have a lot in common. It's more that they fascinate each other. Each wants to see what the other will do next.

EXERCISE 3

Reduce this passage to a succession of simple sentences like the ones in the previous exercise. What effect do your changes have on the writer's voice? You'll find a sample answer on the *Understanding Style* website.

> Attitude clearly matters in fighting cancer. We don't know why (from my old-style materialistic perspective, I suspect that mental states feed back upon the immune system). But match people with the same cancer for age, class, health, and socioeconomic status, and in general, those with positive attitudes, with a strong will and purpose for living, with commitment to struggle, and with an active response to aiding their own treatment and not just a passive acceptance of anything doctors say, tend in a sentence to live longer.
>
> STEPHEN JAY GOULD, *The Median Isn't the Message*

Avoiding Overlong Breath Units

Breath units can be short as you like. Surrounded and outgunned at Bastogne in World War II, General Anthony McAuliffe gave a perfect reply when the Germans demanded his surrender—"Nuts!" But long breath units quickly get out of hand:

> Brooks briefly emerges from this discussion of irony to address the objection of his failure to note the importance of history in the background of literary works.

There's no place to get your breath in this 45-syllable monstrosity. The ideas seem to pile up on one another, not because they're complex, but because the reader must push to get through the breath unit, whether reading silently or aloud. To make the ideas clearer, rewrite the sentence with an internal pause:

> Brooks briefly emerges from this discussion of irony to address an objection:❙ hasn't he overlooked the importance of history in the background of literary works?

This version shrinks the breath units to a manageable 22 and 23 syllables.

Notice the structure of the original sentence about Brooks. Its length comes from a drawn-out daisy-chain of **prepositional phrases**: "*of* his failure to note the importance *of* history *in* the background *of* literary works." A series of similar **dependent clauses** can sound just as bad:

> The simple fact is *that* all of our experiences show us *that* the schools cannot devise any programs *that* will solve the problems *that* sent them emotionally stunted and dangerously distorted people.

Once again, adding a pause buys immediate improvement:

> The simple fact is that all of our experiences show us that the schools cannot devise programs to overcome poor social conditions—❙ the problems of a society that sends them emotionally stunted and dangerously distorted people.

Overlong breath units often go hand in hand with deadwood, as they do here. To take the revision one step further, remove unnecessary words and phrases:

> ~~The simple fact is that all of~~ our experiences show ~~us~~ that ~~the~~ schools cannot devise programs to overcome poor social conditions—| the problems of a society that sends them emotionally stunted ~~and dangerously distorted~~ people.

Now we're down to a sentence that communicates efficiently and moves with an attractive rhythm:

> Our experiences show that schools cannot devise programs to overcome poor social conditions—the problems of a society that sends them emotionally stunted people.

EXERCISE 4

Rewrite the following sentences to break up overlong breath units. Take the revision a step further, if necessary, by cutting deadwood. How do your revisions change the writer's voice? You'll find a sample answer on the *Understanding Style* website.

1. Most teachers would inform you, if you would investigate the real world rather than basing your opinions on publications written by those who probably have never spent a day in the classroom, that wholesale expulsions would not be necessary to purge the classroom of disruptive individuals.

2. Contrarian investment strategy assumes that the behavior of investments is essentially unknowable and therefore when investors are left to their own devices they are as quite as likely to be wrong as right about the direction prices will take from the time an investment is made.

3. Prestigious Greek classical styles of architecture were especially appealing during the period before America's Civil War because the young country was trying to attain a status equal in culture as well as in other ways to that of established countries of Europe like Britain and France.

Using Breath Units to Control Rhythm

Too many breath units of roughly the same length quickly grow monotonous:

> F. Scott Fitzgerald is a magnet for biographers.| He was famous for his drinking.| He fought ferociously with his wife Zelda.| He lived colorfully in Paris.| He spent years in Hollywood.| This was when film making was corrupt.| He had a rivalry with Hemingway.| He was friends with John Dos Passos.| He had extramarital affairs.| He died in the apartment of another woman.| Zelda was languishing in the hospital at the time.|

Not much better:

> For a number of reasons F. Scott Fitzgerald has become a magnet for biographers.| His personal life was made messy and interesting by his drinking and fights with his wife Zelda.| He lived colorfully in Paris and spent years in Hollywood during its most glamorous period.| He was an often bitter rival of Ernest Hemingway and a friend of John Dos Passos.| He was rumored to have had extramarital affairs and died in the apartment of another woman while Zelda languished in the hospital.|

Either of these styles would soon have readers snoring. Combine long and short breath units, and see how the rhythm improves:

> A magnet for biographers,| F. Scott Fitzgerald pursued a messy life made interesting by his drinking and ferocious fights with Zelda,| his wife.| Fitzgerald lived colorfully in Paris.| He was in Hollywood during its most glamorous period.| He was a bitter rival of Ernest Hemingway but loyal and considerate to his friend,| John Dos Passos.| He was rumored to have had extramarital affairs and died in the apartment of another woman,| Sheila Graham,| while Zelda languished in the hospital.|

EXERCISE 5
Rewrite the following paragraph so that each breath unit is at least ten syllables longer or shorter than the one before it. Remember that breath

units don't have to be sentences. There can be several within a sentence. Try to make your short breath units measure five syllables or fewer and the long ones fifteen or more. What effect does your revision have on the writer's voice? You'll find a sample answer on the *Understanding Style* website.

> Loving relationships are fragile. They are often undermined by bad ways of thinking. These ways of thinking make problems seem permanent. Partners may accuse each other of inborn character flaws. Selfishness or immaturity are examples. They may accuse each other of childhood hangups. They may say, "You're not mad at me. You're really still mad at your mother." They may accuse each other of demanding perfection. It's unrealistic to want things to be perfect always. This will never happen. All these ways of thinking have one thing in common. They direct attention away from the couple's immediate problem. A quarrel about how you behaved at a party can be solved. But changing underlying causes seems hopeless. They will still be there the next time there's a falling out. And dwelling on them makes another falling out more likely.

Using Stress to Control Rhythm

Because every breath unit has a nuclear stress that helps determine its character (Chapter 9), stress is another variable that affects rhythm. At the simplest level, nuclear stresses that fall on words of one syllable are stronger and more distinct than those in polysyllabic words. When a high percentage of nuclear stresses fall on strong monosyllables, your sentences sound forceful and clear. This is a trick you can use almost anywhere:

> Margaret spent Tuesdays reviewing the **LEDG**er. On Wednesdays she paid **IN**voices.

> Margaret spent Tuesdays reviewing the **BOOKS**. On Wednesdays she paid **BILLS**.

Adverbs of emphasis also influence nuclear stress. These words—like *also, already, always, barely, finally, hardly, never, only, seldom,* *sometimes*, and *still*—negate verbs or express their frequency or duration. English speakers pronounce them with enough force to make breath units in which they appear seem to have more than one nuclear stress:

> My old Nissan Stanza **FIN**nally quit **RUN**ning.
>
> Mourning doves **NEV**er eat peppe**RON**i.
>
> I **ON**ly have eyes for **YOU**.
>
> AL DUBIN

Short **parenthetical elements** add additional stresses to a clause by breaking it into several breath units:

> That camping trip we TALKed about,| SCOTTy,| will have to be post**PONED**.
>
> The interest RATE,| it SEEMS,| will be higher than they **SAID.**|

In **coordinate series** of three or more items, a nuclear stress falls on each word linked by the construction:

> Paula resolved to EAT,| DRINK,| and be **MER**ry.
>
> FAT, com**POS**ed, and BEAU**tiful**, the baby stared back **PLAC**idly.

Grammatical **transformations** (see Chapter 9) also influence stress:

> It was to appease **HIT**ler that Chamberlain signed the Munich PACT.
>
> It was **CHAM**berlain who signed the Munich Pact to appease HITler.

Finally, rhetorical inversions of one kind or another rearrange stress, but these generally sound too stagy for ordinary writing situations:

> Never a**GAIN** would birds' song be the **SAME**.
>
> ROBERT FROST

So much WRONG could religion in**DUCE**.

Lucretius

He that is WEARy, let him **SIT**.

George Herbert

EXERCISE 6

Rewrite as directed. What effect do your revisions have on rhythm and the writer's voice? You'll find a sample answer on the *Understanding Style* website.

1. Make a monosyllabic word the sentence nucleus:

   Darius the First was the most able king of ancient Persia.

2. Add *surely*, an adverb of emphasis, after *was*:

   Nijinsky was at his best in those early performances of *Sacre du Printemps*.

3. Add "you old hornswoggler" after *Curtis*:

   Curtis, there's no such thing as a left-handed lariat.

4. Create an *it* transformation to emphasize *Jerusalem artichoke*:

   The Jerusalem artichoke is the only economically important root plant to have originated in North America.

5. Invert, putting the direct object "whose woods these are" first:

   I think I know whose woods these are.

Using Long and Short Words to Control Rhythm

Short words bring their own slow rhythm with them; long words generate increasing velocity as a developing sentence unfolds; rhythms created by a mixture of short and long words fall in the middle, neither notably slow or notably fast. Say these sentences to yourself:

The Huns,| who stayed free of other races,| spread their sway across the Steppes and then to China,| where the Great Wall was built to keep them out.

Nomadic Huns,| ethnically separate from neighbor peoples,|
conquered central Russia and invaded China,| where extensive
border fortifications were erected to counteract their offensive
maneuvers.

The Huns,| who stayed ethnically separate from other races,|
spread their empire across the Steppes and then invaded China,|
where the Great Wall was erected to counter their attacks.

The first sentence sounds dramatic and forceful, partly because short
words are strong themselves, but also because of its stately, deliberate
rhythm: you almost hear a voice-over announcer reading the sentence
as an animated montage of the Huns' growing empire spreads across the
screen. The second sentence sounds like a textbook. The voice moves
along at brisk clip without ever seeming deeply involved in the material.
The third is in the middle, where good writers find themselves most of
the time. Its mixture of short and long words, fast and slow rhythms is
like a random sample of ordinary language. It doesn't call attention to
itself.

EXERCISE 7

Rewrite this passage two times: first using as many words of two syllables or longer as you can supply, and then with a mixture of long
and short words. You may need a thesaurus. What effect do your revisions have on the writer's voice? You'll find a sample answer on the
Understanding Style website.

Glass has been made a long time from sand and an alkali heated
in clay ovens to the boiling point, skimmed, and cooled in molds
in the shape of rounded objects like bowls or figures or mugs
or in flat sheets you can see through. Colors can be added while
the glass is molten. To make glass tough, it is heated again and
then cooled very slowly to make the molecules cling to each
other so that the glass is harder to break.

EXERCISE 8

Rewrite this passage two times: first use as many words of one syllable
as you can supply and no words of more than two syllables; next use
a mixture of long and short words. You may need a thesaurus. What

effect do your revisions have on the writer's voice? You'll find a sample answer on the *Understanding Style* website.

> Considering that constantly burgeoning demand for proscribed narcotics has created a voluminous seller's market, while unceasing efforts to interrupt supplies of controlled substances have demonstrated themselves ineffectual, a proposal has materialized for the government to provide free legal narcotic dosages to confirmed addicts. Supply having proven unresponsive to eradication initiatives, this suggestion adopts the alternate approach of expunging demand.

MAKEOVER

Rewrite the following passage, using a variety of breath units and stress-manipulating techniques, and a better balance of long and short words to improve its rhythm. What effect do your revisions have on the writer's voice?

> Asynchronous processors are computer central processing units (CPUs) uncontrolled by clock crystals. Every operation occurring in asynchronous CPUs can proceed at optimal velocity. No job must slow down to the pace of others to keep all operations in step. You would think that a chip on which every job goes as fast as it can would be quicker than one on which one job is held back to keep pace with the others, but this does not seem to be true so far. Indeed, although in asynchronous processors selected operations occur swiftly compared to a variety of others, the processor frequently must wait on the results of laggard operations before forwarding information so the computing process can proceed. But since no clock crystal must send time signals to each part of the chip, clockless CPUs can save up to four-fifths of the power needed for synchronous chips with the same capacities.

Your Writing

Analyze the rhythms of a piece you wrote yourself. Mark the pauses at the end of each breath unit. Mark the emphasized syllables, noting any that are also one-syllable words, and therefore especially strong. Record the syllable/breath unit ratio and the number of syllables in the shortest and longest breath units. Calculate the syllable/word ratio, remembering that the closer this comes to 1:1, the more emphatic your writing will seem, an effect that you don't always want it to have. Most writing for general purposes should have a syllable/word ratio between about 1.4:1 and 2:1, and a syllable/breath unit ratio of around 12:1, with plenty of variation between some breath units in the 20-25 syllable range and others as short as one syllable. How does your piece stack up against these rough parameters? Does the analysis suggest ways its rhythm might be improved?

◇◇

POINTS TO REMEMBER

1. Most writing should contain breath units averaging about 12 syllables, but with a generous amount of deviation between long, short, and medium-length units.
2. A syllable/word ratio of between 1.4:1 and 2:1 is appropriate for most writing. Short words make for slow, deliberate rhythms, especially when a large number of them are stressed.

◇◇

CHAPTER 11

Grammatical Variety

Readers appreciate variety in grammatical structures as well as in sentence rhythms. In fact, the two are related both to each other and to coherence and emphasis. Writing that mixes sentence types and lengths with other syntactical structures in unpredictable ways can't help being rhythmically lively and interesting. Complicated sentences with several internal pauses allow you to make nuclear stresses in your sentences fall where you want them (see Chapter 9). And managing sentences so that important ideas appear in major grammatical constructions gives you a valuable way to make your writing coherent (Chapter 8).

How Sentences Become Complex

Sentences operate in two dimensions, words and grammar. Words are signs for things, actions, and relationships. Grammar is a system of rules telling how these signs may be combined into valid statements. *Grammar* in this sense doesn't mean textbook terminology but the internalized knowledge that teaches even someone who can't tell a noun from a verb that "My bicycle chain is rusty" makes sense and "Rusty my is chain bicycle" doesn't. Native speakers learn grammar at this practical level as children. As their vocabulary grows, they plug new words into known structures to create sentences they can be sure other speakers will understand, sentences like

The Barbary States—Tunisia, Morocco, and Algeria—were named for the Turkish corsair Barbarossa.

According to one theory of language formation, complicated sentences like this are based on simpler statements, called **kernel sentences**. The Barbary sentence conveys all these ideas:

The Barbary States include Tunisia.

The Barbary States include Morocco.

The Barbary States include Algeria.

The Barbary States were named for someone.

That someone was Barbarossa.

Barbarossa was a Turk.

Barbarossa was a corsair.

The same basic ideas can be combined in many other ways:

1) The Barbary States, which include Tunisia, Morocco, and Algeria, were named for the Turkish corsair Barbarossa.

2) The Turkish corsair Barbarossa gave his name to the Barbary States, including Tunisia, Morocco, and Algeria.

3) Comprised of Tunisia, Morocco, and Algeria, the Barbary States derive their name from Barbarossa, the Turkish corsair.

Although you've never seen these words combined this way before, you understand the sentences immediately because you know their grammar (operational rules, not textbook terms). And you can undoubtedly think of still more valid combinations like this one:

4) The Barbary States of Tunisia, Morocco, and Algeria were named for a Turkish corsair. His name was Barbarossa.

In other words, you already have the grammatical expertise you need to vary sentence structures in your writing. Later sections of this chapter discuss specific sentence-combining strategies to consider when you catch your focus wavering or your style slipping into a rut.

Grammatical Variety in Context

Before plunging into the details of combining ideas in sentences, we need some ground rules for judging the results. Once you've discovered several ways to mix and match the same material, how do you choose the best version? Assuming that the emphasis falls on appropriate words (Chapter 9) and that the rhythms check out (see Chapter 10), the answer usually depends on the context, or **sentence cluster**, in which your material figures and what you want it to accomplish. If you can bear it, consider these additional renditions of the Barbarossa sentences:

> Barbarossa, the Turkish corsair, gave his name to the Barbary States—Tunisia, Morocco, and Algeria.

> A Turkish corsair named Barbarossa gave his name to the Barbary States. These include Tunisia, Morocco, and Algeria.

As Chapter 8 explains, most coherent writing focuses on closely linked grammatical subjects throughout a sentence cluster. The first version here, all one sentence with *Barbarossa* as its subject, would work best if the cluster were about the old pirate himself. Possible next sentence: "With the help of his brother Aruj, Barbarossa wrested Algeria from Spain." The second, two-sentence version is more open-ended. The sentence that follows it could still be about Barbarossa, but the first subject in the example is actually not *Barbarossa* but *corsair*, so a sentence about corsairs would fit as well: "The corsairs were only loosely controlled by central authority." On the other hand, either of these situations might leave readers wondering why *These* [Barbary States] merits a sentence of its own: "These include Tunisia, Morocco, and Algeria." They might expect something like this to follow: "As Turkish control lessened, the Barbary States became a hotbed of out-and-out piracy." As you work through the exercises in this chapter, ask yourself what a reader would expect to come next in a sentence cluster after each combined sentence you create. You'll soon begin to see how much context has to do with choosing the right combination.

EXERCISE 1

For each of the numbered versions of the Barbary States material above, write another sentence that might logically follow in a coherent sentence cluster.

EXERCISE 2

Combine the following kernel sentences in five ways resembling the Barbary States sentences.[1] One of your answers should divide the information into two sentences, one long and one short. One of your answers should make de**VEL**opment a **sentence nucleus** (see Chapter 9). Add a sentence to each of your combinations that would logically follow in a coherent sentence cluster. You'll find a sample answer on the *Understanding Style* website.

Federal lands include parks.

Federal lands include wildlife refuges.

Federal lands include marine sanctuaries.

Federal lands include other tracts.

Federal lands are like islands of open space.

These islands are threatened.

These islands are surrounded by development.

Varying Sentence Structure with Nominals

Nouns show themselves through meaning, form, and use.

Noun Meanings. The traditional definition of noun meanings is still the best: a noun is the name of a person, place, or thing:

Beethoven [a person] went deaf.
Vienna [a place] honors him.
The *Archduke Trio* [a thing] is tuneful and exciting.

Noun Forms. With few exceptions, nouns can be made plural, usually by adding *-s* or *-es*, but sometimes in ways carried over from other languages: *spread sheet/spread sheets; walrus/walruses;* but *medium/ media; ox/oxen; focus/foci* (or *focuses*).

Nouns can also follow determiners—words like, *a, an, the, their, its, many, several, each, every*, and *three*. Whenever such a word appears,

---

[1] Most exercises and example sentences in this chapter silently do some combining for you. For instance, "Federal lands include parks," really should be, "Some lands are federal. The lands include something. That something is parks." But combining sentences this simple is no fun. Besides, people tend to think on the "Federal lands include parks" level, performing the really basic transformations subconsciously.

a noun will be along shortly, although one or more other words may intervene:

a *gismo*
that sandy *reef*
her first prom *dress*
five golden *rings*

Noun Functions. Nouns can be **subjects, complements, objects,** or **appositives. Subjects** are the actors of sentences, answering the question "Who or what?" about the verb and the rest of the predicate.

A *gismo* was invented to extract floating pickles from a jar of brine. [What was invented? A *gismo*.]

Her first prom *dress* was excessively demure. [What was excessively demure? Her *dress*.]

Most **noun complements** come after a verb like *is* or *seems* and refer to the subject of the verb. In these sentences the verb functions like an equal sign:

That gizmo is a pickle *extractor*. [*Extractor* identifies *gizmo*.]
Delphine seems a *match* for anyone. [*Match* identifies *Delphine*.]

Nouns can be direct objects, naming the person, place, or thing that receives the action of a verb:

Beethoven wrote the *Archduke Trio*. [The *trio* is what was written.]

After the battle, peasants bludgeoned and pillaged the wounded *knights*. [The *knights* were the ones bludgeoned and pillaged.]

Or they can be indirect objects, naming the person, place, or thing to or for whom something was done:

Willard gave *Kendall* a black eye. [The black eye was given; it's the direct object. *Kendall* was the recipient; he's the indirect object.]

The guidebooks give *Vienna* high marks. [High marks, the direct object, were given *to Vienna*, the indirect object.]

Or they can be objects of **prepositions**, function words like *of, with, in, under, through*, or *between*:

The guide books speak highly of Vienna. [*Vienna* is the object of the preposition *of*.]

She cut the straps off her prom *dress* in the *car*. [*Dress* is the object of *off*; *car* is the object of *in*.]

An appositive comes after another noun and renames it:

My favorite kitchen tool, a Chinese *cleaver*, does every knife job except paring. [*Cleaver* renames *tool*.]

The sloop wrecked on a submerged hazard, a sandy *reef*. [*Reef* renames *hazard*.]

EXERCISE 3

Find the nouns in the following sentences and identify them as subjects, complements, direct or indirect objects, objects of prepositions or appositives. There will be more than one noun per sentence. You'll find a sample answer on the *Understanding Style* website.

   1. Scotland resents any hint of English domination.

   2. Morton often cooks red beans and rice.

   3. Sally painted the upstairs windows shut.

   4. A large Doberman bounded up the marble steps after us.

   5. Tina always eats lunch in the commissary.

Nominals. Nominals play all the grammatical roles nouns do. In addition to nouns, the class includes certain **phrases** and **clauses** that are noun work-alikes.

Most **nominal phrases** are based on gerunds or infinitives, verb forms used to bring more information into a sentence that already has another main verb. Gerunds end in *-ing*; infinitives are usually identified by the marker *to* followed by the basic form of the verb, as in "*to sleep*, perchance *to dream*":

Milking 78 Holsteins every day is a big job. [*Milking 78 Holsteins every day* is a gerund phrase and subject of the sentence. What is a big job? *Milking 78 Holsteins every day*.]

Jennifer decided *to buy the Honda*. [*To buy the Honda* is an infinitive phrase and the direct object. What did Jennifer decide? *To buy the Honda*.]

Nominal clauses are introduced by words like *that, who, whom, which, where, when, why,* and *how*. Unlike phrases, these clauses have subjects and verbs of their own; in fact, the introductory word itself is often the subject:

Garlic is *what gives this stew its special flavor*. [*What gives this stew its flavor* is a noun clause and complement. It identifies *garlic*.]

Why Grant charged remains a mystery. [*Why Grant charged* is the subject of *remains*.]

Transforming Kernel Sentences into Nominals. Notice that all these nominal constructions are another way of putting an idea that could be a kernel sentence by itself: "Something gives this stew its flavor"; "Grant charged for a reason." Nominals are a standard means of combining the information from kernel sentences like these into more complicated constructions:

Something is a big job.

That something is milking 78 Holsteins every day.

Milking 78 Holsteins every day is a big job.

Something gives this stew its special flavor.

That something is garlic.

Garlic is *what gives this stew its special flavor*.

EXERCISE 4

Combine these kernel sentences into sentences with at least one nominal phrase or clause and other constructions as you see fit. Somewhere among your answers be sure to include one of each: a gerund phrase, an infinitive phrase, and a noun clause. Keep the coherence of the passage in mind as you work. You'll find a sample answer on the *Understanding Style* website.

1. Ambrose Bierce grew up in Warsaw, Indiana.

   He enlisted in the Ninth Regiment of Indiana Volunteers.

   He enlisted in 1861.

   He was eighteen.

2. Bierce fought in the Civil War.

   He fought for four years.

He fought more or less continuously.

He fought in West Virginia.

West Virginia was not yet a separate state.

3. Bierce fought at Shiloh.

He fought at Stones River.

He fought at Chickamauga.

He stormed Missionary Ridge.

Missionary Ridge overlooks Chattanooga.

He was wounded at Kennesaw Mountain.

He was wounded in the head.

He was wounded by a sharpshooter.

4. He returned to Indiana.

He returned to convalesce.

He convalesced on his father's farm.

He went back to the war a year later.

5. He returned to the fighting at Nashville.

He also fought at Franklin, Tennessee.

His abilities were limited by his wound.

He was discharged from the army.

He was mustered out in January 1865.

Varying Sentence Structure with Adjectivals

Adjectivals, words and constructions that modify or explain nouns, include adjectives and phrases and clauses that work like adjectives.

Adjectives name qualities like *plump, luscious,* or *courageous.* Adjectives can be compared, or made stronger or weaker, as in *plumper, less luscious, most courageous.* They may appear before nouns, often following a **determiner**, or as adjective complements, following a verb like *is* or *seems* and referring to the subject of the verb:

> Atop the pole hung a *rusty, gray* transformer. [Both adjectives modify *transformer*.]

> These rocks appear *calciferous*. [Adjective complement modifying *rocks*.]

Occasionally adjectives crop up in other positions:

> *Lean* and *hungry*, Cassius averted his glance. [Both modify *Cassius*.]

> The last Neanderthals may have died on Gibraltar, *isolated* and *malnourished*. [These two modify *Neanderthals*.]

An Adjective Test. The *RUSTY* transformer is very *RUSTY*. The *ISOLATED* Neanderthals were very *ISOLATED*. Whenever you find a word that will fit into a sentence like this, it is an adjective. But note that the test won't work with adjectives like *no* or *some,* or with adjectives in the comparative or superlative degree. You can't say "The *MOST ISOLATED* Neanderthals were very *MOST ISOLATED*."

EXERCISE 5

Find the adjectives in the following sentences and identify the nouns they modify. There will be more than one adjective per sentence. You'll find a sample answer on the *Understanding Style* website.

1. Long, ropey strings of orange pulp cascaded from the biggest pumpkin.

2. The furious doctor gave her guilty receptionist a stinging lecture.

3. Geese are large, aggressive birds.

4. Switzerland is often cold and gloomy in May.

5. Cold and gloomy in May, Switzerland is no place for tourists.

Other Adjectivals. Adjectival phrases are usually based on prepositions (The skimpy meals *on the flight* offended Marvin) or participles, which are past or present verb forms that anchor constructions modifying nouns (Marvin, *protesting the skimpy meals on the flight*, berated the attendant; *Still famished after his in-flight meal*, Marvin berated the attendant).

Adjective clauses are introduced by the same words that introduce noun clauses—*that, who, whom, which, where, when, why*, etc. Instead of working like nouns, however, they provide information about a noun already in the sentence:

> Marvin, *who had definite ideas concerning in-flight meals,* lectured the attendant on the skimpiness of his.

> The attendant, *who had listened patiently*, offered Marvin another bag of complimentary peanuts.

Transforming Kernel Sentences into Adjectivals. Ideas that might have been separate sentences can often be expressed by single adjectives:

> Some whales are mothers.
> These pump milk.
> The milk comes from glands.
> The glands are mammary glands.
> The milk comes with force.
> The force is tremendous.
> The milk goes to calves.
> The calves belong to the whales.
> The calves grow fast.
> *Maternal* whales pump milk from their *mammary* glands with *tremendous* force to their *fast-growing* calves.

or by adjectival phrases or clauses:

> Whales *with fast-growing calves* pump milk *from their mammary glands* with tremendous force. [*With fast-growing calves* is a prepositional phrase modifying *whales; from their mammary glands* is a prepositional phrase modifying *milk*.]

> *Nursing their fast-growing calves*, whales pump milk *produced by their mammary glands* with tremendous force. [*Nursing their fast-growing calves* is a participial phrase modifying *whales; produced by their mammary glands* is a participial phrase modifying *milk*.]

> Whales, *who are solicitous mothers*, pump milk from their mammary glands to their fast-growing calves with tremendous force. [*Who are solicitous mothers* is an adjective clause modifying *whales*.]

EXERCISE 6

Combine these kernel sentences into sentences with at least one adjective phrase or clause and other constructions as you see fit. Somewhere among your answers be sure to include one of each: a prepositional phrase, a participial phrase, and an adjective clause. Feel free to write more than one answer sentence per item. Try to make your sentences add up to a sustained passage, with passable internal coherence (Chapter 8), emphasis (Chapter 9), and rhythms (Chapter 10). You'll find a sample answer on the *Understanding Style* website.

1. Samuel Bowles is a behavioral scientist.

   He directs the Behavioral Sciences Program.

   The program is at the Santa Fe Institute.

   Bowles is interested in moral motivation.

   He is interested in economic motivation.

   He is interested in how the two are related.

2. Bowles reported his findings.

   His article appeared in *Science Magazine*.

   His findings were surprising.

   They were based on a study.

   The study concerned a new program.

   The program was put in place by six daycare centers.

   The centers operated in Haifa, Israel.

3. The centers had a problem.

   Parents were picking their children up.

   They were picking them up late.

   The centers imposed a fine.

   Parents had to pay the fine.

   They had to pay for each late pick up.

4. The plan didn't work.

The parents were late more often.

This went against everyone's expectations.

They wanted to know why.

Bowles had an answer.

More than one force was working on the parents.

5. Paying the fine was one force.

A moral obligation was the other.

This obligation was to be on time.

Bowles explained this.

People paying the fine felt free.

They felt they'd paid for being late.

Their fines bought that right.

The moral obligation went away.

6. That left only one question.

It was convenient to come late.

Was the convenience worth the fine?

BASED ON RONALD BAILEY,
Does the Invisible Hand Need a Helping Hand?

Varying Sentence Structure with Adverbials

Adverbials modify clauses, verbs, and other modifiers, answering questions like *when*, *where*, *why*, *how*, and *how much* about the constructions they modify. The class is based on adverbs, many of which end in -*ly*:

The hidden guns rumbled *softly* but *deeply* beyond the horizon. [The adverbs tell *how* about *rumbled*, the verb.]

Her eyes were *intensely* blue. [The adverb tells *how much* about *blue*, an adjective.]

Frankly, my dear, I don't give a damn. [The adverb tells *how* about the following clause.]

Adverbs are especially mobile. You can put them almost anywhere in a sentence, though moving them generally changes the meaning. The carets (^) in the following sentence show where the adverb *only* might be placed. Notice how the meaning changes with each new location:

^Beverly^thinks^Florida's beating^Ohio State^was^a fluke.

Like adjectives, most adverbs can be compared: *less frequently, most advantageously,* etc.

Other Adverbials. Most **adverbial phrases** are based on prepositions.

In October formations of geese and ducks stream *down the flyway.* [*In October* tells *when* about the verb; *down the flyway* tells *where.*]

You might get a yellow daylily *by crossing two red ones.* [Tells *how* about the verb, *might get.*]

But some are based on infinitives (*to* plus a verb) when they carry the sense of "in order to":

I called Houston *to confirm my reservation.* [That is, *in order to* confirm my reservation.]

To see eagles, you must be patient or lucky. [*In order to* see eagles, you must be patient or lucky.]

Adverbial clauses are especially useful because they specify logical relationships, making your ideas easier to follow. "*As the climate changes,* forests advance and recede." "The stock will hold its value *provided that the company makes its earnings estimates.*" The italicized parts of these sentences are adverbial clauses, ordinary sentences made dependent by tacking a **subordinating conjunction** on at the beginning. Common subordinating conjunctions are words like *after, although, as, because,* or *when.* You'll find a much longer list in Chapter 6 (p. 99).

Add one of these conjunctions to a sentence and it is no longer capable of standing alone. It becomes an adverbial clause telling *when, where, why,* or *how* about another clause or verb:

After the regatta ended, squalls swept the bay. [Tells *when.*]

They left a trail of evidence, *as if they wanted to be caught.* [Tells *how.*]

Because I could not stop for Death—He kindly stopped for me. [Tells *why.*]

EMILY DICKINSON

A Note on Branching and Embedding. Because they are so mobile, adverbials may appear at the beginning of a sentence, to the left of the **independent clause**: "*After the regatta ended,* squalls swept the bay" (this is called left-branching), or after the independent clause: "Squalls swept the bay *after the regatta ended*" (right-branching). They can even interrupt in a clause: "Squalls, *after the regatta ended*, swept the bay" (embedded). Choosing the right arrangement for your purpose can involve logic—The regatta ended *and then* the squalls came; shouldn't that be the right order?— or emphasis or formality. While both the left-branching and embedded versions of the regatta sentence place the **sentence nucleus** on **BAY**, the right-branching sentence emphasizes **END**ed. That distinction might be important for your purposes. Each sentence projects a different level of formality as well. Because right-branching sentences are far more common than left-branching or embedded sentences in written and spoken English, right-branching sentences sound less formal than left-branching or embedded ones. Embedded sentences are least common and by far the most formal-sounding of the three.

Transforming Kernel Sentences into Adverbials. Like nominals and adjectivals, adverbial constructions give you a way of combining information from kernel sentences into more complicated constructions:

Howard Head invented the oversized tennis racket.

He wanted more power in his tennis game.

This was in 1976.

Because he wanted more power in his tennis game [adverbial clause telling why] Howard Head invented the oversized racket *in 1976* [adverbial phrase telling when].

Unsightly bags under the eyes can be prevented with Preparation H.

Put a dab on.

Put it under each eye.

The skin is loose here.

To prevent unsightly bags, [adverbial phrase telling why] put a dab of Preparation H *under each eye* [adverbial phrase telling where] *where the skin is loose* [adverbial clause telling where].

EXERCISE 7

Combine these kernel sentences into sentences with at least one adverbial phrase or clause and other constructions as you see fit. Somewhere among your answers be sure to include one of each: a prepositional phrase, an infinitive phrase, and an adverbial clause. Feel free to write more than one answer sentence per item. Try to make your sentences add up to a sustained passage, with passable internal coherence (Chapter 8), emphasis (Chapter 9), and rhythms (Chapter 10). You'll find a sample answer on the *Understanding Style* website.

1. Randolph Nesse and George Williams wrote *Why We Get Sick*.

    This was in 1995.

    The book is based on an approach to medicine grounded in evolutionary theory.

    Richard Dawkins, an evolutionary theorist, figures in the book.

    Dawkins wrote *The Selfish Gene*.

    That was in 1976.

2. Dawkins' ideas on evolution emphasize genes.

    Genes don't serve organisms.

    Organisms serve genes by reproducing.

    Reproducing organisms pass genes on to the future.

    Evolution may be just a mechanism serving genes.

    It may work by promoting reproductive success.

3. Our genes might encourage some illnesses that helped them get reproduced long ago.

    People died young then.

    A gene would want organisms to reach reproductive maturity.

    A gene would want to promote reproduction.

    After that, a gene wouldn't care what happened.

4. Heart disease may have an evolutionary rationale.

Much is brought on by rich diets and inactivity.

Fatty or sweet foods supply a lot of energy.

This energy can be stored in fat deposits.

Inactivity conserves this stored energy.

5. Fatter people may have been more likely to reproduce in the evolutionary past.

Life was hard.

The food supply was uncertain.

Shorter lives meant heart disease had less chance to develop.

The same tendencies are dangerous now.

Food is abundant.

People live longer.

Fat deposits choke modern hearts.

6. Morning sickness may be another example.

Unborn babies are vulnerable to toxic substances in food.

Nausea discourages intake of many foods.

Toxic, strong-flavored foods become distasteful.

This reduces the fetus's risk.

There is a related phenomenon.

Young children are still vulnerable.

They have an aversion to strong flavors.

BASED ON WRAY HERBERT,
Why Do We Get Sick? Ask Your Ancestors

Varying Sentence Structure with Parallel Construction

Parallel construction is a way of linking similar grammatical structures together. You probably used it in combining these kernel sentences from an earlier exercise:

Bierce fought at Shiloh.

He fought at Stones River.

He fought at Chickamauga.

He stormed Missionary Ridge.

However you combined the rest of the sentences, it would seem natural to link those first three place names with an *and*:

After fighting at *Shiloh, Stones Rivers, and Chickamaugua*, Bierce stormed Missionary Ridge.

English allows this sort of linking for almost any constructions in the language, requiring only that the constructions be grammatically similar. In addition to *and*, the conjunctions *or*, *nor*, and *but* can connect parallel elements; or for a change of pace you can even dispense with conjunctions entirely:

Linked Nouns
Give me the *political economist, the sanitary reformer, the engineer*; and take your *saints* and *virgins*, *relics* and *miracles*.
CHARLES KINGSLEY

Linked Verbs
Always do right. This will *gratify* some people and *astonish* the rest.
MARK TWAIN

Linked Adjectives
Our worst enemies are not the *ignorant* and *simple*, however *cruel*; our worst enemies are the *intelligent* and *corrupt*.
GRAHAM GREENE

Linked Prepositional Phrases

…government *of the people*, *by the people*, and *for the people*.
ABRAHAM LINCOLN

Linked Infinitive Phrases

We have talked long enough in this country about equal rights.
We have talked for a hundred years or more. It is time now *to
write the next chapter*—and *to write it in the books of law.*

LYNDON JOHNSON

Linked Dependent Clauses

[They say] Socrates is a doer of evil, w*ho corrupts the youth*
and *who does not believe in the gods of the state.*

SOCRATES

Linked Independent Clauses

We do not ride on the railroad; it rides on us.

THOREAU

Wherever parallel ideas occur in your writing there's a good chance
you can combine them into a parallel construction:

Many forms of marriage are known.

Monogamy involves one husband and one wife.

Polygamy involves one husband and several wives.

Polyandry involves several husbands and one wife.

Among known forms of marriage are monogamy (one husband
and one wife), polygamy (one husband and several wives), and
polyandry (one wife and several husbands).

A softball is 3″ larger than a baseball in circumference.

A softball infield is about 30 square feet smaller than a baseball
infield.

Softball pitchers throw underhand.

Softball games last seven innings.

Softball is very different from baseball.

Because a softball is 3″ larger in circumference than a baseball, because a softball infield is about 30 square feet smaller, because softball pitchers throw underhand, and because games last only seven innings, softball is very different from baseball.

EXERCISE 8

Combine these kernel sentences using parallel construction and other constructions as you see fit. Be sure to include at least one parallel series in each answer. Feel free to write more than one answer sentence per item. Try to make your sentences add up to a sustained passage with passable internal coherence (Chapter 8), emphasis (Chapter 9), and rhythms (Chapter 10). You'll find a sample answer on the *Understanding Style* website.

1. The Hubble Space Telescope has found a belt of comets in orbit around the sun.

   The belt reaches out beyond Pluto.

   It contains many objects.

   Pluto is the farthest planet from the sun.

   The belt reaches out 4 billion miles from the sun.

   It is called the Kuipper Belt.

2. The Kuipper belt was proposed by Gerard Kuipper.

   He made the proposal in the 1940s.

   He thought the solar system did not just end with Pluto.

   He thought debris was orbiting farther out.

   This debris was from the formation of the planets.

3. Seeing these objects was difficult.

   There are millions of them.

   They are composed of ice and rock.

   They are like dirty snowballs.

   They are primarily black.

They reflect little light.

4. Anita Cochran confirmed the belt's existence.

She leads a team of astronomers.

She got the space telescope to record objects in the belt.

She focused on specific areas.

She used long exposures.

She was looking for an object the size of Manhattan.

5. Cochran found what she was looking for.

She recorded images of objects.

Her success was surprising.

It pushed the Hubble Telescope to its limits.

Cochran said seeing the objects was like spotting a 100-watt bulb from 4.3 million miles away.

BASED ON PAUL RECER,
Tiny Comets Surround Solar System

Grammatical Emphasis

A section of Chapter 9 explains how to gain emphasis through **grammatical bulk**, or adding modifiers to a word or idea to give it extra heft in its sentence. A more subtle technique is to construct sentences so that the ideas most important for your purposes appear in major grammatical constructions while less important information is consigned to lesser ones. The ideas most important for your purposes are generally those having most to do with the subject of the **sentence cluster** in which they appear. To elevate such an idea to the highest level of grammatical emphasis, give it a sentence of its own. To play it down, take away its grammatical independence: make it one branch of a **compound sentence**, make it a **dependent clause** and therefore subordinate to some other idea, reduce it to a **phrase** or even a single word. In general, each step away from independence weakens the **grammatical emphasis** you place on the idea. To see the principle at work, consider this complex of kernel sentences about navigation:

Ancient sailors depended on landmarks.

They stayed in sight of land.

Later navigators were more venturesome.

They sailed far from land.

They charted their locations by latitude.

They charted their locations by longitude.

As separate sentences all these ideas get equal, heavy emphasis. Suppose you were writing a piece on the cautious sailors of the ancient world. Here's a way to subordinate what you have to say about the later mariners:

Although later, more venturesome navigators sailed far from land, charting their locations by longitude and latitude, ancient sailors depended on landmarks. They stayed in sight of land.

In another piece you might choose to emphasize the moderns:

While ancient sailors depended on landmarks and always stayed in sight of land, later navigators were more venturesome. They sailed far from land, where locations could be charted only by degrees of latitude and longitude.

In each case, the grammar itself channels readers' attention to the ideas you want to emphasize.

MAKEOVER

Use combining techniques to provide a variety of sentence structures and breath units in this passage. Choose some combinations to promote coherence (Chapter 8), to make nuclear stress fall on important words (Chapter 9), or to ensure that important ideas appear in major grammatical constructions like separate sentences and independent clauses.

Around 1700, the Comanches lived in New Mexico. They were a small tribe. They lived by hunting and gathering. Then they got horses. This changed them. They became fearsome warriors. They were called the "Spartans of the Plains." They resisted European expansion on two fronts. They resisted the Americans. They resisted the Mexicans. By 1750 they controlled all of New Mexico. They dominated Texas. They ruled in parts of Louisiana. They ruled northern Mexico. They lived mainly on buffalo herds. These herds were vast in the early nineteenth century. About 7 million buffalo lived then in Comanche territories. Horses lived there too. Those territories were home to about 2 million wild horses. The Comanches kept another 120,000 domesticated horses. These horses allowed the Comanches to fight effectively. They fought with Europeans. They fought other Indian tribes. The horses allowed the Comanches to kill buffalo. They killed about a quarter of a million buffalo a year.

BASED ON FRANK MCLYNN, *Spartans of the Plains*:
A Review of Pekka Hämäläinen's The Comanche Empire

Your Writing

"De-write" a passage of your own by breaking it down into kernel sentences like those in this chapter's exercises. Choose a passage four or five sentences long and list the kernel sentences in the same order they occur in the original. Now experiment with recombining your kernel sentences in different ways using nominal, adjectival, and adverbial elements and parallel constructions. Think about ways to fit the most important ideas into the most important grammatical constructions. What does this show you about the grammatical variety and emphasis of your original sentences?

◇◇◇

POINTS TO REMEMBER
1. A variety of grammatical constructions, like a variety of breath units, helps make your writing lively and interesting.
2. Putting your most important concepts in the most important grammatical constructions gives them special prominence. Putting less important ideas into lesser constructions keeps them in the background.

◇◇◇

PART SIX

Quick Fixes

CHAPTER 12

Rules of Thumb

Many points about effective sentences can be stated as general maxims. The writing tips in this chapter are loosely organized and may repeat material from other chapters. But all are highly practical. One or two may be just the quick fix you need.

Start Most Sentences with the Subject

The usual order of sentence elements is subject-verb-complement, and good writers structure most of their sentences this way. The **subject** is (or should be) what the sentence is about. Bringing it immediately to the reader's attention makes for clear communication and helps your sentences sound natural and unaffected. A quick survey of professional writers' work in popular magazines and books suggests that they begin about two-thirds of their sentences with the subject. That's a good percentage of subject-first sentences to keep in mind when you write.

When professional writers put something other than the subject first, it's generally an **adverbial**—usually a prepositional phrase, a sentence modifier, or an adverbial clause:

In late October, The McCain campaign swerved in another direction. (prepositional phrase)

Thanks to acid rain, whole mountainsides are covered with ghost forests of dead trees. (sentence modifier)

Although the proposal passed, the margin was slim. (adverbial clause)

You should generally avoid sentences that open with long modifying phrases or clauses and sentences that invert the normal sentence order:

> Originating in the 1920s and dominating public architecture during the 50s and 60s was the angular and severely functional International Style. (This sentence puts the complements first, then the verb, then the subject, *International Style*.)

> A non-metallic element discovered in 1811 by Bernard Courtois and the least active halogen, iodine has important medicinal and industrial uses. (The subject *iodine* is preceded by a long appositive phrase.)

While sentences like these may occasionally provide welcome variety, most can be improved by rewriting to put the subject first. Others can be broken into two or more sentences, each with a subject of its own:

> The angular and severely functional International Style originated in the 1920s and dominated public architecture during the 50s and 60s.

> The non-metallic element iodine was discovered in 1811 by Bernard Courtois. Iodine, the least active halogen, has important medicinal and industrial uses.

EXERCISE 1

Rewrite the following sentences to put the subject at or near the beginning. Start at least one of your revisions with a short adverbial phrase or clause. In another, break the original sentence in two. What effect do your changes have on the writer's voice? You'll find a sample answer on the *Understanding Style* website.

1. Years after founding phenomenology, a painstaking philosophical study of the laws governing conscious experience, Edmund Husserl concluded objects had no existence outside the mind.

2. Outgrowths of follicles arranged in certain tracts and forming a protective, decorative and functional layer outside the skin, birds' feathers may have evolved from the scales of Mesozoic reptiles.

3. Because the United States maintained neutrality during the conflicts between France and Britain brought about by the French Revolution and the Napoleonic Wars and because the angry British began to impress American sailors and confiscate American cargoes in retaliation, the War of 1812 began.

Make Your Subjects Definitely Named Actors

There are two points to remember here: you should name the **subject** of each sentence clearly, and your subjects should be well chosen—the true doers of the actions you're discussing, not just a related idea. Whenever possible these subject-actors should be people.

Suppose you were writing a sentence about Martinique in the West Indies and wanted to explain that French settlers exterminated the native Indians, replacing them with African slaves. Unless you had a special purpose—like recounting European crimes against native Americans—your best subject would probably be the obvious one, *French settlers.* Don't say:

European interests exterminated the native Carib Indians and replaced them with African slaves.

French settlers is much more precise than *European interests.*

Choosing **nominalizations** (nouns made from verbs) for your subjects or using passive constructions (in which instead of doing something the subject has something done to it) makes the sentence even less effective:

Extermination of the native Carib Indians and their *replacement* with African slaves was the work of French settlers. (nominalized subjects in italics)

The native Carib Indians *were exterminated* and African slaves *were brought in* by French settlers. (passive verbs in italics)

The best way around all these problematic choices is to pair a subject that clearly identifies the real actor you have in mind with active verbs that plainly say what the subject did:

> *French settlers exterminated* the native Carib Indians and *replaced* them with African slaves.

Make Your Verbs Name Definite Actions

Strong **verbs** name definite actions—not always physical actions like *hit* or *kick*, but ones with clear meanings: *deceive, rationalize, insist, tolerate*. Avoid **weak verbs** like *concern, establish*, or *have* that are often used in vague ways, and be especially leery of the weakest of them all, *to be*. If weak verbs are undermining your writing, replace at least half of them with stronger choices:

> Not
>
> Poverty *is* an important factor in most social problems.
>
> But
>
> Most social problems *feed* on poverty.
>
> Not
>
> We *acknowledge* a need to *explain* why the mine explosion *occurred*.
>
> But
>
> We *need* to *know* why the mine *exploded*.

EXERCISE 2
Revise the following sentences to provide more definite and expressive actors and actions. If the original wording is so vague you can't tell what it means, make up your own specific meanings. How do your revisions change the writer's voice? (Actors and actions to be replaced appear in italics.) You'll find a sample answer on the *Understanding Style* website.

> **1.** *Certain parties have indicated* that there *may be problems* with the way airbags *deploy* in *various models* in our product line.

2. *A major recording artist has developed a promising marketing concept related to* her latest album.

3. *Native peoples* were *introduced to European disorders* and, lacking antibodies to control these, *succumbed in disproportionate numbers.*

Write Mostly in Independent Clauses

More than half of your sentences should be anchored by one or more **independent clauses** able to stand by themselves as separate sentences. And as a general rule, none of your sentences should have more than three **dependent clauses**, or clauses that need to be attached to an independent clause in order to be complete. Dependent clauses have a grammatical function within another clause. They may function as **nouns** ("Ivan wouldn't say *what was wrong*"), **adjectives** ("The one *that I like best* is blue"), or **adverbs** ("They checked their inventory *while we waited*"). They don't make complete sense on their own.

In his book *A Writer's Companion*, Richard Marius analyzes samples of popular writing to show the number of dependent clauses in each. Examining 95 sentences from current magazines and books, Marius found only 56 dependent clauses. More important, 65 of the sentences—roughly 70%—contained no dependent clauses. No sentence contained more than three dependent clauses.

My own two-hour survey confirmed Marius' results, but I did find a sentence with five dependent clauses in a guide to the *Iliad*. It's pretty bad. The author mentions that Aithra, the mother of Theseus, appears in Troy as a handmaid to Helen and her presence requires an explanation. Then he goes on (dependent clauses in brackets):

> This was forthcoming in the story, known as early as the epic cycle, [that [when Helen was carried off by Theseus and Perithoös, some time [before she married Menelaos,] her brothers Kastor and Polydeukes rescued her]] and, [while doing so, they carried off in reprisal Theseus' mother Aithra,] [who thus became a slave of Helen.]
>
> Malcolm M. Willcock,
> *A Companion to the* Iliad

Willcock is a good writer, and this sentence is not typical of his work, but it could certainly stand simplifying. To loosen a logjam like this, divide it into several sentences, removing some of the dependent clauses in the process (dependent clause in brackets):

> This was forthcoming in a story known as early as the epic cycle. Some time before her marriage to Menelaos, Helen had been carried off by Theseus and Perithoös. [When her brothers, Kastor and Polydeukes, rescued her,] they also carried off in reprisal Theseus' mother, Aithra. Aithra thus became a slave of Helen.

Instead of one sentence with five dependent clauses, the revision offers four sentences with one dependent clause. There is no loss of content and a large gain in readability. This sort of simplification works wonders when dependent clauses pile up too deeply.

EXERCISE 3

Rewrite the following sentences to eliminate half the dependent clauses (in brackets). Change the sentence structure however you like but keep all the major ideas of the originals. Feel free to create new sentences. How do your revisions change the writer's voice? You'll find a sample answer on the *Understanding Style* website.

1. [Because some welfare recipients [who had poor work histories] and [who could make only minimum wages] chose to stay on public assistance indefinitely in Fond du Lac, Wisconsin,] authorities designed a program, [which is called Work Not Welfare,] so [that people [they considered to be welfare-dependent] would take charge of their own lives.

2. [When the program took effect] recipients [who had been on welfare a long time] were told [that they had only two years [in which they could continue to receive benefits]] and [that they had to earn those remaining benefits by performing services [that helped their neighbors and other citizens.]]

3. [Although the program appears to be working for people [who have cooperated with social workers and educators [who have trained them for jobs [which have a future,]]]] costs for training, child care, and other expenses proved far higher [than officials

expected,] and many targeted individuals have not cooperated [because they didn't believe [they could ever hold a good job]] or [because they simply didn't want to.]

Keep Subjects and Verbs Close Together

The vital **actor/action relationship** between **subjects** and **verbs** needs to be as plain as you can make it. Long interruptions between subjects and verbs put readers on hold while they wait for the thought to be completed. The best revision is usually to move the interrupting element to the beginning or the end of the sentence:

Not

Our objective, after we have taken the time to define it clearly and draft a plan of action to bring it about, will be paramount.

But

After we have taken the time to define it clearly and draft a plan of action to bring it about, our objective will be paramount.

Or

Our objective will be paramount after we have taken the time to define it clearly and drafted a plan of action to bring it about.

Another revision technique is to bundle the interrupter off into a sentence of its own:

We must first define our objective clearly and draft a plan of action to bring it about. Then the objective itself will be paramount.

Keep Verbs and Complements Close Together

Verbs sometimes appear by themselves ("Fútbol rules!"), but they are more often followed by adverbials ("Fútbol rules *in much of the world*"); objects ("Fútbol rules *their lives*"); or subject complements ("Fútbol is *number one*"). Don't let long interrupters come between your verbs and these completing elements. Move them to the beginning or end of the sentence or give them sentences of their own:

Not

The Mau Mau uprising in Kenya resulted after a series of highly publicized attacks on Europeans in the relocation of the Kikuyu tribe.

But

After a series of highly publicized attacks on Europeans, the Mau Mau uprising in Kenya resulted in the relocation of the Kikuyu tribe.

Or

The Mau Mau uprising in Kenya resulted in the relocation of the Kikuyu tribe after a series of highly publicized attacks on Europeans.

Or

The Mau Mau uprising in Kenya involved a series of highly publicized attacks on Europeans. These attacks resulted in the relocation of the Kikuyu tribe.

EXERCISE 4

The sentences that follow are marred by awkward interrupters. Revise them in one of three classic ways: (1) move the interrupter to the beginning of the sentence; (2) move it to the end; or (3) give it a sentence of its own. You'll find a sample answer on the *Understanding Style* website.

1. Impedance—the degree to which a circuit resists the flow of electric current, a resistance factor expressed as ohms—is sometimes increased by capacitors.

2. The gene for blue eyes, which is fairly common today and even valued by some for producing what they consider a beautiful eye color, arose as little as eight thousand years ago.

3. Jefferson complained, and this was a complaint he maintained to the end of his life with bitterness that only increased as he grew older, that revisions forced on his Declaration of

Independence by the Second Continental Congress left it a weaker document.

Use Single Verbs with Multiple Subjects. Use Single Subjects with Multiple Verbs

Multiple subjects followed by multiple verbs usually add up to too many ideas to sort out easily. Simplify the **subjects** or the **verbs**:

Not

Jimmy Carter and Bill Clinton threatened and cajoled the Pentagon's big spenders.

But

Jimmy Carter and Bill Clinton threatened the Pentagon's big spenders. When this failed, they tried to cajole them.

Or

Jimmy Carter threatened and cajoled the Pentagon's big spenders. So did Bill Clinton.

Favor the Active Voice

Cast most of your sentences in the **active voice** so that the subject does something rather than has something done to it. **Passive** constructions can be useful when it doesn't matter who performs a certain action ("Foods high in saturated fat should be avoided.") or when you want to emphasize results regardless of who brought them about ("As if bloody civil war weren't enough, Angola was ravaged by AIDS.") But most sentences gain force and directness with active verbs:

Not

The Fourth of July *is regarded* as our chief secular holiday by most Americans.

But

Most Americans *regard* the Fourth of July as our chief secular holiday.

Choose Positive Rather Than Negative Constructions

You save words and communicate more directly when you tell what something is rather than what it isn't:

Not

She was not without charm.

And certainly not

She was not uncharming.

But

She was charming.

You may be tempted to use negative constructions and weak verbs to soften a disagreeable truth. It's usually best to resist:

Not

The company is frequently not in compliance with accepted accounting standards.

But

The company frequently violates accepted accounting standards.

EXERCISE 5

Revise the following sentences to avoid pairing multiple subjects with multiple verbs, to make passive verbs active, and to replace negative constructions with positive ones. Sentences may have more than one problem to correct. How do your revisions change the writer's voice? You'll find a sample answer on the *Understanding Style* website.

1. Sally, her mother, and her cousins wandered through Charleston's historic district, shopped for souvenirs, and had lunch near the water.

2. The university has not been placed under sanctions by the NCAA.

3. The foil, the épée, and the saber—weapons used in sport fencing—are not without an evolutionary relationship to swords once used in actual combat.

Focus Each Sentence on the Ideas Expressed by the Subject and Predicate

A **predicate** consists of a verb plus the modifiers, objects, and comple-ments that go with it. Together, the subject and predicate make a com-plete idea, which everything else in the sentence should support. Don't let unrelated material pull the sentence too far from this central thought:

> Alabama, whose economy was nearly ruined by a boll weevil infestation during the early twentieth century, is a hotbed of stock car racing mania.

The core statement here is "Alabama is a hotbed of stock car racing mania." Unless nearby sentences somehow connect stock car racing with the ravages of the boll weevil, readers will find the digression illogical and confusing. Find the boll weevil a home in a new sentence or elimi-nate him altogether.

Mix Long and Short Sentences

Readers look for the chief actors and actions in each sentence, and these are harder to keep track of in long sentences than in short ones:

> Inside a small cubical enclosure within the Great Mosque at Mecca, rests the Kaaba, or Black Stone, the most highly vener-ated object in the Muslim world and the destination of devout believers' pilgrimages, occupying much the same location it had before the coming of Muhammad, when it was sacred to pagan sects of undetermined antiquity. Infidels are strictly forbidden to approach it.

A page of sentences like the first one would give anyone a head-ache. Combining such sentences with short follow-ups like "Infidels are strictly forbidden to approach it" helps by giving readers a chance to catch their breath:

On the other hand, too many short, simple sentences in a row are as bad as a page full of excessively long ones. One short sentence after another makes writing sound simpleminded, like the uncombined kernel sentences in Chapter 11:

> There is a small cubical enclosure within the Great Mosque at Mecca. Here rests the Kaaba. It is also called the Black Stone. It is the most highly venerated object in the Muslim world. Moreover, it is the destination of devout believers' pilgrimages. It occupies an ancient location. It was there before Muhammad arrived. It was sacred to pagan sects. Infidels are strictly forbidden to approach it.

Even if you chose not to shoehorn all this material into one huge sentence, you could combine the first part into two and still add the short follow-up for contrast:

> Inside a small cubical enclosure within the Great Mosque at Mecca, rests the Kaaba, or Black Stone, the most highly venerated object in the Muslim world. The stone, which is the destination of devout believers' pilgrimages, occupies much the same location it had before the coming of Muhammad, when it was sacred to pagan sects of undetermined antiquity. Infidels are strictly forbidden to approach it.

The point is to combine long and short sentences to give readers the variety they need to stay interested and involved in what you're saying.

Remember, this advice applies to breath units—the words spoken together between pauses in a sentence—as well as to sentences themselves. In the final revision of the Great Mosque sentence above, the phrases "or Black Stone" and "The stone" are very short breath units that contrast with the longer units around them.

End Sentences with a Bang, Not a Whimper

The final few words of a sentence most often receive the greatest emphasis, so it pays to put ideas you most want to leave in readers' minds at the ends of sentences. Imagine trying to convince readers that your firm would be the best choice to underwrite a stock offering because of its history of underwriting successes. You'd want to use the principle of **end focus** to place your company's experience in the position of emphasis:

Not

We have more underwriting experience than any other *firm in the ARea.*

But

No other firm in the area can match our *underwriting exPERience.*

EXERCISE 6

Revise the following sentences as directed. How do your revisions change the writer's voice? You'll find a sample answer on the *Understanding Style* website.

1. As Nelson bent over her tiny hand, a cloud (a towering cumulonimbus, or thunderhead) suddenly obscured the sun. (Remove the digression and use end focus to emphasize *her tiny hand.*)

2. Social thinkers considered gin, made from fermented cereal grains and flavored with juniper berries, the scourge of the poor in eighteenth century London, where gin shops dispensed cheap drinks to a laboring populace so degraded by brutal living conditions that only the oblivion of drunken stupor could relieve them from what Doctor Samuel Johnson called "the pain of being human." (Remove the digression; break up the remainder to provide a short contrasting sentence.)

3. Three sects of Jews have called themselves Hasidim, starting with the conservative pre-Christian group whose resistance to outside forces in Israel culminated in the revolt of the Maccabees, then going on to a community of twelfth and thirteenth century mystics in Germany, and finally to the present movement, begun in Poland but now spread throughout the world, which emphasizes individual goodness over strict observance of rabbinical law. (Break into three or four sentences with some contrast in length.)

MAKEOVER

Use the writing tips from this chapter to revise the passage that follows. Change the grammar and sentence structure however you like, but try to retain all the important ideas. How do your revisions change the writer's voice?

Under the principles of *feng-shui*, or "wind and water," a system for choosing building sites that dates from the Han Dynasty (202 B.C.—A.D. 220), the Chinese—the world's most populous nation—developed what could be called a tradition of mystical surveying. This group, whose country is physically the third largest in the world, adapted themes from their three great religions—Taoism, Buddhism, and Confucianism—which included such things as the yin and yang of Taoism, the five directions and five elements of Buddhism, and the 64 hexagrams of the Confucian *I-Ching*, along with astrological lore, to determine the most auspicious locations for public buildings and private homes. Before building began, a consultant called a *feng-shui hsien sheng*, or "doctor of the vital force" was called in to assess the landscape and lay out the site by studying the shape of surrounding peaks and hills, the location of boulders, the direction of streams and prevailing winds, and other factors in order to pick a site that was aligned in various ways with the vital forces of the place, the seasons, the elements, and the stars. Sometimes the site would be altered on the basis of the *feng-shui hsien sheng*'s findings to obtain results that would not have been possible without human intervention. Trees would be planted, streams diverted, boulders moved, even hills reshaped in an effort to manipulate *feng-shui* values so that a building could be placed where the owner wanted it without incurring the risk of evil forces and bad luck. Some have become convinced that the well-known Chinese expertise in gardening can be traced to these early efforts to alter the *feng-shui* values of building sites.

BASED ON WITOLD RYBCZYNSKI
The Most Beautiful House in the World

Your Writing

Choose a page or two of your own writing to analyze in terms of this chapter's rules of thumb, listed below. Look for tendencies you might need to watch for and avoid, such as failure to mix long and short sentences or too many dependent clauses. Highlight and correct any problems you find. How do your changes affect the written voice?

◇◇◇

POINTS TO REMEMBER
1. Start most sentences with the subject.
2. Make your subjects definitely named actors.
3. Make your verbs name definite actions.
4. Write mostly in independent clauses.
5. Keep subjects and verbs close together.
6. Keep verbs and complements close together.
7. Use single verbs with multiple subjects. Use single subjects with multiple verbs.
8. Favor the active voice.
9. Choose positive rather than negative constructions.
10. Focus each sentence on the ideas expressed by the subject and predicate.
11. Mix long and short sentences.
12. End sentences with a bang, not a whimper.

◇◇◇

A Brief Dictionary of Usage

accept, except *Accept* is a verb meaning "to take." *Except* can be a verb meaning "to exclude," as in "He *excepted* his stamp collection from the bequest," but it is more often a preposition, as in "Everyone was invited *except* me."

access, excess *Access* always involves the idea of approaching or entering, as in "I have *access* to all the files." *Excess* is related to *excessive*: "A hurdler can't afford excess weight."

adapt, adopt *Adapting* something means changing it to fit your needs: "Glen helped *adapt* the play for television." But to *adopt* something means to take it up or take it over: "We *adopted* a little girl," "The school *adopted* my plan."

adverse See *averse*.

advise, advice *Advise* is a verb that means to give counsel to someone; *Advice* is a noun that means the recommendation itself: "She *advised* me to take your *advice*."

affect, effect Most often, *affect* is a verb: "This decision *affects* my future." *Effect* is most commonly a noun: "The *effect* of his decision was to limit my earnings." But this is a slippery pair. *Affect* can also be a noun, meaning a particular emotion, or a verb meaning to pretend: "She *affects* indifference to her father." On rare occasions *effect* can be a verb too. As a verb, *effect* always means "to cause": "The physician *effected* a complete remission."

all ready, already *All ready* is a pronoun and its adjective modifier: "We were *all ready* to begin." *Already* is an adverb of time: "The loaves had *already* risen."

all right, alright *All right* is the correct way to spell this combination no matter how you use it: "By then we were *all right*"; "*All right*, I'll do it your way."

all together, altogether *All together* means gathered in a group: "The boys were *all together* in a corner." *Altogether* is an adverb of degree, meaning *completely:* "Bayard has *altogether* too much confidence in himself."

allude, elude To *allude* to something is to make a quick reference to it: "The prosecuting attorney *alluded* to her violent temper." To *elude* is to evade: "We *eluded* your brother."

allusion, illusion, delusion An *allusion* is a reference to something: "*Allusions* to the Bible flew thick and fast." An *illusion* is a false appearance: "Lowering a car gives the *illusion* of greater length." And a *delusion* is a loss of contact with reality: "It was Jane's *delusion* that her sofa was watching her."

alot Not a word. Always spell this as two words: "a lot."

already See *all ready.*

alright See *all right.*

altar, alter *Altar* is a noun signifying a table or platform for sacrifice: "The bull was slaughtered before a low *altar*." *Alter* is a verb meaning "to change": "We *altered* our plans."

alternately, alternatively *Alternately* is an adverb of time meaning "by turns": "Add flour and water *alternately*." *Alternatively* is an adverb of manner meaning "by way of alternative": "She could shut up and pay, or, *alternatively*, she could go to the police."

altogether See *all together.*

among, between Both words are prepositions, but *among* is generally used with objects consisting of three or more things, while *between* is used with objects that consist of only two: "We wandered *among* the booths"; "Gail stood *between* Tony and his brother." However, *between* can apply to more numerous objects in sentences dealing with agreements: "A contract was drawn up *between* the three heirs."

amoral, immoral An *amoral* person, action, or thing is one to which the whole idea of morality is foreign or irrelevant: a tornado is *amoral* and so are the actions of the criminally insane. An *immoral* person or action is one that should measure up to moral standards but does not: arson is *immoral*.

amount, number *Amount* is a word used of a commodity that cannot be counted: "The *amount* of sediment in the bottom of the glass was alarming." *Number* applies to things that come in countable units: "The *number* of bison in Poland has recently increased."

and etc., A needless doubling. *Etc.* means "and other things"; therefore, *and etc.* can only mean "and and other things." Dump the *and.*

angry with, angry at *Angry with* goes with people: "I am *angry with* my parole officer." *Angry at* applies to situations: "I am *angry at* the way I've been treated."

annual, perennial *Annual* means once a year: "An annual checkup." *Perennial* means "throughout the year," and by extension, "throughout the years," as in "a perennial problem." A perennial plant lasts for years. An annual lasts just one year.

ante-, anti- *Ante-* is a prefix meaning "before," as in *antechamber,* or *antecedent. Anti-* means "against," as in *antibiotic,* or *antifreeze.*

anymore Should always be spelled as two words: "any more."

anyone, everyone, someone Spelled as they are here, each of these is a one-word indefinite pronoun: "*Everyone* needs *someone,* but not just *anyone.*" But each is also capable of being spelled as two words when the emphasis is on the *one*: "Every *one* of his friends attended"; "Some *one* answer must apply to them all." All these pronouns are singular forms and take singular referents. To include males and females, the referents should be *she or he, her or him,* or *his or her*: "Does everyone know *his or her* way? Other solutions include changing the person of the pronouns—" "Do *you* all know *your* way?"—or making the antecedent plural—"Do all the *hikers* know their *way*?"

anyway, any way, anyways As one word, *anyway* is an adverb: "Ted decided to come *anyway.*" As two words, it indicates a noun plus its modifier: "Is there *any way* to relieve the pressure?" *Anyways* is a non-standard form of *anyway.*

as Used between clauses, this word can lead to confusion. The conjunction *as* has a number of meanings, and the one intended may not always be clear: "*As* he washed the windows, I scrubbed the sink." (Does the *as* here mean *while* or *because?*) *As* causes further problems when used incorrectly in place of the conjunctions *whether* or *that*: "I don't know *as* she'll agree with you." It is usually better to pick a more precise conjunction.

As can also be a preposition. In this role it creates yet another sort of problem when used unnecessarily before objective complements: "We considered Disco Dancer *as* a sure thing." There should be no *as* in this kind of construction.

ascent, assent An *ascent* is a climb: "Gail slipped dangerously at the top of her *ascent*." *Assent* can be a noun or verb, but it always has to do with agreement: "She nodded in *assent*"; "She will *assent* to our proposal."

assure, ensure, insure To *assure* means to confirm something: "He *assured* me that the gun was unloaded." Most writers now limit *insure* to matters dealing with insurance policies: "My life is *insured* for fifteen thousand dollars." *Ensure* is left with the general meaning of "make sure": "The net below *ensured* his safety."

averse, adverse *Averse* means "disinclined." It often appears in the negative: "Mark is not averse to keg parties." *Adverse* means "unfavorable," as in "adverse conditions" or "conditions adverse to our plans."

avoid, evade, elude To *avoid* is to stay clear of something: "Thomas is avoiding his ex-wife." To *evade* is to escape through some clever dodge: "Tabitha evaded my question." To *elude* means to throw off through out and out trickery: "Reynard eluded the hounds by doubling back on his tracks."

awhile, a while *Awhile* is an adverb of time: "Sit with me *awhile*." *A while* is a noun plus an article; this is the form you want as the object of a preposition (for *a while* , after *a while*) or in such constructions as "*a while* back" or "*a while* ago."

beside, besides *Beside* means "next to": "Hank stood *beside* the steps." *Besides* means "in addition": "I don't like him; *besides*, he'd steal the keys out of your laptop."

between See *among.*

between you and I Common, but incorrect. Both pronouns are objects of the preposition *between*, so the phrase should be "between you and *me*."

biannual, biennial *Biannual* means twice a year. Something is *biennial* if it happens once every two years.

born, borne A thing is *born* when it comes into the world: "The lamb was *born* at midnight." Something is *borne* when it is carried: "This burden must be *borne*." But remember that a child that is *born* must first have been *borne* (carried) by its mother.

breath, breathe The first word is a noun, the second a verb: "Every time you take a *breath,* you *breathe*."

bust, busted, bursted Only the first of these is a word in standard usage, and it is a noun meaning a woman's chest or a statue of someone's head and shoulders. If you need a verb meaning "break" or "blew up," the word is *burst*.

can, may Strictly speaking, *can* means "is able to," and *may* means "is allowed to." It is acceptable to ask, "*Can* she run a mile?" But *may* is the right choice when permission is involved : "*May* I have the last chicken finger?"

capital, capitol The second of these means the seat of government, generally a statehouse or the Capitol Building in Washington: "They repaired the roof of the Capitol." *Capital* is the form for all other uses, from *capital* letters to *capital* gains.

censor, censure To *censor* something is to cut out offending parts or keep it from appearing: "Censorship would kill my act!" To *censure* is to condemn: "Superintendent Stout was censured for hiring her five cousins."

center around, center about Neither phrase makes sense. (Think about it.) *Center on* is the appropriate combination.

cite, site, sight The first of these is a verb meaning "to refer to": "The senator *cited* our tradition of free enterprise." The second word indicates a place: "The *site* was attractive and well drained." And the last has to do with vision: "You are a *sight* for sore eyes!" "She finally *sighted* the falcon."

clothes, cloths *Clothes* are what you wear, and what you wear is made of various *cloths*. *Cloths* can also refer to pieces of cloth: "We'll need some *cloths* for cleaning the oven."

co-equal, equal Both mean the same. Use *equal*.

complacent, complaisant, compliant *Complacent* people are self-satisfied. *Complaisant* people do what they can to please others, *Compliant* people do as they're told whether it pleases anyone or not.

complement, compliment A *complement* is something that makes a thing complete, as a *complement* of sailors makes up a ship's crew, a grammatical *complement* completes a verb, or a *complementary* angle when added to another makes up ninety degrees. A *compliment*, on the other hand, is an expression of praise or admiration, as is a *complimentary* remark.

comprise, comprised of See *consist of.*

consist of, comprise, comprised of, include A thing *consists* of all its parts: "The first movement of a classical sonata consists of an opening statement of contrasting themes, development of the themes, and a recapitulation." *Comprise* is a verb meaning "is entirely made up of": "A classical sonata comprises several parts." *Comprised of* means the same as *consists of. Includes* often refers to only some parts of a whole: the South *includes* Georgia and Mississippi, but it doesn't *consist of* or isn't *comprised of* Georgia and Mississippi.

continual, continuous Something is *continual* if it keeps coming back: "She was unnerved by the *continual* errors in her play." Something is *continuous* if it never goes away in the first place: "The air conditioner set up a *continuous* roar."

couldn't care less An informal way of saying someone was indifferent. If you use this expression, be sure to phrase it in the negative; expressions like "He could care less" say precisely the opposite of what they are meant to.

could of, may of, might of, should of, would of, and so on All these are misspellings for *could have, may have, might have*, and so on.

council, counsel A *council* is some form of executive or advisory committee: "Gretel appealed to the ruling *council*." *Counsel* is either advice or (in court) the lawyer who gives it: "I ignored their *counsel*"; "Who is *counsel* for the defense?"

credible, creditable A *credible* story deserves belief; something is *creditable* when it deserves praise: "Her account of the UFO seems credible"; "They made a creditable attempt to recycle aluminum cans."

criteria, data, media, phenomena These are all plural forms and demand plural verbs: "Your criteria are remarkably low"; "The media are on a witch hunt." The singular forms *criterion, datum, medium,* and *phenomenon* are familiar enough except *datum*, which is rarely seen. *Media* is often used in the sense of mass media—that is, newspapers, magazines, television, radio. Just remember that each of these by itself, radio, for example, is a *medium*, and singular. They're only *media*, in the plural, when taken together. *Mediums* is an acceptable form as well, but it refers to clothing sizes or spiritualists.

data See *criteria*.

delusion See *allusion*.

descent, dissent A *descent* is a coming down in one sense or another: "The *descent* was more hazardous than the climb up"; "She was proud of her aristocratic *descent*." *Dissent* means disagreement: "Progress shall not bow to the forces of *dissent*!"

device, devise *Devise* is the verb form; it means "to invent." *Device* is a noun: "A *device* is something someone has *devised*."

differ from, differ with To *differ from* means "to be different from": "Apples *differ from* oranges." To *differ with* is to disagree: "Pete always *differs with* his father."

discreet, discrete *Discreet* people behave tactfully and keep secrets: "My landlady is most *discreet*." *Discrete* means "separate": "Philosophy and religion are *discrete* disciplines."

disinterested, uninterested *Disinterested* means impartial: "Her decision was wholly *disinterested.*" *Uninterested* means "indifferent": "I am completely *uninterested* in your cell phone plans."

dissent See *descent.*

distinct, distinctive Something is *distinct* when you can't miss it: "His testimony produced a distinct impression of guilt." *Distinctive* means "characteristic": "Her distinctive walk gave her away."

dominating, domineering A *dominating* person or thing is clearly superior: "Shaq was a dominating center." *Domineering* always carries the **connotation** of "bossy" or "bullying": "I hate my domineering sister, Portia."

effect See *affect.*

elder, older *Elder* applies only to people: "elder brother." *Older* can apply to anything capable of ageing: "the older explanation."

elementary, elemental *Elementary* means basic: "Elementary, my dear Watson!" *Elemental* means "stripped to a raw essence": "the elemental thunder of kettledrums."

elude See *allude* and *avoid.*

emotional, emotive To be *emotional* is to be driven by emotion: "an emotional farewell." *Emotive* means "appealing to the emotions": "an emotive issue."

ensure See *assure.*

etc., short for *et cetera,* "and others." Do not overuse. Two other points to keep in mind are that *etc.* already has a built-in *and* (see *and etc.*) and that the "others" the word indicated must be clear to the reader, Use *etc.* only to avoid listing the obvious, not when you yourself cannot think of anything to add.

evade See *avoid.*

everyday, every day *Everyday* is an adjective meaning "commonplace": "I wore my *everyday* clothes." *Every day* is a noun plus its modifier. This second form is the one you want after a verb: "She practices with her rifle *every day.*"

everyone, every one See *anyone.*

except See *accept.*

excess See *access.*

facet, factor, feature, function These words tend to be overused and misused. A *facet* is one of many plane surfaces, as in a cut diamond. A *factor* is a contributing cause. A *feature* is an especially conspicuous portion of something. And a *function* is a characteristic activity. These meanings are precise and limited, so none of these words should be used when you mean something as vague as "part."

factor See *facet.*

farther, further Use *farther* when real physical space is involved: "Portland is *farther* than Seattle." Use *further* for other kinds of distance: "Nothing could be *further* from her mind."

feature See *facet.*

feel badly Almost always wrong. If you're unhappy or regretful, you feel *bad.* You'd feel *badly* (perform the act of feeling in a deficient way) only if your fingers were numb.

fewer, less *Fewer* is for things that can be counted: "Pickles have *fewer* calories than pancakes." *Less* applies to quantities that must be measured some other way: "Lawn mowers use *less* fuel than jetliners."

firstly *First* is always a better choice than *firstly,* as *second* is better than *secondly,* *third* better than *thirdly,* and so on.

flare, flair *Flare* carries the sense of fire: "Put out some *flares*"; "*flare* up." *Flair* means "talent": "She has a *flair* for blackjack."

flaunt, flout To *flaunt* means to "make a show of": "Sylvester *flaunts* his sexuality." To *flout* is to "scoff at": "Each Saturday they *flout* the noise ordinance."

former, latter The *former* is the first of two things you have previously mentioned; the *latter* is the second. When more than two things are involved, use "the first" and "the last."

forth, fourth The first of these indicates a direction ("Go *forth*!"), while the second is an ordinal number or a fraction: "This is my *fourth* cup"; "She inherits a *fourth* of the estate."

fortunate, fortuitous *Fortunate* means "lucky": "Wanda envied the *fortunate* heir." Something is *fortuitous* when it occurs by chance: "Our *fortuitous* meeting may prove unfortunate."

fulsome *Fulsome* means "sickening." *Fulsome* praise is so overdone it makes you want to throw up.

function See *facet.*

further See *farther.*

healthful, healthy *Healthful* things make you *healthy*: "Carrots are loaded with *healthful* vitamins"; "*Healthy* lambs can survive a frost."

idea, ideal An *idea* is a notion or concept, any notion or concept. As a noun, an *ideal* is a notion as well, but always a notion of perfection: "I have an *idea* she's his *ideal.*" *Ideal* can be an adjective too, in which case it means "perfect": "Becky has landed the *ideal* job."

illusion See *allusion.*

immoral See *amoral.*

imply, infer To *imply* is to hint: "Manning *implied* something odd was going on at the mayor's office." To *infer* is to guess or conclude, usually on the basis of a previous implication: "We may *infer* that the ship was already sinking, since the lifeboats had been lowered before she was sighted."

include See *consist of*.

incredible, incredulous *Incredible* means "unbelievable": "Ricardo has *incredible* balance." *Incredulous* means "unbelieving": "She answered my story with an *incredulous* look."

infer See *imply*.

ingenious, ingenuous *Ingenious* means "inventive" or "clever"; it is usually the word you want: "The float valve was an *ingenious* device." *Ingenuous* means "innocent": "The boy convinced everyone by his *ingenuous* expression."

in regards to Should be *in regard to* or, better, *regarding*.

insure See *assure*.

irregardless Nonstandard form of *regardless*.

is because Often misused in explanations. A construction such as "The reason *is because* it is durable" should be rephrased to say "The reason *is that* it is durable" or "The reason is its durability."

is when, is where Misused in definitions such as "A strike *is when* all the pins are knocked down" or " A cafeteria *is where* people eat." Try to be precise in definitions: "A strike is scored by knocking over all the pins with one's first roll in a frame of bowling"; "A cafeteria is an eating place in which customers serve themselves, usually from a line of steam tables."

its, it's The *its* without the apostrophe is the possessive form of *it*: "My canary has been neglecting *its* water." *It's* is the contraction for "it is" or "it has." "*It's* well known that *it's* been getting colder each year."

lay, lie To *lay* something is to put it somewhere. You can *lay* bricks or silverware or books on the table. To *lie* (when it doesn't mean *deceive*) means to recline. You *lie* in the sun. The past tense and past participle of *lay* is *laid*: "Rita *laid* her hand on my arm." "Henrietta has *laid* a clutch of eggs." The past tense and past participle of *lie* are *lay* and *lain*. "Yesterday Juan *lay* in bed until noon." "The pliers have *lain* there since Easter."

less See *fewer*.

lie See *lay*.

like This word produces many problems. Do not use *like* as a filler-word in writing, the way people sometimes do in speech: "He was *like* fifteen years old." (Drop the *like*.) Remember, too, that when it is not a verb *like* is a preposition, not a conjunction. Its proper role is to introduce nouns: "I collect all sorts of things, *like* old license plates." It should not be used in place of *as, as if,* or *that* to introduce clauses: "You look *as if* (not *like*) you could use some Gatorade"; "She feels *that* (not *like*) the season will be a success."

loose, lose Ninety-eight percent of the time *loose* is an adjective meaning the opposite of *tight. Lose* is a verb meaning to misplace or suffer the loss of something: "These pants are so *loose,* I'm afraid I'll *lose* them."

maybe, may be The single word *maybe* means perhaps: "*Maybe* she didn't hear you." As two words, *may be* is always a verb: "He *may be* lying."

may of See *could of.*

media See *criteria.*

might of See *could of.*

must of See *could of.*

myself Use only as an intensive/reflexive pronoun to add emphasis or to show that the actor of a clause also receives the action: "I *myself* prefer chocolate"; "I blame only *myself.*" *Myself* is unacceptable as a grammatically timid substitute for *I* or *me.* Do not write "Donna and *myself* are looking forward to seeing you" or "This has been a great day for Rex and *myself.*" The word is part of the subject of the first sentence; the phrase should be "Donna and *I.*" In the second sentence, the object of the proposition *for* should be "Rex and *me.*"

number See *amount.*

off of, off from These phrases can always be reduced to the more standard *off:* "Roger, get *off* (not *off of* or *off from*) the trampoline."

O.K., ok, okay These spellings are all acceptable. Choose one and stick with it.

older See *elder.*

passed, past *Passed,* with the -ed, is a verb form, the past tense of *pass:* "Hooray! I *passed* calculus!" "Later we *passed* through Little Rock." *Past* is a noun or an adjective having to do with former times: "The *past* is the key to the future"; "He should not be judged for his *past* mistakes."

perennial See *annual.*

personal, personnel The word with one *n, personal,* means "private" or "individual": "She took off three days for *personal* business." With two *n's, personnel* means "employees." But it can sound pompous to talk about "personnel" when you mean employees in a general sense, The word works best when you are talking about people in the military.

phenomena See *criteria.*

plain, plane *Plain* is an adjective meaning "ordinary" or a noun meaning a flat stretch of land, like the Great *Plains*. A *plane* can be a tool for smoothing wood, an air*plane*, or a mathematically level surface, as in *plane* geometry. Moral *planes*, rising to a new *plane*, etc. are metaphors based on the geometrical concept.

plus *Plus* is usually a preposition, not a conjunction: it can be used before nouns but not before clauses. Avoid expressions such as "I don't feel well, *plus* I am tired." Replace the *plus* with *and* or *besides:* "I don't feel well; *besides*, I am tired."

preplan, advance planning No different from *plan* and *planning*. Prefer the shorter forms.

principal, principle The second of these, *principle*, is a noun meaning "a basic truth or doctrine": "Martin is devoted to the *principle* of fair play." This is the form that ends in *-le*, like *rule*, a word of similar meaning. All the other uses of the word—including such meanings as "leader," "sum of money," or "foremost"—require the spelling *principal*: "Ed was sent to the *principal's* office"; "Add the interest to the *principal*"; "Greed is his *principal* motive."

raise, rise These words are rather like *lie* and *lay*. *Rise* is something a subject does by itself: bread, the sun, sleepers, and hot air *rise*. *Raise* is something a subject does to something else: you *raise* crops, children, the flag, or Cain.

real, really *Real* is an adjective meaning "genuine": "This is *real* gold." *Really* is an intensifier (an adverb that modifies other modifiers): "Cara is *really* frightened." Be on guard against using *real* where *really* is required: "The night was *really* (not *real*) dark."

reason why The *why* is rarely necessary: "Haste was the *reason* (not the *reason why*) he made those errors."

respectfully, respectively Both words are adverbs, but *respectfully* means "with respect," and *respectively* means "each in its own way." "I must *respectfully* disagree"; "Beans fill the stomach and hyacinths the soul, *respectively*."

restless, restive A *restless* person can't settle down, often for no particular reason. A *restive* person is peevish about something definite: "The children grew *restive* when asked to take their naps."

sensual, sensuous *Sensual* is usually disapproving. It means "given over to the senses": "She looked the other way to avoid his *sensual* leer." *Sensuous* simply means "appealing to the senses," with no value judgment involved: "The *sensuous* glide of water over mossy stone set up a low murmur."

sentiment, sentimentality A *sentiment* is a feeling or opinion rooted in any emotion: "The crowd was buoyed by courageous *sentiments*, *sentiments* of justice." *Sentimentality* is a feeling rooted in sloppy emotions: "The greeting card oozed *sentimentality*."

set, sit Another confusing pair of verbs. *Set* usually takes an object and means "put," as in "He *set* the toaster on the counter." But *set* can also appear without an object in various constructions: "It took all day for the concrete to *set*"; "That hen will not *set*"; "The sun will *set* at 6:45." *Sit* is simpler: it always means "assume a sitting position" and rarely takes an object: "I like to *sit* in the sun."

shall, will, should, would There is a fading tradition that *shall* and *should* (its past tense) ordinarily go with first person subjects (*I* or *we*), while *will* and *would* are the forms to use with all others: "I *shall* be delighted," but "They *will* be delighted." If you wish to be forceful, however, you may reverse this relationship: "I *will* prevail!" "You *shall* listen to me!" These rules are commonly disregarded except in questions, Most writers still prefer "*Shall* we (or *I*) answer this letter?" to "*Will* we answer this letter?"

should of See *could of.*

sight See *cite.*

sit See *set.*

site See *cite.*

so One problem with this word concerns its use as a conjunction. Used to connect clauses, *so* should mean "therefore": "I am faster than she is, *so* I got home first." But when there is a sense of intention (that is, when a subject does something in one clause in order to make possible the action expressed in another), the two-word subordinating conjunction *so that* is more precise: "She mowed the lawn *so that* her brother would be free to practice for his recital."

So can also cause trouble when used as an intensifier to modify other modifiers: "Barbara is *so* polite." The *so* in a sentence like this one demands a *that* clause to complete the thought: "Barbara is *so* polite *that* she makes my hair curl." Another solution is to replace the *so* with *very* or *overly*, intensifiers that do not demand a *that* clause.

societal No different from *social.* Prefer the shorter form.

someone, some one See *anyone.*

sometime, some time As one word, *sometime* is an adverb: "She wanted to visit him *sometime*." As two words, it is a noun plus its modifier: "She demanded *some time* to herself."

such Used before an adjective, *such* works the way *so* does as an intensifier. It demands a *that* clause to complete the thought it starts: not "They are *such* good friends," but "They are *such* good friends *that* they even dress alike."

temerity, timidity A set of opposites. *Temerity* is foolhardy boldness: "She had the *temerity* to make fun of his vest." *Timidity* means fearful caution: "Her Pekingese was untroubled by *timidity*."

than, then *Than* is used in comparisons: "Your toes are longer *than* mine." *Then* is the word you want when you mean "next" or "afterwards": "He cleared his throat; *then* he blew his nose."

that, which, who *Who* refers to people, *which* refers to things that are not people, and *that* can refer to anything at all. It is as bad to talk about "the girl *which* you saw" as it is to say "the building *whom* I entered." Some writers distinguish between *that* and *which*, using *that* for **restrictive** clauses and *which* for **nonrestrictive** ones: "Hair *that* is naturally curly can never be completely straightened" (restrictive); "Helium balloons, *which* are lighter than air, can lift considerable weights" (nonrestrictive).

then See *than*.

there, their, they're *There* works either as an expletive or to indicate a place: "*There* are no carrots in my stew"; "You should dig over *there*." *Their* is the possessive form of *they*: "They found a bomb in *their* car." And *they're* is a contraction of "they are": "I think *they're* on the wrong track."

thusly Not a word. Use *thus*.

to, too, two *To* is either a preposition meaning "toward" or the sign of an infinitive: "Wendy went *to* the dog show"; "I want *to* live." *Too* is an adverb that can be used as an intensifier or in the sense of "also": "She was *too* weary to care"; "We, *too*, have a say in the matter." And *two* is always a number: "I'll have *two* orders of fries."

uninterested See *disinterested*.

used to Be sure you spell this out completely: "Joy *used to* (not *use to*) work on transmissions."

utilize *Use* is shorter and better.

venial, venal A *venial* sin is not very serious (as opposed to a mortal sin). *Venal* means open to bribes: "Bustable would make a *venal* chief of police."

wander, wonder To *wander* is to roam with no clear destination. *Wonder* can be a noun for something marvelous or a verb meaning "to think about": "I *wonder* who's kissing her now."

which See *that.*

who See *that.*

who, whom *Who* is the form to use for subjects: "*Who* is coming?" "*Who* cares?" *Whom* is for objects: "*Whom* did he call?" "I wondered *whom* she means." "To *whom* was this addressed?"

Both words frequently introduce dependent clauses, appearing as the first word regardless of their function in the clause. To pick the right form, consider what the word is doing in the clause it introduces. The easy way is to examine the clause for a subject. If no other subject is available, *who* is the form you want: "The dean asked *who was interested.*" If there is another word in the subject slot (naming the person or thing performing the action of the verb) you're dealing with an object, and *whom* is the right choice: "The dean asked *whom he could send.*" "The dean asked *from whom we had gotten his number.*"

whose, who's *Whose* is a possessive pronoun: "*Whose* truck were you driving?" *Who's* is a contraction for "who is" or "who has": "*Who's* qualified so far?" Even though it's a form of *who*, *whose* can refer to nonhuman or inanimate antecedents: "the building *whose* door was ajar." We have no other possessive pronoun for that sort of construction.

will See *shall.*

would See *shall.*

would of See *could of.*

your, you're *Your* is a possessive pronoun: "I don't know how *your* notes got in my locker." *You're* is a contraction for "you are": "Dennis still thinks *you're* interested in him."

Alphabetical Guide to Punctuation

While sharp-eyed readers will find exceptions to many of the "rules" listed here, taken together they add up to a system of punctuation in general American use. No one who follows these guidelines should be accused of bad punctuation.

Apostrophes (')

1. Use an apostrophe plus *s* (*'s*) to indicate ownership or grammatical possession with indefinite pronouns and most nouns:

   the *rat's* tail   the *statue's* patina
   a *day's* work   *Japan's* industry
   someone's buckle   the *heat's* effects

2. Use an apostrophe by itself to form the possessive of plural nouns ending in *s* sounds:

   trees'   Navahos'
   boys'   necessities'
   tableaux'   computers'

3. Use either *'s* or an apostrophe by itself to form the possessive of singular nouns ending in *s* sounds, depending on how many *s*'s you hear when you pronounce the word:

   nucleus's   Moses'
   class's   oasis'
   Jones's   Dickens'

4. Use an apostrophe to mark the omission of letters or numbers from contractions:

don't	o'clock
can't	'76
we've	she'll

5. Use an apostrophe to form plurals of letters, numbers, and words used for their own sake.

misshapen *B*'s	crazy *8*'s
too many *whereas*'s	demure *ahem*'s
if's, *and*'s, and *but*'s	count by *10*'s

Brackets ([])

1. Use brackets to enclose your own additions or comments within a quotation:

   "We wasn't [sic] frightened."
   "It [the Army of the Potomac] is only McClelland's bodyguard."
   "Hast thou clothed [the horse's] neck with thunder?"

2. Use brackets to mark a parenthesis within parentheses:

   I doubled down (thinking that was the right move [It wasn't!]).

Capital Letters

1. Capitalize the first word in a sentence.

2. Capitalize the first word in quoted complete sentences:

   Malory's account is unforgettable: "Whoso pulleth out this sword of this stone and anvil is rightwise King born of all England."

3. Capitalize the pronoun *I* and the interjection *O*.

4. Capitalize proper nouns:

Robby Alford	Delaware	*Apollo 13*
Methodism	Monday	Easter
the Potato Famine	Bell Telephone	Psychology 100

5. Capitalize proper adjectives:

Jeffersonian	Pleistocene	Anglican
Socratic	French	Roman
Latin	Elizabethan	Virginian

6. Capitalize genus names, but not species names, in scientific nomenclature:

Canis lupus   *Quercus alba*   *Salmo gardineri*

7. *Do not* capitalize names of seasons, colors used to refer to races, or the names of academic areas that are not proper adjectives (like French or Japanese) or part of the title of a particular course.

black pride   astronomy   autumn

8. Capitalize the first and last and all other words in titles except the determiners *a, an,* and *the;* the conjunctions *and, but, or, nor, for* or *yet*; and prepositions that contain fewer than five letters:

Catcher in the Rye   *The Songs of Christmas*
"A Dialog Between the Soul and Body" *Stereo Review*
Washington Crossing the Delaware   "The Track of My Tears"

9. Capitalize titles and forms of address that come before a person's name:

Doctor Shirley Ores	Judge Landon
Cousin Kenneth	Reverend Mills
Professor Goldfarb	Dean Smithers

10. Capitalize direction names only when they indicate an area you could point to on the map:

The Southwest has developed a culture all its own.
But
Marvella struck out to the southwest along the ridge.

Colons (:)[i]

1. Use a colon to set off a long appositive at the end of a clause, especially when the appositive involves a list:

Vote for Prokbroom: a man of vision, tenacity, and integrity.

---

[i] When typing, leave only one space between a colon and the word that follows it.

Butch was a big pointer: a long-striding animal with the stamina to hunt all day.
There are several important steps in serving: 1) get the proper grip; 2) make a high, consistent ball toss; and 3) follow through.

2. Use a colon to separate independent clauses when the second clause explains the first:

Dot Shadburn was irritated: her husband refused to vote Democratic.
I noted a curious optical illusion: the truck appeared to be floating on air.

3. Use a colon to introduce block quotations, but only when the quoted material is grammatically independent.

Charles Handy describes the dependency of the rich:

Paradoxically, rich societies seem to breed dependency. If you are poor, you are forced into self-sufficiency. As you get rich, it is easier and more sensible to get other people to do what you do not want to do or cannot do, be it fixing the roof or digging the garden.

The Age of Unreason

But

Charles Handy maintains that large accumulations of wealth

seem to breed dependency. If you are poor, you are forced into self-sufficiency. As you get rich, it is easier and more sensible to get other people to do what you do not want to do or cannot do, be it fixing the roof or digging the garden.

The Age of Unreason

4. Use a colon for salutations in formal letters, Bible references, times of the day, publication data in bibliographical references, and between titles and subtitles:

To Whom It May Concern:	1 Chronicles 15:25–27
5:07 P.M.	Boston: Allyn and Bacon
John Donne: Life, Mind, and Art	Ezekiel 17:23 (New English Bible)

Commas (,)

1. Use a comma with a **coordinating conjunction** to separate **independent clauses**:

   The *Odyssey* seems to be based on the real geography of the Mediterranean, *and* scholars enjoy debating which islands and coasts Odysseus visited.

   Peace is a yellow blend, First Prize is pink, *and* Mr. Lincoln is dark red.

2. Use a comma to set off long introductory clauses or phrases:

   Across the top of the table by the front door, a selection of magazines fanned out like a card hand.

   Although the clone is genetically identical to its adult "mother," their experiences of life will never be the same.

3. Use commas to set off transitional phrases that modify a whole clause:

   Second, we rely on your professional discretion.

   I did very well on my evaluations, incidentally.

   Our objections, in other words, remain unanswered.

4. Use a comma to set off introductory modifiers based on **verbals**:

   To love, one must first understand.

   Satisfied, he leaned back against the rough wall.

   Sighing with boredom, Max fiddled with his buttons.

5. Use a comma after an introductory element that would otherwise be momentarily confusing:

   Beneath the tree, frogs croaked despondently.

   Besides, John was the only contestant from Ohio.

   When the dog smells, air freshener covers the odor.

6. Use commas to separate three or more words, phrases, or clauses in a series:

> She is tall, willowy, attractive, and unscrupulous.

> Ed boxed the gift, wrapped it, and left it on Mike's desk.

> Custom can make the unknown familiar, the exception the rule, and innovation the hallmark of a new status quo.

7. Use commas to set off **nonrestrictive** and other parenthetical elements.

> Chicago, which was settled about the same time, monopolized shipping.

> Hardwoods, for example walnut, are much more expensive.

> Father Murphy, after all his study of canon law, should have an answer.

8. Use commas to set off most **appositives:**

> I'll ask Father Murphy, a well-known expert on canon law.

> My favorite activity, snorkeling, affords only moderate exercise.

> Efficient predators, grizzlies, help keep elk populations down.

9. Use commas to set off words in direct address:

> Yes, Virginia, there is a Santa Claus.

> My deluded darling, I fear you're mistaken.

> Attention, troop, this is not the Cub Scout way!

10. Use commas in dates, addresses, and geographical names:

> They were married on June 2, 1993, in Saginaw, Michigan.

> Steve lives as 325 Center, Orlando, Florida, The United States, North America, Western Hemisphere, Earth, Our Solar System, Milky Way Galaxy, The Universe.

We moved from West Grove, Pennsylvania, to Beaverton, Oregon.

11. Use a comma between coordinate adjectives (these modify the same noun directly and can switch positions with each other or be separated by *and*):

her nervous, frightened son   a plump, tender turkey

But

his final spring vacation   my new wool skirt

12. Use commas to set off quotations associated with "credit tags":

"S[hadwell]," wrote Dryden, "never deviates into sense."

Thomas said, "This plant can only be *Trifolium dubium*."

But

Dryden charged that Shadwell "never deviates into sense."

Thomas identified the plant as "*Trifolium dubium*."

13. Use commas to set off the salutation of informal letters and follow the complimentary close of any letter:

Dear Gillian,   Truly yours,

Dashes (—)[ii]

1. Use a dash to set off a surprising appositive or summary at the end of a clause:

He did not invent much—just the aerosol can.

She has one wholly dedicated enemy—her father.

But

There was my oldest friend, Howard Zermatt.

It was a delicious apple, crisp and tart.

[ii] Type as two hyphens between consecutive words. No spaces.

2. Use dashes to set off abrupt interruptions or changes of thought:

> Owls—their hearing as overdeveloped as their enormous, light-gathering eyes—are superb night hunters.

> The Big Mac—billions sold—is an enduring marketing triumph.

Ellipses (...)*iii*

1. Use ellipses to show you have omitted words from a quotation:

> According to Smythe, "Nineteenth century economics were...more influential than scientific developments like the theory of evolution."

2. If your ellipsis bridges two or more sentences, mark it with four periods, the first unspaced, like a regular period at the end of a sentence, and the others spaced:

Material to be quoted:

> Collins was always attached to his older sister, the beloved "Sis" of his autobiography. He felt he owed her everything and constantly referred to her generosity.

Quotation:

> According to the reviewer, "Collins was always attached to his older sister....and constantly referred to her generosity."

3. Use ellipses to show hesitation or an unfinished thought:

> Well...uh...if you're sure...it *would* be a great help if you looked after Diablo for me.

> "Don't count on it," she said. "You know 'There's many a slip...'"

Exclamation Points (!)

1. Use an exclamation point to mark an emphatic sentence or expression:

> I've been chosen queen of the Kohlrabi Festival!

---

iii Type as three spaced periods with a space before the first and after the last. That's five spaces in all.

Ouch!

Down with tyrants!

2. Use an exclamation point (informally) to indicate surprise:

They hooked twelve tarpon (!) but landed none.

Hyphens (-)

1. Use a hyphen to mark a word divided between two lines of text.

2. Use in hyphenated compounds (when in doubt consult the dictionary):

mother-in-law   acid-washed
all-nighter   voice-over

3. Use hyphens to join combination modifiers before a noun:

fast-approaching   well-schooled
aggressive-sounding   top-of-the-line

Major exception: when the first word ends in -*ly* don't hyphenate.

explicitly political   apparently unconcerned

4. Use hyphens as needed to head off confusion:

small-appliance salesman   small appliance-salesman
fast-opening number   fast opening-number

5. Use hyphens in writing out numbers from twenty-one to ninety-nine and to separate numerators from denominators in spelled-out fractions:

thirty-seven   five-eighths
eighty-ninth   four-fifths

Italics (*italics*)

1. Italicize titles of books, magazines, newspapers, works of art, plays, musicals, televisions shows, record albums, and other major works issued separately.

Moby Dick   *The Thinker*   *Saving Grace*

Road & Track	*Damn Yankees!*	*The Mikado*
The Last Supper	*King Kong*	*Abbey Road*

2. Italicize names of ships, planes, trains, and spacecraft:

The Spirit of St. Louis	*Mariner I*
H.M.S. Bounty	the *Santa Fe Chief*

3. Italicize letters, numbers, and words used for their own sakes:

   He had not crossed a single *t* in the whole essay.

   Is that an *XVIII* or a *XVII?*

   Taradiddle is a good term for such foolishness.

4. Italicize foreign words and phrases (consult the dictionary about what counts as foreign):

coup de grâce	*miles gloriosus*	*Übermensch*

5. Italicize scientific names for plants and animals.

Micrurus fulvius, the coral snake	*Juglans nigra*, the black walnut
Myrmecophaga jubata, the ant bear	*Vultur gryphus*, the condor

6. Italicize words that carry special stress (use sparingly):

   That model had not four or six but *five* cylinders.

   She had it in her head that I was *Russian*.

Parentheses ()

1. Use parentheses to set off interruptions or changes of thought less abrupt than those indicated by dashes but more marked than those requiring only commas:

   When I got home (utterly exhausted by work) I still had to cook dinner.

   Nestor said he was sorry (though no one believed him).

Periods (.)

1. Use a period to mark the end of a sentence or an intentional fragment.

   Remember to get margarine at the store.

   Divaney has been with us for fifteen years.

   Gray sky and water. Cold gray wind.

2. Use periods with most abbreviations:

Sue Jones, D.V.M.	B.C.	cont.
Jr.	Ph.D.	Ind.
etc.	Feb.	Blvd.

Question Marks (?)

1. Use a question mark at the end of a direct question:

   Who was that masked man?

   Did the bishop lead the singing?

2. Use a question mark to transform a statement into a question:

   She chained herself to his Porsche?

   There's fresh water under the South Pole?

3. Use a question mark with interpolated or quoted questions:

   Jefferson—wasn't it Jefferson?—planned the Lewis and Clark Expedition.

   He asked, "Aren't there antelopes in South America?"

4. Use a question mark to indicate uncertainty:

   Genghis Kahn (1167?-1227) raided Eastern Europe.

I believe Dr. Mohr said it was a matter of valence (?) electrons.

Quotation Marks (" ")

1. Use double quotation marks to enclose word-for-word quotations from any written or spoken source:

    He said he had given up coffee "for medical reasons."

    "My dedication to the team," she said, "is second to none."

    The task Milton set himself was to "justify the ways of God to men."

2. Use double quotation marks to enclose titles of poems, songs, short stories, chapters, or articles in books, magazines, newspapers, or other longer works.

    Kilmer's "Trees" remains popular in spite of critics' disdain.

    "Yesterday" is my favorite Beatles song.

    Chapter 11, "Glimpses of the Future," concludes the work.

    Martin contributed an article called "New Hope for the Blind."

3. Use double quotation marks to enclose specialized jargon, words of dubious propriety, or words or phrases used ironically:

    Many "liberal" people prefer animal rights to human rights.

    She "flamed" me for not reading the "FAQ" file.

    He referred to his hair piece as a "rug."

4. Use double quotation marks with the second term in formal definitions or translations:

    The word *turgid* means "in a state of distention."

    Dis aliter visum, says Vergil: "The gods thought otherwise."

Single Quotation Marks (' ')

1. Use single quotation marks for quoted material within another quotation:

He stuck to his story: "The doctor told me, 'Drink as much as you like.'"

"The word *turgid*," she said, "means 'in a state of distention.'"

Punctuation to Introduce Quotations

1. Use commas with credit tags that introduce quotations:

Trevonna said, "I don't know what you're talking about."

Wilde lamented, "I can resist everything except temptation."

2. Use a colon (:) to introduce long or formal quotations or ones preceded by independent clauses:

Generalizing, perhaps falsely, from his own experience, Wordsworth proclaims: "Nature never did betray the heart that loved her."

Samuel Johnson saw the dangers of brevity: "In all pointed sentences, some degree of accuracy must be sacrificed to conciseness."

3. In capitalizing the first word of your quotations, be guided by your original:

She said, "You keep changing the subject!"

But

She accused me of "changing the subject."

As Edward Young said: "By night an atheist half believes a God."

But

Edward Young maintained that "by night" even atheists have some faith in God.

Punctuation at the End of Quotations

1. Place commas and periods inside final quotation marks:

   Renney approved of what she called "the God scene."

   "Only a few more minutes," she said.

2. Place colons and semicolons outside final quotation marks:

   She vowed she would "never drive again": her brakes had failed halfway down Corkscrew Mountain.

   Leonard may not have meant it when he said, "You can kick me if you want"; however, I took him at his word.

3. Place question marks, exclamation points, and dashes inside quotation marks when they punctuate the quotation, outside when they do not:

   He asked, "Why do you keep following me around?"

   Did he say, "Stop following me around"?

   Grandpa was beside himself: "Enough of this tomfoolery!"

   Don't say "cool," when all you mean is "I think I understand"!

   "The theme of the novel is the same throughout—" the speaker insisted, "freedom."

   Bill is devoted to his "old lady"—meaning my cousin Jennifer.

4. Quotations containing exclamation points or question marks keep them no matter where the quotation appears:

   Lucy shouted, "Look out!" and ran for cover

Of course, "Who do you think you are?" seldom leads to a constructive answer.

5. Quotations that would ordinarily end in periods lose their end punctuation when they appear at the beginning or in the middle of another sentence:

"It has begun to rain harder," he announced.

Every few minutes Joan complained, "I can't make up my mind," and went back to biting her nails.

Semicolons (;)

1. Use a semicolon between two independent clauses not linked by **coordinating conjunctions**:

His wife is fascinated by violent movies; he is horrified by them.

Wine was the drink of the upper classes; beer and ale were good enough for the workers.

2. Use a semicolon between two independent clauses linked only by **conjunctive adverbs**:

I thought I had won; consequently, I was surprised to hear Nina's name announced.

Ollie will be back next fall; then we'll have some major parties again.

3. Use semicolons to separate three or more items in a **coordinate series** when the items contain internal punctuation:

When he got to the store, he found the shelves were bare, having been stripped by bargain hunters; the clerk, in a nervous panic, had no idea what to do; and the manager was nowhere to be seen.

Waiting for me were Kenny; Don; Mike, the office boy; and Maureen.

GLOSSARY

Abstract: Language that appeals more to the mind than to the senses. *Color* is abstract, a category name that covers every specific color there is. *Mustard Yellow* is **concrete**; close your eyes and you can see it. Abstract language includes **nouns** (*courage, worthlessness*), **verbs** (*engage, consider*), **adverbs** (*rationally, efficiently*), and **adjectives** (*direct, undependable*).

Abstraction: An abstract noun like *honesty, megalomania,* or *abundance.*

Actor-action relationship: The pivotal relationship between the **subjects** of **sentences** and **clauses** and their **verbs.** Good writers make most of their subjects name specific people or things, not vague **abstractions,** and make most of their verbs express definite actions, with special attention to replacing **weak verbs** with strong ones. It's also good to keep subjects and verbs close together so the actor-action relationship is not obscured by intervening words and phrases.

Adjectival: A word or word group used to modify **nouns** and other **nominals**:

Her *ballpoint* pen was leaking. (noun as an adjectival)

I want the one *in the display case.* (adjectival phrase)

The man *we saw* was much fatter. (adjectival clause)

Adjective: A word whose function is to modify **nouns** or other **nominals.** Aside from descriptive adjectives naming qualities (*solid, fast, puny*), adjectives include subtypes such as determiners, possessives, and proper, demonstrative, and interrogative adjectives.

What Italian composer dedicated *his final* opera to *a* woman of *that* name?

Most descriptive adjectives are capable of comparison, undergoing form changes that show differences in degree: *good, better, best; strong, stronger, strongest; intelligent, less intelligent, least intelligent.*

Adverb: A word whose function is to modify a **verb,** an **adjective,** another **adverb,** or a whole **clause** or **sentence**:

Finally, heavily loaded trucks *quickly* destroy even *very well* constructed roads.

Any one-word modifier that does not modify a **noun** or other **nominal** is an adverb.

Adverbial: Words or word groups used to modify **verbs, adjectives, adverbs,** or whole **clauses** or **sentences**:

We started *home.* (**noun** used adverbially)

She thinks the answer appears *in the manual.* (adverbial phrase)

They'll sue *when all other approaches are exhausted.* (adverbial **clause**)

Adverbs of emphasis: A class of adverbs like *also, already, always, barely, finally, first, hardly, never, only, seldom, sometimes,* and *still* that negate statements or express the frequency, order, or duration of a verb or other target word. Such words are exceptions to the principle of **end focus**: they are stressed wherever they appear in a sentence.

Apostrophe: Besides naming the punctuation mark (') used to indicate possessives and contractions, an apostrophe is a figure of speech in which a writer or speaker addresses an imaginary hearer, who may not be human: "O liberty! What crimes have been committed in thy name!"

Appositive: A word or phrase that follows a noun or other nominal to define, identify, or rename it:

Hidalgo, *a seven-year-old quarter horse*, was her obsession.

A third man, *Thompson*, was watching the entrance.

Branching: Adding **adverbial** elements to an **independent clause** before the clause (left-branching) or after it (right-branching). In addition to being a basic technique for expanding sentences, left- and right-branching helps determine where the main emphasis or **sentence nucleus** falls:

> When Tyrone smelled gas, he lit the **PI**lot light. (left-branching)
>
> Tyrone lit the pilot light when he smelled **GAS**. (right-branching)

Breath units: Units of language made up of words spoken together without taking a breath. These may vary somewhat from speaker to speaker. Good stylists mix long and short breath units and rarely let any unit exceed 25 **syllables**.

Clause: A group of related words containing a **subject** and a **predicate**. **Independent clauses** can stand alone as complete sentences. **Dependent clauses** refer to or form parts of other clauses. They cannot stand alone. Dependent clauses may do the work of **adjectivals**, **adverbials**, or **nominals (nouns)**:

> Independent clause: Tyrone smelled gas.
>
> Dependent clauses: That was the day *that Tyrone smelled gas.* (*adjectival*)
>
> *When Tyrone smelled gas*, he relit the pilot light. (**adverbial**)
>
> She said *that Tyrone smelled gas.* (**nominal**)

Clichés: Trite phrases that replace original language with lackluster formulas. These may be dead figures of speech like *happy as a clam*, literary allusions like *much ado about nothing*, or simply popular phrases that people employ without much thought—for example, *global perspective, viable alternative*, or *software solution*. Although no one avoids clichés entirely, careful writers edit them out, especially when they are concerned to make every word count.

Colloquial English: Language too informal for most public **writing situations**. Colloquial English includes abbreviated forms like *DC* for Washington, slang words like *nerdy*, and popular phrases of the moment (*"I was like, 'Duh!'"*). Because the category is fluid, deciding what is or isn't colloquial can be difficult. *Gimmick* was considered colloquial fifty years ago. Today it is **standard English**. *Geek* is colloquial today. Tomorrow it may be standard English, too.

Comma fault, Comma splice: Linking two **independent clauses** with a comma and no conjunction:

> I patted his knee right back, he had the grace to blush.

Usually corrected by adding a coordinating conjunction or by making one of the clauses **dependent:**

> I patted his knee right back, *and* he had the grace to blush.

> *When* I patted his knee right back, he had the grace to blush.

Complement: The **verb** or verbs of a **sentence** along with their objects, modifiers, or other words that "complete" the sentence by filling out the comment it makes about its **subject.** In most sentences the subject (which may also be several words long) comes first, followed by the verb(s) and complement(s).

Complete subject: The **simple subject** of a clause and all the words that go with it: *"She /* did exercises at her desk." *"The newly hired botanist /* did exercises at her desk."

Complex sentence: A **sentence** containing one **independent clause** and one or more **dependent clauses:**

> A submarine volcano which has been active for several years is in the process of forming a new Hawaiian island.

Compound sentence: A **sentence** containing two or more **independent clauses,** usually joined by a **coordinating conjunction** (compare **simple sentence** and **complex sentence**):

> Hawks swoop down and kill other birds openly, but shrikes sidle up and kill by stealth.

Compound-complex sentence: A **sentence** containing two or more **independent clauses** (which makes it compound) and one or more **dependent clauses** (which makes it complex):

> Nero fiddled while Rome burned, and the Christians were blamed for the fire.

Concrete: Nouns, verbs, and **adjectives** that help you imagine specific sensations or form mental pictures. *Tomato, scrabble,* and *akimbo* have this effect. *Vegetation, activity,* and *posture* don't. Used judiciously, concrete words add life to your writing. But beware of straining too hard for concreteness, which can make you sound like a victim of overheated imagination:

Her freshly laundered petunia-pink apron waved winningly in the warm, gentle breeze.

Conjunctive adverb: An adverb that connects and relates two **independent clauses**. Between clauses, conjunctive adverbs call for semicolon punctuation, not just a comma:

Frank was widely respected; *however,* his financial forecasts were seldom accurate.

Other common conjunctive adverbs: *consequently, furthermore, likewise, moreover, nevertheless, then, therefore,* and *thus.*

Connotation: The emotional charge that attaches to some words and causes readers or hearers to react not just to their dictionary meaning but to the value orientation they carry. Thus, people who listen to all sides might be *fair-minded* if you approve of them, *wishy-washy* if you don't. Not all words have a strong connotation. Most, like *jacket* or *rectangle,* are more or less neutral.

Coordinate series: Combining technique through which similar grammatical elements are melded into a unit using **coordinating conjunctions.** Coordination can be applied to everything from **independent clauses** (see **compound sentences**) to single words. Particularly interesting from the point of view of style are coordinate series of three or more elements. Constructions of this kind are separated by pauses (usually marked by commas in written sentences), which vary the rhythm of a sentence by breaking it up into several **breath units.** Coordinate series of three or more elements also introduce additional **nuclear stresses** which fall on the words linked by the construction: "OF the people, BY the people, and FOR the people"; "READy, WILLing, and Able"; "Marcel RAN to the window, THREW open the shutters, and CALLed out into the **STREET.**"

Coordinating conjunctions: *and, but, or, nor, for, so,* and *yet.* These connect grammatical equals: "She and Alex were weary *but* exhilarated" (two **adjectives**); "The past is important, *for* it determines the future" (two **independent clauses**). Correlative coordinating conjunctions like *neither … nor,* or *both … and* work in pairs: "*Not only* Romans *but* Greeks contributed to 'Roman Art.'"

Denotation: The objective, dictionary meaning of words. A *mule* is the sterile offspring of a male donkey and a female horse. That's the word's denotation. Mulish stubbornness and relative lack of value are part of its **connotation.**

Dependent clause: A **clause** that functions as an **adjectival, adverbial,** or **nominal** in another clause:

Kandinsky, *who was reputed to be a great teacher,* painted abstractions. (**adjectival**)

Though he later specialized in abstractions, Kandinsky began by painting scenes from Russian folk tales. (***adverbial***)

Harrison thought *Kandinsky had painted it.* (**nominal**)

Determiners: Grammatical road signs that may have a meaning of their own, but serve also to begin noun phrases. Determiners include articles (*a, an, the*); possessives like *their* and *Ron's*; demonstrative pronouns (*this, that, these, those*); indefinite pronouns such as *some, no,* or *every*; quantifiers like *many* and *several*; and numbers: "*the four* brothers," "*our many* projects," "*these* hubcaps."

Diction: A writer's choice of words, which should be suited to the topic and the **writing situation.** Effective word choice requires you to consider the **denotative** and **connotative** meanings of words, and also the range of language options from formal to informal diction. See **formal English, colloquial English,** and **standard English.**

Doublespeak: Using vague, high-flown language to obscure one's real meaning, as when a boss offers an employee "an opportunity to further evaluate career options without the distraction of continuing employment pressures." In other words, "You're fired."

Emphasis: Tendency in English for one **syllable** in a **breath unit** to be pronounced with more force and therefore attract more attention than the others. Because of the principle of **end focus,** this highlighted syllable usually appears at the end of its breath unit: "My favorite was peppermint SCHNAPPS." "Rocked in the bosom of ABraham." Careful writers structure their sentences to emphasize words that reinforce the points they are making. Two other forms of emphasis are **grammatical emphasis,** or assigning important ideas to major grammatical elements, and **grammatical bulk,** adding modifiers to a word or idea to magnify its importance.

End focus: Predisposition of English speakers to postpone the **nucleus** or most highly **stressed syllable** to the end of a **breath unit** or **sentence.**

Carries over to writing because readers also tend to stress the last significant word of each breath unit when they **subvocalize**. Important
for dealing with questions of **coherence** and **emphasis**.

Euphemism: Language that attempts to take the sting out of a harsh
reality—for example, *stout* for "obese," *dysfunctional* for "deranged,"
or *rightsizing* for laying off workers.

Figurative language: Language, usually involving comparison, that is
not literally true but provokes the imagination of the reader to make an
unfamiliar connection. When Shakespeare's Iago wants to underscore
his idea that our minds, not bodies, should control our actions, he says
"Our bodies are our gardens, to the which our wills are gardeners." Not
really true, but a vivid way of making his point. Not all comparisons
are figurative, only those it takes an imaginative leap to understand.
"Ash lumber looks much like white oak" is not figurative because it is
literally true. Figurative language can become laughably illogical when
two or more comparisons clash. Modern readers are less willing to tolerate this than Shakespeare, who once let a character say, "Trust none;
for oaths are straws, men's faiths are wafer-cakes, and hold-fast is the
only dog, my duck." At least the character who said it was drunk.

Formal English: The language of political oratory and commencement
addresses. Has little place in writing, unless you are composing epic
verse.

Fragment: Something less than an independent clause treated as if it
were a sentence. A mistake in punctuation unless it is an **intentional
fragment**. Spot fragments by adding them to this construction—
"Have you heard that..." For instance, to check out "The girl who
told me about the concert," ask yourself whether you could say "Have
you heard that the girl who told me about the concert?" No? Then the
sentence would have to be something that passes the test, like "Stella
is the girl who told me about the concert."

Grammar: A system of rules for constructing sentences that native
speakers recognize as typically English. *Grammar* should be distinguished from "correctness," which is a sort of linguistic etiquette governing which grammatical constructions are appropriate to particular
situations. Telling the mayor in a public meeting that if she'd support
your proposal you "might could support her'n" would be grammatical. She would know what you meant and recognize it as English. But
it probably wouldn't be right for the occasion.

Grammatical bulk: Adding modifiers to a word or concept you want
to emphasize. "A spectacle unfolded before her" might produce these

more emphatic revisions: *"An* awe-inspiring *spectacle unfolded before her"; "A* thrilling, awe-inspiring *spectacle unfolded before her"; "A* thrilling, awe-inspiring *spectacle,* the like of which she had never seen, *unfolded before her."* A little of this goes a long way.

Grammatical emphasis: The principle that the closer a sentence element is to an **independent clause** the more important readers will expect its content to be and the more attention they will focus on it. Grammatical emphasis ranges from **independent clauses** (emphatic) through **dependent clauses** and **phrases,** down to single words. With each step the idea expressed becomes less strongly emphasized—for example, the concept of fright in the following sequence:

> Many soldiers were frightened by the horrors of battle. (independent clause)

> *Because they were frightened by the horrors of battle,* many soldiers never fired a shot. (dependent clause)

> *Frightened by the horrors of battle,* many soldiers never fired a shot. (phrase)

> Many *frightened* soldiers never fired a shot. (single word)

Hyperbole: Figurative language that depends on overstatement for rhetorical effect: *"I've asked you a million times to stop cracking your knuckles!" "You're the most beautiful girl in the world!"*

Impersonal subject: Abstract, often disembodied subjects that replace the real actors in many a vague sentence. Commonly associated with unnecessary **passive verbs**:

Original Sentence:

> Spring was not a time of abundance in the prehistoric Eastern forests because game was scarce then and nuts were far from ripe, but by 6,000 years ago, fast-ripening "weed" plants like sunflowers helped make up the difference; preserved droppings show that sunflower seeds often made up a quarter of the Indians' diets.

> BASED ON WILLIAM H. MACLEISH, *The Day Before America*

Rewritten with impersonal subjects:

> Abundance was not notable in spring in prehistoric Eastern forests because of the scarcity of game then and the immaturity of foods

like nuts, but by 6,000 years ago, the difference was made up by fast-ripening "weed" plants like sunflowers; analysis of preserved droppings shows that a quarter of Indians' diets was often made up of sunflower seeds.

Independent clause: A **clause** that can stand alone as a complete sentence. This designation includes clauses connected by **coordinating conjunctions** within **compound sentences**:

Identification cards can already contain all sorts of electronic information. (one clause)

I like dark beers, but Mona drinks only pale, light ones. (compound sentence)

Informal English. See **colloquial English**.

Intentional fragment: Part of a **sentence** punctuated as if it were complete in keeping with common practice in the spoken language. "They say we missed our last estimated payment. Not so." Used occasionally in the right circumstances, intentional fragments can enliven your style.

Jargon: Specialized vocabulary of a profession or other interest group—for instance, *client* for "patient" (counseling); *boot* for "start" (computers); and *defective socialization* for "bad manners" (education). While jargon may put off outsiders and so should be kept to a minimum in writing for general audiences, it may be essential in professional communications, partly for its frequent precision, and partly because it shows you are a member of the group, someone to be taken seriously.

Kernel sentences: Basic **subject-predicate** statements from which many more complex sentences can be built. For instance: *"Many German Jews put money in Swiss banks. This happened often. This happened before World War II. They thought the money would be safe. They sensed trouble on the horizon."* could become *"Sensing trouble on the horizon before World War II, many German Jews put money in Swiss banks, where they thought it would be safe."* Of course all sorts of other configurations are possible. Thinking of sentences this way—as combinations of basic building blocks—frees you to rearrange elements to achieve different **rhythms** and patterns of **emphasis**.

Latinate diction: Words borrowed directly or indirectly from Latin (or less often from Greek) that retain their bookish savor. Latinate terms can often be paired off against homier synonyms: *domicile/house,* *contiguous/touching, expectorate/spit.* Latinate words tend to be suited to formal or impersonal **writing situations**; however excessive Latinate diction is a hallmark of the **official style**. In most writing, a mix of Latinate and plainer words works best.

Metaphor: Figurative language that involves a comparison just as **simile** does, but dispenses with *like* and *as* to simply assert that something is what it's really not. W.H. Auden once said crowds on the street, anonymous and moving unreflectively toward death, "were fields of harvest wheat." William Morris played the comparison another way. Thinking of a dead friend at dawn, he imagined nature shared his reverence. He spoke of "the tender, bowed locks of the corn," comparing the wheat field around him to a congregation in church, which is an example of **personification** also.

Metonomy: Naming one thing when you really mean something else associated with it: "No one was there but *stuffed shirts.*" "These figures were released by *the White House.*"

Mixed metaphors: Illogical combination of **figurative** comparisons. Often associated with **clichés**, which writers get used to tossing about carelessly. "If you think she remained *innocent as a lamb* while climbing the *ladder of success,* you can't *smell a rat* when you see one."

Nominal: A noun or other construction functioning as a noun. This includes noun *clauses* (*How she came to know his salary* is the main question), some infinitive phrases (*To be truly objective* is difficult), and gerund phrases (*Climbing alone* was forbidden).

Nominalization: A process of transforming verbs into abstract nouns that robs writing of specific weight and vigor. Thus, "We hope you'll attend" might become "We look forward to your *attendance* with *anticipation.*"

Nonrestrictive modifier: See **Restrictive and nonrestrictive modifiers.**

Noun: A noun names a person, place, or thing (*trooper, provocation, Minnesota Mining and Manufacturing*). Most nouns form plurals by adding -s or -es to the singular form (*class, classes*). Nouns can follow determiners, words like *the, his,* or *nine:* "the *hat,*" "his *scruples,*" "nine *editions.*"

Nucleus, nuclear stress: Syllable in a **breath unit** pronounced with the most force and therefore drawing the most attention. Because of the principle of **end focus**, this syllable tends to occur in the last significant word in the breath unit: "Dragonflies can take off BACKward, fly 35 miles an HOUR, and turn at right angles without BANKing." The last stressed syllable in this sentence, "BANKing," is the **sentence nucleus**, the single most strongly stressed syllable in the sentence.

Official style: Pompous, windy language dear to officials hoping to magnify their own importance or forestall debate. Depends heavily on **formal English, clichés, nominalization**, and **passive voice**:

> Today when the institution is threatened with financially straightened circumstances we have no choice but the continuation of maintenance of a viable and competitive athletic program that hopefully offers the prospect of making a contribution to the university's fiscal well-being at some future point in time.

Overwriting: Bad style that results from trying too hard to be impressive or creative. The key feature of either form is excess, blowing out of proportion something that could be simply stated:

> Alternative organizational options notwithstanding, administrative officials have determined to adhere to a top-down, nonparticipatory model. (*No more advisory committees.*)

> Beneath my size 36 alligator belt keen pangs radiate from the pit of my empty stomach to tireless neural receptors in my brain. (*I'm hungry.*)

Paradox: Figurative language that seems self-contradictory until you come to understand it in the special sense the writer intended: "There's no such thing as bad weather." "It's a great art to saunter." (Thoreau)

Parallel series: Items of equivalent function and importance appearing in the same type of grammatical constructions:

Althea was blessed with *friends*, *health*, and *contentment*.

Kids let off steam by *running*, *jumping*, and *swinging upside down*.

Fish gotta swim, birds gotta fly, I gotta love that man till I die.

OSCAR HAMMERSTEIN

Parenthetical elements: Interrupters of all kinds that occur within other grammatical constructions or breath units: "No, | *Lawrence,* | there's plenty more"; "My intentions, | *however,* | are entirely honorable"; "Aunt Theresa, | *who found everything funny,* | could barely speak." Because they add pauses, parenthetical elements help vary a sentence's **rhythm** and provide additional opportunities to assign **nuclear stress**.

Passive verbs: Verbs constructed with some form of *to be* which rearrange sentences so that the subject is the receiver, not the doer, of the action:

> Her life *was cut* short.

> At one time warts *were thought* to be caused by toads.

Personification: Describing something not human as if it were: "rosy-fingered dawn," "The World Bank is in bed with the European Union."

Phrase: A group of words that works together to perform a single grammatical function. Unlike **clauses**, phrases do not have subjects and verbs. Typical examples include **prepositional phrases** used as **adjectivals** ("the man *by the bridge*") or **adverbials** ("rebounding *off the wall*") and various **nominal** phrases: "*Riding the clutch* causes excessive wear"; "Helen wanted *to master Middle Eastern cooking.*"

Predicate: One of the two principal parts of a sentence, the comment the sentence makes about its **subject**. The predicate includes the **verb** along with any **complements** or **adverbials** that go with it. In most sentences the subject (which may also be several words long) comes first, and all the words that follow make up the predicate.

Prepositional phrase: Prepositions include words like *in, of, by, with, over, around, through,* and *like* that come before a nominal, creating **phrases** that can be used in **sentences** to serve different grammatical roles—usually as adjectivals or adverbials:

> The girl *in the flowerbed* is Garvin's date. (adjectival)

> No one scales a carp *like Uncle Charlie.* (adverbial)

Relative clause: An **adjectival clause** introduced by one of the relative pronouns (*who, whose, whom, which, that, whoever,* etc.) or relative adverbs (*where, when, why*). "Sylvia commended the doctor *who assisted her.*" "The formation *[that]* we saw was spectacular." As the second example demonstrates, the relative pronoun *that* can often be omitted.

Restrictive and nonrestrictive modifiers: Terms used to describe **adjectival** modifiers. Restrictive modifiers *restrict* the meaning to a subset of the **noun** or **nominal** they modify. For example, in the sentence "Little children who misbehave are unwelcome," the writer does not mean all little children are unwelcome—only those who misbehave.

The statement is restricted to little children who misbehave. Compare "Little children, whose hands are smaller than adults', have trouble playing many chords." Here the modifying clause does not restrict the subject. All little children have small hands, and all of them have trouble playing some chords. This modifier is nonrestrictive.

Because they are essential to a sentence's meaning, restrictive modifiers do not become separate **breath units** and are not set off by punctuation from the rest of the sentence. Because they supply only extra information and are not essential, nonrestrictive modifiers are treated as interruptions or **parenthetical elements**. They are pronounced as separate breath units and are set off by punctuation, usually commas, before and after the modifier.

Rhythm: Determined by the length and speed of **breath units** in a writer's sentences. The length of breath units is measured in **syllables**. Although it is fine to have as few as one or two syllables per breath unit on occasion, the upper limit for most purposes is around 25. Speed is a function of the **syllable/word ratio**. Breath units made up of long, polysyllabic words tend to be spoken or **subvocalized** quickly. Short words make for a slower, weightier effect. Good style calls for a variety of lengths and speeds to keep the writing from becoming monotonous.

Sentence: Free standing grammatical unit containing at least one **subject** and **predicate** combined into an **independent clause**. Sentences start with a capital letter and end with a period or other terminal punctuation.

Sentence cluster: A group of related sentences focusing on the same point, usually one step in a longer presentation. One or more sentence clusters may exist in the same paragraph.

Sentence nucleus: The strongest stressed syllable in a sentence. Because of the principle of **end focus** this tends to appear in the last significant word of the sentence. "Andre Dumas' father was the son of a black slave and her owner, a SUGar planter." Most sentences can be restructured to make the sentence nucleus fall on various syllables. Writers with special points to emphasize might prefer these versions of the sample sentence: "Andre Dumas' father was the son of a sugar planter and his black SLAVE." "The son of a sugar planter and his black slave became the father of Alexander DuMAS."

Sentence structure: The grammatical makeup of a sentence. Can range from simple ("Malcolm cheats.") to quite complicated, with multiple **clauses** and other elements like **adjectivals** and **adverbials**.

Simile: Figurative language in which one thing is overtly compared to another, generally in a construction using *like* or *as*. A famous simile is Langston Hughes' question about a deferred dream: "Does it dry up/like a raisin in the sun?" Describing a flirtatious heroine's glances, Alexander Pope combined two similes: "*Bright as the sun*, her eyes the gazers strike/And, *like the sun*, they shine on all alike."

Simple sentence: A sentence composed of one independent clause only: "Hubert slept"; "Mung beans can be cooked, not just cultivated for sprouts."

Simple subject: The **nominal** or nominals at the heart of a clause's subject; the part left behind when all modifiers are stripped away: "A dark, stony *ravine* led down to the plain." "Bright green *shamrocks* and *leprechauns* decorated the banner."

Sound qualities: Patterns of **sentence structure** (simple or complicated?) and **diction** (plain or polysyllabic?) along with effects of **rhythm** and **emphasis** that readers hear in their heads as they **subvocalize** what they are reading. An important factor in judging a writer's **voice**.

Standard English: The language of most good writing from memos to articles to grant proposals. As this range of examples suggests, there are many levels of standard English. Contractions, for instance, may be fine in less formal situations, but not when you must tread carefully addressing an unfamiliar audience. Try to match your language to the **writing situation.**

Stress: The degree of force with which syllables are pronounced. While linguists distinguish several degrees of stress, this book is concerned only with the heavy **nuclear stress** placed on the most prominent word in a **breath unit** or **sentence.** The principle of **end focus** dictates that in most cases nuclear stress falls on the last significant word in a unit. Controlling stress is the most effective way of putting **emphasis** in a breath unit or sentence exactly where you want it.

Subject: The topic of a sentence, invariably a **nominal** that answers the question "Who or what?" asked about the **predicate.** "The emir is happy with his gift camel." "Who or what is happy with his gift camel?" *"The emir."* "Holding hands in the hallways was forbidden." Who or what was forbidden?" *"Holding hands in the hallways."* Notice that subjects often include several words, and that in **passive** sentences like the second example, instead of acting itself the subject has something done to it.

In writing arranged for maximum **coherence**, the grammatical subjects in a given **sentence cluster** all refer to "known" concepts. See Chapter 8.

Subordinating conjunctions: words like *because, whether, since, if,* or *while,* which show the subordinate status of **adverbial dependent clauses**: "*Because* it was raining, she postponed her usual run."

Subvocalising: Going through the mental processes of generating speech but not actually making the sounds. A reader's tendency to subvocalize explains why the **sound qualities** of writing have such an impact on its stylistic effect even when the words are not spoken aloud.

Suffix: A construction added to the end of a word to change its meaning (*laundry, launderette*), its part of speech (*home, homeless*), or its inflection (*gibbon, gibbons; stodgy, stodgier*). Be wary of *-tion* or *-sion*, a suffix commonly involved in excessive **nominalization**.

Syllables: Words or parts of words spoken as uninterrupted units. Marked in dictionaries by raised periods (*e·pis·te·mol·o·gy, stro·ga·noff*). Some syllables are single vowels; others combine vowels and consonants. Syllables provide a basic unit for measuring the complexity of a writer's **diction** by its **syllable/word ratio** and its **rhythm** by the length of its **breath units** in syllables.

Syllable/word ratio: In general, keep this between 1.4 and 2.0 syllables per word, and closer to 1.4:1 than 2:1 if possible. While an occasional emotional, punchy passage might justify a lower ratio and technical subjects might call for a higher one, a most writing situations call for a middling approach.

Synecdoche: Figurative language using a part of something to stand for the whole thing: "hired *hands*," "what elegant *threads*!"

Topic sentence: A **sentence** that introduces the main idea or point of a **sentence cluster**. All the other sentences in the cluster should explain or support the assertion made in the topic sentence. Topic sentences usually appear at the beginning of their clusters, but may be placed elsewhere or occasionally just implied. Paragraphs with more than one sentence cluster may have more than one topic sentence.

Transformations: Standard techniques rooted in English **grammar** for transforming one construction into another. Transformations of whole sentences redistribute **emphasis**. For example a *what* transformation could shift the emphasis from **FLOOR** to **JACK** in the following pair of sentences: "Paul used a hydraulic jack to lift the sagging **FLOOR**"; "What Paul used to lift the sagging floor was a hydraulic **JACK**."

Other notable transformations include *there* transformations ("*There is* the JACK Paul used to lift the sagging **FLOOR**"; "*There* is the FLOOR Paul **LIFTED.**"); *it* transformations ("*It* was PAUL who lifted the sagging **FLOOR.**"); and passive transformations ("The sagging FLOOR *was* lifted with a hydraulic **JACK.**")

Transitions: Connections between one idea, **sentence, sentence cluster**, or paragraph and the next. Transitions range from sentences ("*Stealth is another important objective of submarine warfare.*") to single words used to indicate relationships like addition (*and, too, also, furthermore*, etc.), cause and effect (*therefore, consequently, as a result*), comparison (*likewise, similarly*), specification (*for example, for instance, in particular*), summation (*in conclusion, to sum up*), time (*afterwards, then, meanwhile, next, later, soon, immediately*), and contrast (*but, however, on the other hand, nevertheless, still*). Although transitions help promote coherence, they can be overdone. Ask yourself whether each one you use is really necessary.

Understatement: Figurative language at the opposite end of the spectrum from **hyperbole.** Understatement says something with less emotional emphasis than most people would think it deserves: "His appearance was not improved by losing his nose." "It's late to apologize when you're lying in the grave."

Verb: A part of speech that expresses an action or a state of being like *is* or *seems*. Verbs can be recognized by their form. Every verb has an *-s* and an *-ing* form, most have an *-ed* form, and all can be combined with auxiliaries like *is* and *have* to indicate changes in time. Typical sequences: *walk, walks, walking, walked, has walked; think, thinks, thinking, thought, has thought.* **Subjects** and verbs are the basic building blocks of **sentences.**

Verbals: Nonfinite verbs (that is, verbs that indicate general or ongoing rather than specific actions). These function alone or in phrases as **nominals, adjectivals**, or **adverbials**:

The swiftly *running* brook disappeared into a cave. **(adjectival)**

We waited there *to see* the fireworks. **(adverbial)**

To run a mile in four minutes is difficult. **(nominal)**

Voice: Your sense of the person speaking in a piece of writing, produced by the writer's grammar and diction, which combine to produce **sound qualities** you hear in your imagination as you read.

Weak verbs: Verbs that express only vague actions or none at all. By far the commonest weak verb is *to be* in any of its many forms—*am, is, are, was, were, shall be, have been,* etc. Other weak verbs include *appear, cause, concern, consider, develop, establish, examine, have, occur,* and *seem,* especially when these are paired with **abstract** or **nominalized subjects**: *"Exploitation of every advantage appears to be a necessary element in our survival."* Edit sentences like this by exhuming the original verbs: "To *survive,* we must *exploit* every advantage."

Writing situation: Determined by the topic and the relationship between writer and readers. Informal, friendly discourse addressed to equals calls for one style and level of logical support, but standards might be quite different for writing addressed to readers who will sit in judgment on your ideas. Easy topics call for an easygoing style (which may not be all that easy to get right). Difficult ones ("Wagner's Views on Race") require more formal treatment.

Index

CPSIA information can be obtained at www.ICGtesting.com
Printed in the USA
BVOW04s1216300714

360991BV00006B/13/P